Road-Tripping the
South Atlantic League

Road-Tripping the South Atlantic League

A Guide to the Teams, Ballparks and Cities

WALTER TRIEBEL

McFarland & Company, Inc., Publishers
Jefferson, North Carolina

ISBN 978-0-7864-9811-6 (softcover : acid free paper) ∞
ISBN 978-1-4766-2041-1 (ebook)

LIBRARY OF CONGRESS CATALOGUING DATA ARE AVAILABLE

BRITISH LIBRARY CATALOGUING DATA ARE AVAILABLE

Front cover illustration © 2016 Thinkstock

Printed in the United States of America

McFarland & Company, Inc., Publishers
Box 611, Jefferson, North Carolina 28640
www.mcfarlandpub.com

Table of Contents

Preface

The goal of this book is to provide a comprehensive guide for planning minor league baseball road trips. The primary focus is on the teams, stadiums, and cities of one specific league—the South Atlantic League, an A-level minor league affiliated with Major League Baseball.

But, the book does not limit travel to just attending games at the home ballparks of South Atlantic League teams. A chapter is devoted to travel plans that include games of teams in other minor leagues that overlay the regional footprint of the South Atlantic League. These include the International League (Triple A), Eastern League (Double A), Carolina League (Advanced A), and Appalachian League (Rookie). It also describes how your travel plans can be tailored so that readers can attend games played by the minor league affiliates of a favorite major league team or add stops at stadiums of other teams in towns and cities along the various travel routes.

Many baseball travel books focus primarily on the stadiums and their amenities. Baseball travel, after all, is about seeing the stadium, the game, and the players. But after having traveled a long distance to attend a game and maybe staying overnight in the town or city, the baseball tourist might want to sample the flavor of their destination. This book is designed with this broader perspective in mind, with the aim of providing a much richer baseball travel experience. At the same time, the book is designed to serve as a functional guide for planning a baseball road trip adventure. It reviews how-to skills and travel tips needed to plan an efficient, cost effective baseball road trip.

With this primary theme in mind, the book offers an expanded view of the South Atlantic League, its teams, stadiums, players, and the history of baseball in the cities that host its teams today. The book

• Traces the origin, evolution, and history of the modern South Atlantic League and its predecessors—the Western Carolinas League, Tar Heel League, North Carolina State League, and Western Carolina League.

• Highlights the history of the league, its teams, and their major league affiliations and identifies players who led the league in a traditional batting or pitching statistic in a recent season.

• Provides a detailed profile of each of the current South Atlantic League teams that includes a review of the history of baseball in the town or city, stadium information, and highlights of the teams and players who played in the city.

• Suggests Durham, North Carolina, as a hub city from which to originate South Atlantic League travel; looks at the rich history of baseball in the city; identifies baseball related and other attractions in or near Durham; and recommends a wide assortment of interesting eateries in the city and surrounding communities.

• Outlines the methodology for developing a baseball road trip plan in addition to offering detailed suggestions for day trips, two-day, three-day and longer routes that may be used to create an efficient and rewarding overall South Atlantic League travel itinerary.

• Highlights baseball-related and other attractions as well as places to eat in or near the interesting, attractive, and in some cases historic small cities that are the homes of today's South Atlantic League teams.

A secondary theme in the book is that minor league baseball travel offers an opportunity for the baseball tourist to see a number of the top up-and-coming prospects for the major leagues, potentially some of the top 20 prospects of one's favorite team, and maybe a few of tomorrow's major league stars. The individual team profiles offer insight and anecdotes regarding players who tuned their batting, fielding, or pitching skills in A-level ball on the field of a South Atlantic League team. The book indentifies more than 300 players who made a stop to play their early ball on the field of a South Atlantic League team and then went on to have long, successful major league careers.

The list includes retired players such as Craig Biggio (Asheville Tourists, 1987), Trevor Hoffman (Charleston Wheelers, 1990), and Derek Jeter (Greensboro Hornets, 1992–93) as well as many of today's top players. For instance, current San Francisco Giant stars outfielder Hunter Pence (Lexington Legends, 2005), Red Sox second baseman Dustin Pedroia (Augusta GreenJackets, 2004), and Phillies first baseman Ryan Howard (Lakewood BlueClaws, 2002) all tuned their baseball skills in the league. The minor league or major league careers of a number of these players are highlighted in the book. For example, during the 2008 season, current Atlanta Braves first baseman Freddie Freeman set the all-time hits, runs batted in, and slugging percentage records of the Rome Braves. That same season, San Francisco Giants lefty ace Madison

Bumgarner set the all-time earned run average record by a starter for the Augusta GreenJackets. During a South Atlantic League baseball road trip, a traveler will surely see a number of prospects who will turn into tomorrow's major league stars.

Over the years I have done extensive baseball travel that has taken me to most of the major league ballparks. Moreover, I have focused on attending minor league games with the intent of seeing up-and-coming top prospects play during the early years of their professional careers. During the 2013 baseball season, I attended a home game of each of the South Atlantic League teams as well as the league's All-Star game at FirstEnergy Park, home of the Lakewood BlueClaws in New Jersey, and to see the Hagerstown Suns play in both Northern Division and South Atlantic League Championship Series games at Municipal Stadium in Hagerstown, Maryland. This book is based on those travel experiences.

The primary sources of historical and statistical information for the book were the Baseball-Reference.com website, baseball related articles on the web, and a number of baseball history- and travel-related books. In an effort to improve accuracy, baseball statistical information was cross-referenced with that available on the MiLB.com, MLB.com, and thebaseballcube.com websites. The information on leagues, teams, and players introduced in the book is current through the end of the 2014 baseball season. Updates for 2015 and future seasons will be provided through the book's Facebook.

Introduction—Planning a Baseball Road Trip

What is a baseball road trip? The expression could mean many different things to different people. For example, it might suggest that one is planning to take a trip to attend a series of baseball games. These games could be played by major league teams, minor league teams, independent league teams, college summer league baseball teams, or even college teams. However, it could also mean they are going to visit another type of baseball destination, such as a museum, or even that the goal is to actually play in a baseball game or watch friends or children participate in a baseball league.

The definition that I am using for baseball road trip is specific. I mean a trip of which the primary intent is to attend one or more baseball games. But this trip could include other baseball activities, such as to see historical sites associated with baseball, or even visits to non-baseball tourist attractions along the route.

Baseball Road Trip Options

The duration of the baseball road trip will vary depending on its goal. For instance, it could simply be a day trip to attend a game played by the major league baseball team that one roots for or maybe a game of one of its local minor league affiliates. Alternatively, the plan for the road trip could be to see games played by one team on consecutive days or games by different teams at different locations. This might mean that one stays for one or two nights near one of the destinations. Finally, the plan could be for an extended baseball road trip that would take one to a series of towns and cities to attend games played by a number of different teams. In this latter case, the baseball road trip could be viewed as simply a multi-day vacation of which the primary theme is to attend baseball games and possibly some baseball-related attractions along the route.

Next I will look at some options for baseball road trips. The well-publicized ultimate baseball road trip is to attend a game played by each of the major league baseball clubs at their home stadium. This is the dream baseball road trip of many a fan, but the accomplishment of a few. However, their travels have been well documented with articles, blog posts, and books. In fact, Holiday Inn has fostered a relationship with Major League Baseball as the official partner of MLB road trips. During the 2006 baseball season, Holiday Inn ran an Ultimate Baseball Road Trip Sweepstakes. For that promotion, Holiday Inn equipped a bus with baseball displays and other baseball-related items of interest. The Big Green Bus traveled from stadium to stadium, and fans attending the games were let onboard. At the completion of the Holiday Inn baseball road trip, one fan won an ultimate baseball road trip that included accommodations, travel, and two tickets to a game at each of the thirty Major League Baseball stadiums.

The ultimate baseball road trip requires a large commitment of both time and money. After all, there are fifteen teams in both the National League and the American League and there are great distances between the home stadiums of those teams. A similar but somewhat less lofty goal would be to see a home game of all of the teams in the league of one's favorite team. For instance, a New York Yankees fan could eventually attend a game at the stadium of each of the fifteen American League baseball clubs or to attend a game when the Yankees are the visiting team in each of those American League cities. This could be achieved by planning a number of independent trips over a number of years, but it would require a lot of time and financial resources.

Baseball Road Trips for the Fan of a Specific Team

Planning the ultimate baseball road trip as a vacation or the primary focus of one's free time might not be realistic. Seeing a favorite team play a game at the home stadium of each of the other teams in their league may also offer too much of a challenge. However, there are many other less demanding baseball expeditions that could be planned as an interesting and fun individual, group, or family adventure. I'm going to offer a list of ideas of some road trips that require a varying scope of commitments.

• See a favorite team either at home or away play all of the teams in the region.

- National League example: Philadelphia Phillies fan—attend games in which they play the Mets, Nationals, and Pirates
- American League example: Chicago White Sox fan—attend games in which they play the Tigers, Indians, and Twins
- Attend a home game of each of a favorite team's closely located minor league affiliates.
  - National League example: Atlanta Braves fan—Gwinnett Braves (AAA), Mississippi Braves (AA), and Rome Braves (A).
  - American League example: Boston Red Sox fan—Pawtucket Red Sox (AAA), Portland Sea Dogs (AA), and Lowell Spinners (A-).
- Attend the opening day of a favorite major league team and most or all of its minor league affiliates.
  - National League example: San Francisco Giants fan—Fresno Grizzlies (AAA), Richmond Flying Squirrels (AA), San Jose Giants (A+), Augusta GreenJackets (A), Salem-Keizer Volcanoes (A-), and AZL Giants (Rk).
  - American League example: New York Yankees fan—Scranton/Wilkes-Barre RailRiders (AAA), Trenton Thunder (AA), Tampa Yankees (A+), Charleston RiverDogs (A), Staten Island Yankees (A-), and GCL Yankees (Rk).

Baseball Road Trip Ideas for Baseball Enthusiasts

Fans of a specific team with a broader interest in the baseball have other options for creating interesting and viable road trips. Using the model of the ultimate baseball road trip, it is possible to plan a similar, but less demanding minor league baseball road trip. Most of the lower level minor leagues (A+, A, A-, and Rk) have all or at least most of their teams concentrated in states associated with a specific region of the county. For example, each of the ten teams of the California League (A+) plays its games at a home stadium located in a city in California. At the class A level, the South Atlantic League has nine of its fourteen teams tucked into North Carolina, South Carolina, and Georgia. Finally, at the A- level six of the eight teams of the Northwest League play their home games in cities that are in either Washington or Oregon.

Some minor league baseball road trip ideas:

- Fans living near a minor league team—or, even better, a minor league affiliate of their favorite major league team—can attend an away game of each of the other teams at the local team's stadium.

• Attend a game at the home stadium of each of the teams in the league associated with a nearby minor league team.

General Baseball Road Trip Planning Tips

1. To reduce the number of nights of lodging, arrive in the city of the first game early on the day of the game and attend an evening game.

2. To save a night of lodging, try to attend a day game on the return date.

3. For major league teams, always have tickets to the game in advance of departure. This is not typically necessary for a minor league game unless it is a special event game or on a holiday.

4. If flying, allow sufficient time to get a rental car, check in at the hotel, and get to the game on time on the day of arrival. When departing, be sure there is enough time to return the car and to check in for your flight. Finally, do not select the last flight of the day for your transportation.

5. Consider attending two games in intriguing cities played by teams of particular interest. These may be cities to which it would be difficult to return.

6. Check the schedules for day or night game opportunities to see two games in the same day—a two-city double header. This may reduce the duration of the road trip by a day or two.

7. When planning the sequence of cities to be visited during a road trip, check the team schedules for Monday through Thursday games. They are the most frequent days that teams might not have a game scheduled. Therefore, games available on those days might dictate the order for traveling.

As pointed out in the Preface, the primary theme of this book is to advocate baseball travel, and the vehicle for achieving this is to attend a home game at the ballpark of each of the teams for one specific league—the South Atlantic League. Today, the South Atlantic League fields fourteen teams in seven states along the eastern seaboard. The core of the South Atlantic League—four teams: the Greensboro Grasshoppers (Marlins), Hickory Crawdads (Rangers), Kannapolis Intimidators (White Sox), and Asheville Tourists (Rockies)—resides in North Carolina. However, six more of the league's teams are located in the neighboring states. South Carolina hosts the Charleston RiverDogs (Yankees) and Greenville Drive (Red Sox); Georgia has the Savannah Sand Gnats (Mets), Augusta GreenJackets (Giants) and Rome Braves (Braves); and there's the West Virginia Power (Pirates).

Often the focus of baseball road trips is on the experience of watching a game played in a series of specific ballparks rather than on the players or teams that are participating in the games. But baseball travel should and can offer much more than that. Using the baseball road trips outline in the book, the fan could

- Attend a game or games at all of the stadiums of the South Atlantic League teams.
- Possibly see a home game played by a favorite team's South Atlantic League class A affiliate—and possibly also see that team play in some away games as well.
- Watch a number of their favorite team's current Major League Baseball ranked top twenty prospects play in games at an early point in their professional baseball careers.
- Observe the play of top prospects of other major league clubs and maybe even some of the top ranked prospects in all of professional baseball.
- Attend games played at historic ball fields, such as McCormick Field, Asheville, North Carolina; William L. Grayson Stadium, Savannah, Georgia; and Municipal Stadium, Hagerstown, Maryland.
- Visit other baseball attractions along the route, such as the North Carolina Baseball Museum, Wilson, North Carolina; Eastern Shore Baseball Hall of Fame Museum, Salisbury, Maryland; and Shoeless Joe Jackson Museum and Reading Center, Greenville, South Carolina.

The footprint of the South Atlantic League, which reaches from Lakewood, New Jersey to the north to Savannah, Georgia, in the south and Lexington, Kentucky, to the west, is rich in baseball teams affiliated with Major League Baseball. In addition to the fourteen teams of the South Atlantic League, twenty-five other minor league clubs are located in these states. For example, North Carolina is home to five more teams—the Durham Bulls (Rays) and Charlotte Knights (White Sox) of the International League (AAA), the Carolina Mudcats (Braves) and Winston-Salem Dash (White Sox) of the Carolina League (A+), and the Burlington Royals (Royals) of the Appalachian League. As mentioned in the Preface, this opens opportunities to customize one's road trip plan for other goals, such as to attend games of other minor league clubs of a favorite team that play in the region or blend in some games of teams from other leagues to expand its overall scope.

I have outlined in the book how a fan could include games of other minor league affiliates of their favorite team that play in leagues, such as the International league (AAA), Eastern League (AA), Carolina League (A+), or Appalachian League (Rk), along the South Atlantic League travel route to tailor the trip based on interest. In fact, ten of the forty-four teams from these four leagues are located within a day-trip drive of Durham, North Carolina— the city I propose as the hub for South Atlantic League travel. They include five teams that are located within 100 miles of Durham—the local Durham Bulls (International League), Carolina Mudcats (Carolina League) in Zebulon, North Carolina (39 miles), Burlington Royals (Appalachian League) in Burlington, North Carolina (45 miles), Danville Braves (Appalachian League) in Danville, Virginia (70 miles), and Winston-Salem Dash (Carolina League) in Winston-Salem, North Carolina (90 miles).

Moreover, the remaining teams of these leagues travel into these more accessible towns and cities for away games. The major league affiliates of six South Atlantic League teams (Yankees, Pirates, Braves, Orioles, National, and Yankees) have another minor league club in three of these other leagues. For example, a New York Yankees fan could plan a trip around dates when the Scranton/Wilkes-Barre RailRiders (International League) are playing the Durham Bull in Durham, North Carolina, the Pulaski Yankees (Appalachian League) are visiting the Burlington Royals in Burlington, North Carolina, or the Trenton Thunder (Eastern League) are playing an away game versus the Richmond Flying Squirrels in Richmond, Virginia. This would potentially enable one to see more of a favorite team's minor league clubs and a larger group of that team's players that are ranked as top up-and-coming prospects.

This book provides all the information to plan a much broader, richer baseball road trip experience.

The Origin and Evolution of the South Atlantic League

Even though a South Atlantic League existed on and off in some form from as early as 1892 and through 1962, the roots of today's version of the league are not derived from any of those earlier leagues. In fact, the South Atlantic League name lay dormant from 1963 through 1979. Instead the modern South Atlantic League evolved out of the Western Carolina League and North Carolina State League of the early 1950s.

Team	Location	Miles from Charlotte
Granite Falls Graniteers	Granite Falls, NC	63 NW
Lenoir Red Sox	Lenoir, NC	74 NW
Lincolnton Cardinals	Lincolnton, NC	36 NW
Marion Marauders	Marion, NC	95 NW
Morganton Aggies	Morganton, NC	76 NW
Newton-Conover Twins	Newton, NC Conover, NC	41/45 NW
Rutherford County Owls	Forest City, NC	64 W
Shelby Farmers	Shelby, NC	45 W

Table 1-1. Western Carolina League teams—1951.

The Roots of the Modern South Atlantic League—the Western Carolina and North Carolina State Leagues

In the 1951 baseball season, the Western Carolina League, which was founded in 1948 as a D class minor league, was made up of the eight teams listed in Table 1-1. All of these teams were located in the western half of North

Carolina and resided in small towns less than 100 miles west or northwest of Charlotte. The westernmost team in the league was the Rutherford County Owls, who played in Forest City, and the easternmost team was the Lincolnton Cardinals. The distance between these two towns was just 42 miles. Likewise, the distance between the northernmost team, the Lenoir Red Sox, and the southernmost team, the Shelby Farmers, was 50 miles.

During this era of professional baseball, minor league team rosters were primarily formed from young prospects; however, sometimes they included a number of more senior former major league players. That is the case for the Shelby Farmers, who won the 1951 Western Carolina League championship. The Farmers roster had just one player that ever played at the major league level. He was second baseman and shortstop Danny Reynolds. However, Reynolds was thirty-one years old in 1951 and had played briefly in

Team	Location	Miles from Charlotte
Concord Sports	Concord, NC	23 NE
Hickory Rebels	Hickory, NC	74 NW
High Point-Thomasville Hi-Toms	High Point, NC Thomasville, NC	85/71 NE
Landis Spinners	Landis, NC	32 NE
Lexington Indians	Lexington, NC	59 NE
Mooresville Moors	Mooresville, NC	28 N
Salisbury Pirates	Salisbury, NC	43 NE
Statesville Owls	Statesville, NC	42 N

Table 1–2. North Carolina State League teams—1951.

the majors for the Chicago White Sox seven seasons earlier in 1945.

In that same summer, the North Carolina State League—in its eighth consecutive season of play—also fielded eight teams all located in North Carolina. Table 1–2 lists the members of the league at the start of the 1951 season. This table shows that the Hickory Rebels were located to the northwest of Charlotte, but the rest of the teams were to either the north or northeast of the city. Note that the host towns of these teams are also all within 90 miles of Charlotte. The most northern and eastern team was the High Point–Thomasville Hi-Toms. High-Point was located approximately 87 miles from the westernmost team, the Hickory Rebels, and about 59 miles from the southernmost team, the Concord Sports.

The High Point–Thomasville Hi-Toms, who played in the North Carolina State League from 1948 through 1952, finished with the best record in the league four out of those five seasons. During those seasons, the Hi-Toms played their home games at Finch Field in Thomasville, which was built in 1935. The renovated version of this historic ballpark is still in use today by a team with a similar name—the High Point–Thomasville HiToms—that plays its games in the Coastal Plain League.

Figure 1–1. Team photograph of the 1949 High Point-Thomasville Hi-Toms (courtesy North Carolina Baseball Museum).

A photo of the team's 1949 roster is shown in Figure 1–1. The Hi-Toms were a D-class minor league team of the Boston Braves of the National League. During that season a forty-two-year-old former major leaguer, Cliff Bolton, led the team's offense. Bolton had played in the American League with the Washington Senators and Detroit Tigers during parts of seven seasons from 1931 through 1941. Bolton led the North Carolina State League for the season in batting with a .399 average. Twenty-two-year-old right-hander Lynn Southworth led the league with an exceptional 21W:1L pitching record. They led High Point–Thomasville to a league leading 90W:34L record and in the postseason won the North Carolina State League Championship.

However, there was one other player that played a key role in the success of the 1949 Hi-Toms. A seventeen-year-old Eddie Mathews, who went on to have a Hall of Fame career at the major league level, played his first season of professional ball with the team that season. Even though he appeared in just 63 games, the young third baseman hit 17 home runs to rank third in the league in that offensive statistic for the season. The two players that ranked above him hit 21 and 22 homers, respectively, but hit them in almost twice as many at-bats.

Mathews debuted as the Boston Braves' third baseman on April 15, 1952, at the age of 20 and stayed to play in the majors for seventeen seasons with the Braves in Boston, Milwaukee, and Atlanta, as well as playing for the Houston Astros and Detroit Tigers. The left-handed power-hitting third baseman led the National League in home runs with 46 in 1953 and 47 in 1959. During his career Mathews compiled a total of 512 home runs, which today ranks him tied for twenty-first on the list of all-time major league home run hitters.

During the 1951 season, High Point–Thomasville led the North Carolina State League for the season with a 90W:36L record. That season the Hi-Toms were led by nineteen-year-old right-hand starter Tom Brewer. He pitched to an exceptional 19W:3L record for the season to lead the Hi-Toms to another NCSL title. Brewer went on to pitch eight seasons in the majors for the Boston Red Sox.

Prior to the 1952 season, both leagues contracted to just six teams, and during that year's off-season they combined to form a new D-class league known as the Tar Heel League. During its inaugural season, 1953, this new western North Carolina based league fielded ten teams. Nine of them were located in towns of either a former Western Carolina League or North Carolina State League ball club. They included Hickory, Lincolnton, Shelby, and Statesville from the Western Carolina League, and High Point–Thomasville, Lexington, Marion, Mooresville, and Salisbury from the North Carolina State League. But this new league was not long lived. For the start of the second season, the league contracted to just four teams, and it folded before the completion of the 1954 season.

Many of the towns that participated in the Tar Heel League remained without a baseball team for the rest of the 1950s, and a few of them, Lincolnton, Marion, and Mooresville, never fielded a team again. Then, in 1960 the Western Carolina League was revived with eight teams mostly located in towns associated with former Tar Heel League teams. They included the Hickory Rebels, Lexington Indians, Salisbury Braves, Shelby Colonels, and the Statesville Owls. The three new teams were the Gastonia Rippers, Newton–Conover Twins, and Rutherford County Owls.

During the 1961 season, the Salisbury Braves, which was a D-class minor league team of the Houston Colt .45s, led the new Western Carolina League during the regular season with a 64W:38L record. Figure 1–2 shows a photo of the players that made up the 1961 Braves roster. The team's first baseman, 19-year-old Aaron "Hawk" Pointer, had an outstanding season with the bat. He led the league for the season with a .402 batting average. This

SALISBURY BRAVES
WESTERN CAROLINA LEAGUE

First Row: Nicky Cosmidis.
Second Row, left to right: Leon Hartless, Lee Roy Hyman, Nick Sessoms, Dick Loughridge, Tommy Murray, Alex Cosmidis Guy Conti, Charlie Word.
Third Row, left to right: John Harms, Ray Armstrong, Bob "Beaver" Martin, Paul Roberts, Wilbert Bragg, Sammy Fountain Marv Dutt, Fred White, Aaron Pointer, Jim Zwergel, Richard Aird, Frank Glenn, Davey McKee.

Figure 1–2. Team photograph of the 1961 Salisbury Braves (courtesy North Carolina Baseball Museum).

batting average still stands as the record for the highest single regular season batting average of the South Atlantic League. Pointer also led the league for the season in a number of other offensive categories, including runs (R)—117, hits (H)—129, triples (3B)—14, stolen bases (SB)—42, total bases (TB)—197, on base percentage (OBP)—.530, slugging percentage (SLG)—.614, and on base percentage plus slugging (OPS)—1.144.

Pointer is the only member of that season's team that went on to play in the major leagues. He made his debut with the Houston Colt .45s on September 22, 1963, at the age of 21. Pointer's major league career was short. During the 1963, 1966, and 1967 seasons, he appeared in a total of just 40 games—all with the Colt .45s, and as a corner outfielder, not as their first baseman. For his accomplishments as a player with the 1961 Salisbury Braves, Pointer was inducted into the South Atlantic League Hall of Fame in 2006.

The renaissance of the Western Carolina League was also short-lived. Prior to its third season of operation, the league shrank and just four teams participated in games during 1962.

Western Carolinas League

The revival of the Western Carolina League turned out to be the gateway for a new and more successful league that eventually emerged as today's South Atlantic League. The next season—1963—the teams from Lexington, Salisbury, Shelby, and Statesville were joined by another North Carolina based team—the Gastonia Pirates—to form a new variant of the league—the Western Carolinas League.

The "s" added to Carolina signaled a big change. The new alignment included the first out-of-state teams—

Team	Location	Affiliation
Gastonia Pirates	Gastonia, NC	Pittsburgh Pirates
Greenville Braves	Greenville, SC	Milwaukee Braves
Lexington Giants	Lexington, NC	San Francisco Giants
Rock Hill Wrens	Rock Hill , SC	---
Salisbury Dodgers	Salisbury, NC	Los Angeles Dodgers
Shelby Colonels	Shelby, NC	New York Yankees
Spartanburg Phillies	Spartanburg, SC	Philadelphia Phillies
Statesville Owls	Statesville, NC	---

Table 1–3. 1963 Western Carolinas League teams and their affiliations (source: www.baseball-reference.com).

the Greenville Braves, Rock Hill Wrens, and Spartanburg Phillies—all residing in towns located in South Carolina. Rock Hill and Spartanburg were former baseball towns that did not have an active baseball team for many years. Table 1–3 lists each of the Western Carolinas League inaugural season teams, the city they played in, and their affiliate major league club. Note that the Rock Hill and Statesville teams were independent—not supported by any major league club. The league was designated to play at the single A (A) level of the major leagues' minor league system.

During the 1963 season, the Gastonia Pirates (Pittsburgh Pirates) led the league with 73 wins and 52 losses. A 19-year-old left-handed pitcher, Jim Shellenback, led the Gastonia pitching staff for the season with a 17W:3L record. His 17 wins tied him for the most wins in the Western Carolinas League, and his .850 winning percentage led the league for all pitchers with more than 10 W/L decisions. Shellenback made his major league pitching debut with the Pittsburgh Pirates in 1965 at the age of 22. He went on to pitch in parts of eight major league seasons for the Pirates, Washington Senators, Texas Rangers, and Minnesota Twins.

The Gastonia offense was led by right-hand-hitting first baseman Bob Oliver. Oliver led the team in hits with 141 and home runs with 13. Oliver played parts of eight seasons in the majors with five different clubs, including three seasons with both the Kansas City Royals and California Angels.

Two players that pitched in the Western Carolinas League during the

GP	GS	W	L	IP	H	R	ER
476	305	145	113	2231.1	2272	1069	949

SO	BB	ERA	WHIP	H/9	BB/9	SO/9	SO/BB
1141	847	3.83	1.354	9.2	3.0	4.6	1.52

Table 1-4. Jack Billingham's Major League career pitching stats.

1963 season went on to have longer than 10-year major league careers. Twenty-year-old Jack Billingham pitched for the Salisbury Dodgers and went 9W:6L for the season. The big right hander made his major league debut with the Los Angeles Dodgers on April 11, 1968. Billingham went 145W:113L over the next thirteen years. He had his best seasons with the Cincinnati Reds where he won 19 games in both 1973 and 1974. The pitching statistics in Table 1-4 summarize his solid major league career pitching stats.

GP	GS	W	L	IP	H	R	ER
445	277	103	125	2099	2188	979	882

SO	BB	ERA	WHIP	H/9	BB/9	SO/9	SO/BB
957	695	3.78	1.335	9.4	2.6	4.1	1.56

Table 1-5. Dave Roberts' Major League career pitching stats.

The other pitcher—18-year-old lefty Dave Roberts—went 9W:3L for the Spartanburg Phillies. His 1.79 earned run average (ERA) and .897 walks + hits per inning pitched (WHIP) were the lowest of any pitcher that had pitched more than 100 innings during the 1963 season. Roberts made his major league debut with the San Diego Padres on July 6, 1969. His most productive season was 1973 when he went 17W:11L as a starter for the Houston Astros. A summary of the pitching stats for his thirteen seasons in the major leagues is given in Table 1-5.

Over the next seventeen years, the new Western Carolinas League blossomed and thrived. Fans of the teams of the league got to see many baseball players that went on to have very successful careers at the major league level—Larry Bowa (1966 Spartanburg Phillies), Dusty Baker (1968 Greenwood Braves), Dwight Evans (1970 Greenville Red Sox), Dave Parker (1971 Monroe Pirates), Willie Randolph (1973 Charleston Pirates), Dale Murphy (1975

Greenwood Braves), and Dave Righetti (1977 Asheville Tourists), to name just a few. They even got to see a few players that were later elected to the Baseball Hall of Fame—Steve Carlton (1964 Rock Hill Cardinals), Nolan Ryan (1966 Greenville Mets), and Ryne Sandberg (1979 Spartanburg Phillies).

Northern Division		
Team	**Location**	**Affiliation**
Asheville Tourists	Asheville, NC	Texas Rangers
Gastonia Cardinals	Gastonia, NC	St. Louis Cardinals
Greensboro Hornets	Greensboro, NC	New York Yankees
Shelby Pirates	Shelby, NC	Pittsburgh Pirates
Southern Division		
Team	**Location**	**Affiliation**
Anderson Braves	Anderson, SC	Atlanta Braves
Charleston Royals	Charleston, SC	Kansas City Royals
Macon Peaches	Macon, GA	---
Spartanburg Phillies	Spartanburg, SC	Philadelphia Phillies

Table 1–6. 1980 South Atlantic League teams and their affiliations.

As the league evolved, it engaged with teams in some larger markets—Charleston, South Carolina, in 1974; Asheville, North Carolina, in 1976; and Greensboro, North Carolina, in 1979. This set the stage for the re-launch of the South Atlantic League.

The Launch of the Modern South Atlantic League

During the 1979 offseason, the Western Carolinas League changed its name to the South Atlantic League for the 1980 season—a league name that had remained unused for seventeen years. For the inaugural season, the league consisted of eight teams arranged in two divisions—the Northern and Southern divisions. Table 1–6 shows the teams in each division and their affiliate major league baseball club. With the addition of the Macon Peaches, the league now spanned three states—North Carolina, South Carolina, and Georgia. Note that the Spartanburg Phillies were the only original Western Carolinas League team that survived through all of the transitions that took place during the evolution to the modern South Atlantic League (SAL).

The division winners for the 1980 season were the Greensboro Hornets

G	AB	R	H	2B	3B	HR	RBI
133	494	92	177	32	5	9	105

TB	BB	SO	AVE	OBP	SLG	OPS
246	59	33	.358	.422	.498	.920

Table 1–7. Don Mattingly's 1980 batting stats with the Greensboro Hornets.

(82W:57L) and Charleston Royals (78W:61L). The Hornets beat the Royals in the final round of the postseason playoffs to become the 1980 South Atlantic League champions.

During the regular season, the Greensboro offense was led by New York Yankees great Don Mattingly. The outfielder–first baseman of the Hornets led the league for the season with a .358 batting average (AVE) and was also the league leader in both hits (H) with 177 and on-base percentage (OBP) .422. A summary of Mattingly's 1980 offensive stats is given in Table 1–7. Note that he also had 32 doubles (2B), 105 runs batted in (RBI), and an excellent .920 on-base plus slugging percentage (OPS). Mattingly was a September 1982 call-up of the New York Yankees and he made his major league debut on September 8 at the age of 21. He entered the game as a late innings defensive replacement in left field. In 1984, Mattingly took over as the Yankees' regular first baseman and he went on to have an excellent fourteen year major league career and retired as a New York Yankee after the 1995 season.

Right-handed starter Byron Ballard headed up the Greensboro starting rotation with a league leading 17W:6L record. He also led all pitchers in the league in complete games with 15. Ballard went on to play for seven seasons in the minor league organizations of the Yankees, Padres, and Mets, but never got promoted to the majors.

A few of the other 1980 season South Atlantic League batting leaders that went on to have 10 year plus major league careers are:

• Brook Jacoby (Anderson Braves): led the league with 108 RBI and in doubles with 40.

• Otis Nixon (Greensboro Hornets): led the league in three offensive categories—124 runs scored, 67 stolen bases, and 113 bases on balls.

• Marvell Wynne (Charleston Royals): led the league with 15 triples and 256 total bases.

The new name better articulated the plans of the SAL. The league spread southward to start the 1984 season by adding the Savannah Cardinals in Georgia. To begin the 1987 season the league expanded eastward with the Myrtle Beach Blue Jays in South Carolina and also northward with the Charleston Wheelers in West Virginia. The South Atlantic League had expanded to four states along the Atlantic Coast and was poised to move into others.

2

Today's South Atlantic League

Up to now I have focused on the early history of the South Atlantic League, how it evolved out of the Western Carolina League and North Carolina State League and then spread from teams tightly grouped in western North Carolina to a South Atlantic League which encompassed teams in four states. The South Atlantic League is also affectionately identified as the Sally League—a name that has been passed on from an earlier vintage of the SAL. Here I will look more closely at the organization and makeup of the league and its teams, some of the transitions that led to the South Atlantic League of today, the makeup of an A-level team roster, a few of the players

Northern Division		
Team	Location	Affiliation
Delmarva Shorebirds	Salisbury, MD	Baltimore Orioles
Greensboro Grasshoppers	Greensboro, NC	Miami Marlins
Hagerstown Suns	Hagerstown, MD	Washington Nationals
Hickory Crawdads	Hickory, NC	Texas Rangers
Kannapolis Intimidators	Kannapolis, NC	Chicago White Sox
Lakewood BlueClaws	Lakewood, NJ	Philadelphia Phillies
West Virginia Power	Charleston, WV	Pittsburgh Pirates
Southern Division		
Team	Location	Affiliation
Asheville Tourists	Asheville, NC	Colorado Rockies
Augusta GreenJackets	Augusta, GA	San Francisco Giants
Charleston RiverDogs	Charleston, SC	New York Yankees
Greenville Drive	Greenville, SC	Boston Red Sox
Lexington Legends	Lexington, KY	Kansas City Royals
Rome Braves	Rome, GA	Atlanta Braves
Savannah Sand Gnats	Savannah, GA	New York Mets

Table 2–1. South Atlantic League teams and their affiliations.

that have passed through the SAL on their way to successful major league careers, and a number of recent players that have stood out during their play in the league.

The Current SAL Towns and Teams

As shown in Table 2–1, the South Atlantic League is currently made up of fourteen teams arranged into two seven-team divisions, which are still known as the Northern Division and Southern Division. Note that teams have been added in Maryland, New Jersey, and Kentucky so that the league as presently constituted touches seven states. This lineup of teams has not changed since 2010.

Today's SAL spans a much larger area of the Atlantic Coast. The northernmost boundary of the league is set by the Lakewood BlueClaws, Lakewood, New Jersey, a Northern Division team and the Philadelphia Phillies A-level affiliate; the southernmost team is the Savannah Sand Gnats, Savannah, Georgia (Southern Division—New York Mets affiliate), and the westernmost team is the Lexington Legends, Lexington, Kentucky (Southern Division—Kansas City Royals). Now the distance between the southernmost team in Savannah, Georgia, and northernmost team in Lakewood, New Jersey, is approximately 790 miles and the new western boundary set by the Lexington Legends is close to 600 miles from the Atlantic Coast. But the highest concentration of teams—nine of them—still remains in North Carolina, South Carolina, and Georgia.

Over the years, teams from the various towns and cities often changed names, formed a new major league affiliation, relocated to a new city, or in some cases ceased to continue operating. In fact, the transition to a new major league affiliate often initiated the renaming of the team. Table 2–2(a) lists each of the current teams of the South Atlantic League, the year that they joined the league, and the duration of their tenure. The Asheville Tourists are an exception. Asheville, North Carolina, is the host city of the current SAL team—the Asheville Tourists—that has the longest continuous participation in the modern South Atlantic League. The Tourists joined the Western Carolinas League in 1976 and made the transition to the South Atlantic League in 1980. The 2014 baseball season marked the Tourists' thirty-fifth consecutive year as a member of the South Atlantic League and the thirty-eighth since it entered the Western Carolinas League. Yes! A team that did not change its name, relocate, or just disband.

Charleston, South Carolina, is the city that has the longest overall asso-

Team	First year	Total Years
Asheville Tourists	1976/1980	35/39
Hagerstown Suns	1993	22
Hickory Crawdads	1993	22
Augusta GreenJackets	1994	21
Charleston RiverDogs	1994	21
Delmarva Shorebirds	1996	19
Savannah Sand Gnats	1996	19
Kannapolis Intimidators	2001	14
Lakewood BlueClaws	2001	14
Lexington Legends	2001	14
Rome Braves	2003	12
Greensboro Grasshoppers	2005	10
West Virginia Power	2005	10
Greenville Drive	2006	9

Team	Affiliation	Years
Asheville Tourists	Colorado Rockies	21
Delmarva Shorebirds	Baltimore Orioles	18
Kannapolis Intimidators	Chicago White Sox	14
Lakewood BlueClaws	Philadelphia Phillies	14
Rome Braves	Atlanta Braves	12
Greensboro Grasshoppers/Bats	Miami Marlins	12
Augusta GreenJackets	San Francisco Giants	10
Charleston RiverDogs	New York Yankees	10
Greenville Drive/Bombers	Boston Red Sox	10
Hagerstown Suns	Washington Nationals	8
Savannah Sand Gnats	New York Mets	8
Hickory Crawdads	Texas Rangers	6
West Virginia Power	Pittsburgh Pirates	6
Lexington Legends	Kansas City Royals	2

Top: Table 2–2(a). Entry year of the current SAL teams and their consecutive years of tenure. *Above:* Table 2–2(b). Current major league affiliates.

ciation with the modern South Atlantic League. It entered the Western Carolinas League in 1973 as the host city of the Charleston Pirates. However, Charleston did not field a team for the 1979 season. Therefore, 2014 was Charleston's forty-first year as the home of a team that was a member of the

Western Carolinas League or South Atlantic League—but this has not been forty-one consecutive years.

The Charleston team has changed names many times over this series of years. They were known as the Charleston Pirates (1973–75, 1978), Charleston Patriots (1976–77), Charleston Royals (1980–84), Charleston Rainbows (1985–93), and finally since 1994 the Charleston RiverDogs. During these forty-one baseball seasons, the team has also been affiliated with a number of different major league clubs—Pittsburgh Pirates, Kansas City Royals, San Diego Padres, Texas Rangers, Tampa Bay Rays, and now the New York Yankees.

Table 2–2(a) shows that the moniker of the Charleston team has been the RiverDogs for the last twenty-one years. But during this period, the River-Dogs have been an affiliate of three different major league clubs: Texas Rangers (1994–96), Tampa Bay Devil Rays (1997–2004), and as identified in Table 2–2(b) the New York Yankees for the last ten baseball seasons.

Table 2–2(b) also shows that among the current SAL teams the Asheville Tourists have the longest ongoing association with their current major league baseball club. The Tourists have been the A-level affiliate of the Colorado Rockies since 1994—the last twenty-one years. However, right behind them is the Delmarva Shorebirds, who have represented the Baltimore Orioles for eighteen seasons.

On the other hand, the Greenville Drive—the Boston Red Sox A-level affiliate—is the newest member of the league. This team entered the SAL in 2005 as the Greenville Bombers and changed its name to the Drive in 2006. So as shown in Tables 2–2(a) and (b), 2014 was their ninth season using the name Greenville Drive and tenth representing the Red Sox in the South Atlantic League. The Drive replaced the Greenville Braves, who played as the Atlanta Braves AA affiliate in the Southern League for many years. It is interesting to note that Greenville, South Carolina, was the home of a team in many of the earlier leagues known as the South Atlantic League. In fact, the Greenville Spinners fielded a baseball team in the original South Atlantic League during twenty-three baseball seasons between 1919 and 1953.

The information in Tables 2–2(a) and (b) suggests that, unlike during its earlier years of operation, the makeup of the South Atlantic League has been very stable over the last decade. Through the 2014 season, thirteen of its fourteen teams have participated in the league for ten or more consecutive years and nine of them were affiliated with the same major league club for a decade or more.

Other Cities That Played Home to SAL Teams

Over the years, South Atlantic League baseball has touched many more people than those located in or near the cities associated with its current

North Carolina	
Gastonia	Gastonia Cardinals (1980-82), Gastonia Expos (1983-84), Gastonia Jets (1985), Gastonia Tigers (1986), Gastonia Rangers (1987-92)
Shelby	Shelby Pirates (1980), Sheby Mets (1981-82)
Fayetteville	Fayetteville Generals (1987-96), Cape Fear Crocs (1997-2000)
Wilmington	Wilmington Waves (2001)
South Carolina	
Anderson	Anderson Braves (1980-84),
Spartanburg	Spartanburg Phillies (1980-81), Spartanburg Traders (1982), Spartanburg Spinners (1983), Spartanburg Suns (1984-85), Spartanburg Phillies (1986-94)
Florence	Florence Blue Jays (1981-86)
Greenwood	Greenwood Pirates (1981-83)
Columbia	Columbia Mets (1983-92), Capital City Bombers (1993-2004)
Sumter	Sumter Braves (1985-90), Sumter Flyers (1991)
Myrtle Beach	Myrtle Beach Blue Jays (1987-1990), Myrtle Beach Hurricanes (1991-92)
Georgia	
Macon	Macon Peaches (1980-82), Macon Redbirds (1983), Macon Pirates (1984-87), Macon Braves (1991-2002)
Columbus	Columbus Indians (1991) Columbus Red Stixx (1992-2002), South Georgia Waves (2003), Columbus Catfish (2004-08)
Albany	Albany Polecats (1992-95), South Georgia Waves (2002)
Kentucky	
Bowling Green	Bowling Green Hot Rods (2009)
Ohio	
Eastlake	Lake County Captains (2003-09)

Table 2–3. Other cities that have hosted South Atlantic League franchises (source: www.baseball-reference.com).

fourteen ball clubs. Since 1980, another sixteen towns or cities have hosted SAL franchises. Table 2–3 lists these cities state by state and identifies each team and the years during which they played in the city. For instance, former SAL teams have been located in four other North Carolina cities—Gastonia, Shelby, Fayetteville, and Wilmington. Note that Gastonia played home to five different ball clubs over the thirteen-year period from 1980 to 1992: Gastonia Cardinals (1980–82), Gastonia Expos (1983–84), Gastonia Jets (1985), Gastonia Tigers (1986), and Gastonia Rangers (1987–92). From the names of these teams, it is clear that most of them were affiliated with a major league club. However, over the years a few SAL teams were independent and had no major league sponsorship. The Gastonia Jets are an example of a team that did not have an affiliation with a major league team.

Even more cities in South Carolina—a total of seven—were the home of former South Atlantic League teams. Table 2–3 shows that Spartanburg, South Carolina, fielded four different named teams over the fifteen baseball seasons from 1980 to 1994. However, the Spartanburg Phillies, Traders, Spinners, and Suns were all affiliates of the same team—the Philadelphia Phillies. In fact, Philadelphia's A-level team—the Spartanburg Phillies—was one of the original members of the Western Carolinas League and played in this predecessor to the SAL continuously from 1963 through 1979. Therefore, a Philadelphia single-A team played in this city for 32 consecutive seasons. However, prior to the start of the 1995 season, Philadelphia moved their A-level affiliate to Kannapolis, North Carolina, as the Piedmont Phillies. The next year they renamed the team the Piedmont Boll Weevils.

Table 2–3 lists three towns or cities of former South Atlantic League franchises in Georgia. Of them, Macon had the longest history of South Atlantic League teams. This city has a rich baseball past and was the home of an SAL team for twenty of the twenty-three seasons between 1980 and 2002. During the 1980 South Atlantic League inaugural season, the Macon Peaches were an independent team. However, for the 1981 and 1982 seasons they represented the Detroit Tigers. The Peaches were followed by the Macon Redbirds (St. Louis Cardinals) for just one season (1983) and the Macon Pirates (Pittsburgh Pirates) the next four seasons (1984–87). But then the Atlanta Braves came to town in 1991 and things stabilized. The Macon Braves team set up shop at historic Luther Williams Field for the next twelve seasons. After the 2002 season, the Braves moved their team to a new stadium at their current South Atlantic League single-A location, Rome, Georgia.

One more interesting fact can be observed from Table 2–3. This is that the South Atlantic League had expanded to an eighth state—Ohio—for a period during the 2000s. From 2003 to 2009 the Cleveland Indians had their single-A affiliate—the Lake County Captains—located in Eastlake, Ohio, as a member of the Northern Division of the SAL. That minor league franchise is still located there, but after the 2009 season the Indians engaged the team with the Midwest League.

The Makeup of a South Atlantic League Roster

Figure 2–1 illustrates the current classifications of teams in the Minor League System of Major League Baseball. New players typically enter at a lower level—rookie (Rk), single A- (A-), or single A (A)—where they work on refining their offensive, defensive, or pitching skills. Over a number of seasons they work their way up through the higher levels, single A+ (A+), double A (AA), and triple A (AAA), with the hope of eventually being promoted to the major leagues. Players at the AAA level may be viewed as being major league ready and poised to be called up to the majors. But that still depends upon whether or not their parent major league club has an open position to fill.

Since its inception as the Western Carolinas League, the South Atlantic League has participated at the single-A (A) level of the Minor League Baseball (MiLB) pyramid. Figure 2–1 shows that A level is one of the lower level classifications of a major league baseball team's minor league system.

The rosters of South Atlantic League teams are typically formed with players that are participating in their first or second season of professional baseball. That is, either high school or college prospects that were signed in the current or prior years' First-Year Player Draft. This draft, which is also referred to as the Rule 4 Draft or June Amateur Draft, is the process used by the teams of Major League Baseball to select prospects

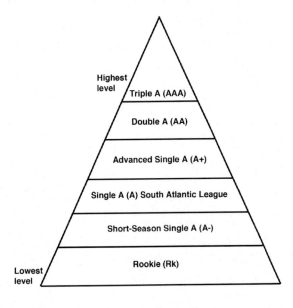

Figure 2–1. Pyramid of levels in the MiLB system.

from the United States and Canada. To be eligible to participate in the draft, a prospect must be:

- A graduate of high school who has not yet attended a college
- A 4-year college student who has completed his junior or senior year of school or reached 21 years of age
- A junior college student independent of the number of years of school he has attended or his age

Once a player is selected, he must be signed by the team that chose him prior to 5 PM (EDT) on July 12 of the current year. A player that is selected by a ball club but chooses to not sign a contract with that major league team is able to participate in the next year's draft as long as he still satisfies the earlier outlined eligibility criteria.

Many of the prospects signed through this draft, start their professional baseball careers at the rookie (Rk) or short season single-A (A-) level. However, some enter directly at the single-A (A) level. For instance, college players, who are more experienced and typically advance more quickly through the various levels of the minor league system, often play their first season of professional ball with a team of an A-level league, such as the South Atlantic League.

Most prospects play at least three years in the minors before gaining the experience and skill needed to be called up to play in the majors. Occasionally, a player makes his major league debut earlier—after two or fewer seasons of professional ball. But it is more common that prospects spend more than three seasons in the minors before getting the call and a majority of them never make it to the big leagues at all.

SAL Players Who Went On to Successful Major League Careers

Over the years many players that later became very successful made a stop with a team of the South Atlantic League on their way to the major leagues. Here is a sampling of some of those baseball players:

1985 Season:

- Roberto Alomar played second base for the Charleston Rainbows (San Diego Padres) and Sandy Alomar was the Rainbows catcher for the entire season.
- Ron Gant played second base for the Sumter Braves (Atlanta Braves) and Tom Glavine was in the Sumter starting rotation.

• John Smiley was assigned to the Macon Pirates (Pittsburgh Pirates) mid-season and pitched in their starting rotation until the end of the season.

1990 Season:

• Ryan Klesko played the first half of the season as the Sumter Braves (Atlanta Braves) first baseman and batted .368, and Vinny Castilla was the shortstop for the Sumter Braves before being promoted late in the season.

• Sterling Hitchcock was a starter with the Greensboro Hornets (New York Yankees) for the full season.

• Tim Worrell was a member of the Charleston Rainbows' (San Diego Padres) starting rotation.

1995 Season:

• Vladimir Guerrero played the full season for the Albany Polecats (Montreal Expos) and led the SAL with a .333 batting average.

• Todd Helton played his first season of professional baseball as the first baseman of the Asheville Tourists (Colorado Rockies).

• Andruw Jones patrolled the outfield for the Macon Braves (Atlanta Braves), and Kevin Millwood pitched as both a starter and reliever at Macon.

2000 Season:

• Josh Hamilton and Carl Crawford played the full season in the outfield of the Charleston RiverDogs (Tampa Bay Rays).

• Brett Meyers pitched as a starter for the Piedmont Boll Weevils (Philadelphia Phillies).

• Erik Bedard was in the starting rotation of the Delmarva Shorebirds (Baltimore Orioles).

2005 Season:

• Ryan Braun was promoted to the West Virginia Power (Milwaukee Brewers) where he played third base and batted .355 in 37 games.

• Ben Zobrist played shortstop during the first half of the season for the Lexington Legends (Houston Astros), and Hunter Pence played the outfield for the Legends.

• Phillip Hughes pitched in the starting rotation of the Charleston River-Dogs (New York Yankees) until he was promoted late in the season.

2010 Season:

• J. D. Martinez played right field for the Lexington Legends (Houston Astros) and hit .362 in 88 games before being promoted.

• José Altuve played second base for the Lexington Legends (Houston Astros) and batted .308 until he was promoted late in the season.

• Robbie Ross was a starter for the Hickory Crawdads (Texas Rangers) until being promoted after mid-season.

Earlier I mentioned that Ron Gant and Tom Glavine were teammates on the 1985 Sumter Braves. This team not only had Gant and Glavine, but also Jeff Blauser as shortstop and Mark Lempke at second base. Gant, Glavine, and Blauser were called up to the Atlanta Braves in 1987 and Lempke in 1988. This quartet of players went on to be part of the early core of an Atlanta Braves team that won the Eastern Division of the National League in eight of the ten seasons during the 1990s. Between them they played at the major league level in the Braves uniform in forty-five seasons, with Tom Glavine accounting for seventeen of them.

The Sumter Braves must have been a shoo-in to win the 1985 South Atlantic League Championship. Not the case! The Braves lost to the Greensboro Hornets in the first round of the playoffs. Interestingly, the 1985 Hornets roster had only one player, right-handed pitcher Jim Corsi, who went on to have a ten year career in the majors.

Recent Major League Players Who Led the South Atlantic League in a Batting or Pitching Stat

A number of current major league players led the South Atlantic League in either batting or pitching statistics for the season. A listing of some of the recent players who had a league leading batting or pitching statistic follows. The major league club identified with the player is the one for which he currently plays, not the affiliate of the minor league team during the season in which he played in the South Atlantic League.

2011 Season:

• Corey Dickerson (Colorado Rockies–Asheville Tourists) led the league in home runs (32), slugging percentage (.629), and on base plus slugging percentage (.986).
• Marcell Ozuna (Miami Marlins–Greensboro Grasshoppers) led the league with 87 runs scored.

2010 Season:

• J. D. Martinez (Detroit Tigers–Lexington Legends) led the league with a .362 batting average, .433 on-base percentage, and .598 slugging percentage.

• Robbie Erlin (San Diego Padres–Hickory Crawdads) led all regular starters in the league with lowest earned run average (2.12) and walks plus hits per innings pitched (0.924).

2009 Season:

• Matt Moore (Tampa Bay Rays–Bowling Green Hot Rods) led all pitchers in the league with 176 strikeouts.
• Derek Norris (Oakland Athletics–Hagerstown Suns) led the league with 90 bases on balls and a .413 on-base percentage.

2008 Season:

• Giancarlo Stanton (Miami Marlins–Greensboro Grasshoppers) led the league in home runs (39), slugging percentage (.611), and total bases (286).
• Madison Bumgarner (San Francisco Giants–Augusta GreenJackets) led the league in wins with 15 and strikeouts with 164.

2007 Season:

• David Robertson (New York Yankees–Charleston RiverDogs) led all full time relievers in the league with a 0.77 earned run average and 0.851 walks plus hits per inning pitched.

2006 Season:

• Lorenzo Cain (Kansas City Royals–West Virginia Power) led the league with 162 hits.
• Eric Young (New York Mets–Asheville Tourists) led the league with 87 stolen bases.

2005 Season:

• Carlos Gomez (Milwaukee Brewers–Hagerstown Suns) led the league in stolen bases with 64.
• Matt Harrison (Texas Rangers–Rome Braves) led all regular starters in the league with lowest walks plus hits per inning pitched (1.084).

Recent No-Hitters Thrown by Pitchers of the Current SAL Clubs

The dream of every pitcher is to someday pitch a no-hitter. In fact, throwing a no-no during the early part of one's professional carrier can punch the pitcher's ticket for the major leagues. Well, maybe not really! But it will sure raise the focus of the parent club on the player and elevate his rank among the team's up and coming prospects.

What is a no-no? The major league definition of a no-hitter is that the pitcher or pitchers of one team must pitch 9 complete innings and not give up a hit. Runners could get on base other ways, such as a walk, error, hit by pitch, etc., and even the opposing team could score a run or runs. It is the norm at the major league level that if a pitcher is throwing a no-hitter the manager would not take him out of the game until either the game is complete or the no-hitter is broken up by someone getting a hit. Things like a pitcher's limiting pitch count or saving the pitcher's arm for his next start typically go out the window. So we usually think of a single pitcher throwing a no-hitter.

Most seasons there are one or more no-hitters thrown by pitchers of teams in the South Atlantic League. Just like in the majors, these games garner

Starter	Reliever(s)	Team	Date	Opponent	Final Score	Inn.
Sergio Romo	Osiris Matos, David Quinowski	Augusta	8/10/06	Rome	5-0	9
Carlos Carrasco	Andrew Barb	Lakewood	8/13/06	Lexington Legends	2-1	9
Daniel Bard	Ryan Phillips	Greenville	6/11/2007	Kannapolis Intimidators	5-0	7
Bruce Billings	None	Asheville	7/23/2008	Lakewood	10-0	9
Martin Perez	Tyler Tufts, Fabio Castillo	Hickory	4/11/2009	Bowling Green	5-0	7
Hunter Strickland	Diego Moreno	West Virginia	7/27/2009	Charleston	4-0	9
Matt Wickswat	Jake Petricka, Taylor Thompson	Kannapolis	8/20/2010	Hickory	1-0	7
Jose Fernandez	Greg Nappo, Kevin Cravey	Greensboro	4/24/2012	Hickory	6-0	9
Mickey Pena	Hunter Cervenka, Tyler Lockwood	Greenville	5/8/2012	Rome	1-0	9
Chris Devenski	None	Lexington	9/1/12	Rome	10-0	9
Luis Parra	Keone Kela, Ryan Bores, Alex Claudio	Hickory	5/19/2013	Delmarva	1-0	7
Braulio Ortiz	Adam Lopez, Joseph Dvorsky	Kannapolis	6/5/2013	Hagerstown	11-0	7
Daniel Stumpf	None	Lexington	7/2/2013	Greenville	1-0	7
Jeb Stefan	Ramon Oviedo, Chris Burgess	Lakewood	7/12/2013	Rome	1-0	9

Table 2–4. List of recently pitched no-hitters in the South Atlantic League.

a lot of attention and extra exposure in the media. It is as exciting for a fan to see a no-hitter thrown by an up and coming pitching prospect in the minor leagues as one in the major leagues.

Table 2–4 lists the no-hitters thrown by pitchers from the current South Atlantic League teams since 2006. Included are the name of the pitcher(s), the name of their team and the opposing team, date of the game, the final score, and number of innings of the game. Reviewing this data we find a few interesting insights about minor league no-hitters. First, the starting pitcher went all the way in just three of the fourteen games. In the other eleven games, a reliever and in many cases relievers finished up the game. In the minor leagues, pitch count is more consistently enforced and the pitch counts are even lower for A-level pitchers. For example, in the no-hitter started by Luis Parra of the Hickory Crawdads on May 19, 2013, versus the Delmarva Shorebirds at Arthur W. Perdue Stadium in Salisbury, Maryland, three relievers were used to complete the game. In that game, Para's pitch count was limited to just 35 pitches. He was removed after 3 innings of play. Since the one batter he walked was thrown out stealing, Parra faced the minimum of 9 batters. But, since Parra did not pitch five full innings, reliever Ryan Bores got the win.

In some of these games, even though the pitcher was throwing a no-hitter they were removed early because they were having control issues and that elevated their pitch count. An example is the game pitched by Carlos Carrasco of the Lakewood BlueClaws on July 27, 2009, against the Lexington Legends at FirstEnergy Park in Lakewood, New Jersey. Carrasco did go 7 innings, but he walked 5 batters and hit another. In fact, in the top of the first inning, he walked two batters, hit a batter to load the bases, and then issued another walk to force in a run. The BlueClaws won the no-hitter by a score of 2–1.

Another observation is that six of the fourteen games went seven innings instead of the regulation nine. In the major leagues a game in which a pitcher has not given up a hit that is shortened to fewer than 9 innings due to rain or some other event is not recognized as a no-hitter. But in the minor leagues, each game of a doubleheader is seven innings, not nine. For this reason, a seven inning game can be a complete game. This was the case for most of these shorter games. However, the no-hitter pitched by Daniel Bard for the Greenville Drive at Fieldcrest Cannon Stadium in Kannapolis, North Carolina, on June 11, 2007, is an exception. Bard went five full innings—did not give up a hit, but walked 6 while striking out 5. He was replaced by reliever Ryan Phillips to start the sixth. But the rains came and the game was called after Greenville batted in the top of the seventh inning. The Drive won the rain shortened game 5–0. Even though the losing team, the Kannapolis Intimidators, had not batted to complete the seventh, Bard and Phillips were awarded a no-hitter.

Finally, none of these no-hitters was a perfect game—that is, a nine inning game in which the pitcher or pitchers faced the minimum of 27 batters and none of them reached base. However, the no-no pitched by starter Sergio Romo and relievers Osiris Matos and David Quinowski at State Mutual Stadium in Rome, Georgia on August 10, 2006, was the closest to being perfect of these fourteen games.

After retiring the first two batters in the top of the first, Romo hit the Rome Braves' number three batter, catcher Cody Clark, with a pitch. But then he went on to retire the next seventeen batters in a row to complete seven innings. Romo was replaced by relievers Matos and Quinowski, who both pitched a perfect inning to close out the 5–0 victory for the Augusta Green-Jackets. The one base runner on the HBP is all that separated this no-hitter from a perfect game.

Six of these starting pitchers—Romo, Carrasco, Bard, Billings, Perez, and Fernandez—have played in games at the major league level. Romo, Carrasco, and Bard have played in the majors during multiple seasons and appeared in a larger number of games than the other three pitchers. Sergio Romo, who debuted with the San Francisco Giants on June 26, 2008, settled in as their closer during the second half of the 2012 season. He saved 38 games for the Giants in 2013. During the 2014 season, he pitched as both San Francisco's closer and as a set man.

Carlos Carrasco has pitched both as a starter and reliever for the Cleveland Indians. During the 2011 season, he started 21 games and went 8W:9L. However, he missed all of the 2012 season due to having Tommy John surgery. Carrasco split the 2013 season between the Cleveland Indians and their AAA minor league affiliate the Columbus Clippers, but he was back full time with the Tribe in 2014.

Of the remaining pitchers, Jose Fernandez and Martin Perez have more recently established themselves in starting roles for the Miami Marlins and Texas Rangers, respectively. Two thousand thirteen was the breakout year for both pitchers. Fernandez made his major league debut on April 7, 2013, and in his first major league season moved to the top of the Marlins starting rotation. Fernandez (12W:6L) led the team's pitching staff in wins (12), games started (28), innings pitched (172.2), ERA (2.19), SO (187), and WHIP (0.98) for the season. After getting off to a good start in 2014, Fernandez experienced elbow problems that resulted in his undergoing season ending Tommy John surgery.

Perez made his first major league appearance with the Rangers on June 27, 2012. He came on strong for the Rangers in the second half of the 2013 regular season and finished with a 10W:5L record in 19 starts. However, after going 4W:3L in April and May of 2014, he too underwent Tommy John surgery and was out for the balance of the season.

3

Profiles of the South Atlantic League Teams

Asheville Tourists

McCormick Field
30 Buchanan Pl., Asheville, NC 28801
www.milb.com/index.jsp?sid=t573

Professional baseball has been played in Asheville, North Carolina, since 1897. In fact, the town has served as the home for a baseball team in all but 25 of the 118 seasons since then. Table 3–1 ASH shows that over this period the town was formally represented by five different teams. The Asheville Moonshiners were the first team to call the town home. The Moonshiners first played in Asheville in 1897 as a member of the Southeastern League, but the league folded at the end of that season.

Professional baseball did not return to Asheville until 1910 when the Southeastern League was revived and the city once again fielded a team called the Moonshiners. Unlike many leagues of the day, the teams of the Southeastern League were distributed over a large regional area. The league had six teams that were located in four states—Tennessee, North Carolina, Georgia, and Alabama—with three of them residing in Tennessee. The distance between the southernmost team, the Gadsden Steel Makers in Alabama, and the northernmost team, the Johnson City Soldiers in Tennessee, was about 300 miles. The Moonshiners were located toward the northern boundary of the league's footprint, close to the teams in Tennessee and just 60 miles from Johnson City.

Prior to the 1911 season, the Asheville Moonshiners joined the three Southeastern League teams from Tennessee and relocated to a newly formed league—the Appalachian League. During the league's inaugural season, it fielded four teams in western Tennessee, one in southwestern Virginia, and the Moonshiners in Asheville, North Carolina. This alignment consolidated

Team Name	1st Year	Years	Leagues
Asheville Moonshiners	1897	2	Southeastern League
Asheville Moonshiners	1911	2	Appalachian League
Asheville Mountaineers	1913	2	North Carolina State League
Asheville Tourists	1915	3	North Carolina State League
Asheville Tourists	1924	7	South Atlantic League
Asheville Tourists	1931	11	Piedmont League
Asheville Tourists	1946	10	Tri-State League
Asheville Blues	1946	3	Independent Negro League
Asheville Tourists	1959	5	South Atlantic League
Asheville Tourists	1964	3	Southern League
Asheville Tourists	1967	1	Carolina League
Asheville Tourists	1968	3	Southern League
Asheville Tourists	1971	1	Dixie Association
Asheville Orioles	1972	4	Southern League
Asheville Tourists	1976	4	Western Carolinas League
Asheville Tourists	1980	35	South Atlantic League

Table 3–1 ASH. Teams that have played in Asheville, NC (source: www.baseball-reference.com).

the teams into a much smaller area. Three of the teams—the Bristol Boosters (Virginia), Johnson City Soldiers, and Knoxville Appalachians—were located within a 100 mile radius of Asheville. The Moonshiners remained a member of the Appalachian League and played a second season in Asheville during 1912.

For the 1913 and 1914 seasons an Asheville Moonshiners team joined the North Carolina State League. This league, which was also playing its inaugural season, consisted of six teams that were all located in North Carolina. Asheville set the westernmost boundary of the league. The remaining teams were located in cities to the east: Winston-Salem, Greensboro, Charlotte, Durham, and Raleigh. Raleigh, which was the easternmost team, was less than 250 miles away. The teams of this league played at the class-D level of minor league baseball. That transition marked the end of the first and a very short era of professional baseball in Asheville.

The next era of baseball in Asheville is all about the Asheville Tourists. Table 3–1 ASH shows that the first local team with the nickname Tourists played ball in the city during the 1915 season as a member of the North Carolina State League. At that point, Asheville, which is located in the mountains of North Carolina, had already become a very popular tourism destination. That is the origin of Tourists as the long-running moniker of the Asheville baseball club.

Since 1915, the city of Asheville has hosted a team known as the Tourists in eighty-two of the one hundred baseball seasons. However, Table 3–1 ASH shows that during that span of years the Tourists traveled from league to league. In fact, they were members of ten different leagues and played their games in the original South Atlantic League during two different periods. A number of these transitions between leagues were initiated by the failure of the league. For instance, the North Carolina State League folded after the 1917 season. This event ushered in another period during which professional baseball was not played in the city of Asheville for a number of years.

The Tourists and professional baseball did not return to Asheville until 1924. But, in preparation for the team's return, the city had built a new baseball stadium—McCormick Field. For that season, a new Asheville Tourists team engaged with an ongoing league—the original South Atlantic League. At that moment, the Sally League, which played its games at the B level, was in its twentieth consecutive season of play. That season the league's alignment also included teams in Charlotte, North Carolina; Greenville and Spartanburg, South Carolina; and Augusta and Macon, Georgia. All of these cities eventually hosted teams associated with the modern South Atlantic League.

But the Sally league disbanded after the 1930 season. This event set in motion a series of engagements between the Asheville Tourists and a number of different leagues over the next forty-one years. As shown in Table 3–1 ASH the Tourists moved to a new home, the Piedmont League (B level), for the start of the 1931 season.

From the mid–1930s through today, there has been a strong connection between the teams that played in Asheville and teams of Major League Baseball. For example, from 1935 through 1942 the Tourists were the B-level affiliate of the St. Louis Cardinals in the Piedmont League. For this reason, some of the changes of league participation in the coming years were driven by the major league club. This was not the case with the Cards. During the World War II years, many of the major league teams reduced their participation with lower level minor league clubs. The Cardinals dropped most of their teams, including the Asheville Tourists.

Baseball was not played in the city from 1942 through 1945, but in 1946 an Asheville Tourists baseball club was back in business as a member of the Tri-State League. Nineteen forty-six was the first season of a revival of this league, which had existed for a short period in the early 1900s. Now the Tourists were the B-level member of the Brooklyn Dodgers' minor league organization. During those years, baseball fans in Asheville got to see a number of players who eventually went on to play for the Dodgers at Ebbets Field in Brooklyn, New York, or the Los Angeles Memorial Coliseum in Los Angeles,

California: pitcher Clem Labine (1947), first baseman Norm Larker (1951), and catcher Joe Pignatano (1953). The new Tri-State League folded after the 1955 season; the connection between the Dodgers and the Tourists was broken, and professional baseball was not played in the city for a few years.

The Asheville Tourists returned to a revival of the South Atlantic League (now A level) for the start of the 1959 season. During this five season stint, the Tourists were first an A-level minor league club of the Philadelphia Phillies and then starting in 1961 the Pittsburgh Pirates. Pittsburgh Pirates great Willie Stargell played in the Tourists' outfield for the 1961 season. He went on to debut with the Pirates on September 16, 1962. Stargell appeared as a pinch-hitter in that game and struck out. However, a few days later he was Pittsburgh's starting right fielder, batted cleanup, and got his first hit at the major league level—an RBI triple.

Stargell went on to star as a left fielder and first baseman in Pittsburgh. During his career, he played 21 seasons in the Pirates uniform, took the field in over 2100 games, and hit 475 home runs. Today Stargell remains the Pittsburgh Pirates' all-time home run leader. In fact, he is also the Pirates' all-time leader in runs batted in and bases on balls. Willy Stargell was elected to the Baseball Hall of Fame in 1988.

The South Atlantic League was elevated to the AA level by Major League Baseball in 1963 but folded after that season. The Asheville Tourists remained an affiliate of the Pittsburgh Pirates in 1964, but the team was relocated to the Southern League (AA). After the 1966 season, the Pirates moved their double A affiliate to Macon, Georgia, as the Macon Peaches.

The vacancy left behind by the Pirates' departure was filled immediately by the Houston Astros, who relocated one of their single-A teams to the city as the Tourists and a member of the Carolina League. However, that team stayed for just the 1967 season. The new vacancy was filled in time for the 1968 season. The Cincinnati Reds moved their double-A team in the Southern League from Knoxville, Tennesse, to Asheville. Sparky Anderson was at the helm of the Tourists for the Cincinnati Reds during the 1968 and 1969 seasons before moving on to manage their major league club in 1970.

During the 1969 season, Anderson had future Cincinnati Reds star Dave Concepcion fielding the shortstop position for him in Asheville. On Opening Day of the 1970 season Sparky Anderson penciled Concepcion into the Cincinnati Reds starting lineup as his shortstop and number seven batter. That was Concepcion's major league debut. Over the next nine seasons, Anderson managed the Big Red Machine to two World Series championships with Concepcion as his starting shortstop.

Concepcion played his complete nineteen season major league career in the Reds uniform. He appeared in close to 2500 games for Cincinnati and

2178 of them at shortstop. Concepcion played his last game at Riverfront Stadium in Cincinnati on September 15, 1988, at the age of 40. He represented the Reds on the National League All-Star team nine times.

The Tourists remained Cincinnati's AA affiliate in the Southern League through the 1970 season. The Chicago White Sox relocated their Dixie Association AA team to Asheville as the Tourists for the 1971 season but then moved it to Knoxville in the Southern League for the 1972 season.

Prior to the 1972 season, the Baltimore Orioles moved their AA affiliate in the Dixie Association—the Dallas–Fort Worth Spurs—to Asheville. The arrival of the Orioles brought about a big change. A long-standing tradition was broken—the team was renamed the Asheville Orioles. The 1972 season was the first time in twenty-six years that a team with a nickname other than the Tourists took the field in the city of Asheville. During the next three seasons, the Orioles were managed by Cal Ripken, Sr., and those teams featured future Baltimore Orioles players, such as center fielder Al Bumbry (1972), third baseman Doug DeCinces (1972), and left-handed starter Mike Flanagan (1974).

But the Orioles played in Asheville for only four seasons. Their departure after the 1975 season marked the end of a second era of professional baseball in Asheville—the pre-modern South Atlantic League era. But, at the same time it set the stage for the return of the Asheville Tourists and their entry into the modern South Atlantic League.

During the 1975 season, the Texas Rangers had two A-level minor league affiliates—the Lynchburg Rangers in the Carolina League and Anderson Rangers in the Western Carolinas League. Prior to the 1976 season, they consolidated their single A teams by eliminating the Lynchburg team and relocating their Western Carolinas League team to Asheville as the Asheville Tourists. At that point, the Western Carolinas League was in its eleventh season of operation. During the 1979 offseason, the league changed its name to the South Atlantic League. The journey of the Asheville Tourists to the modern Sally League was complete. The 2014 season was the thirty-fifth consecutive baseball season that the Asheville Tourists have been a member of the modern South Atlantic League and thirty-ninth season since they entered the Western Carolinas League.

The Home of the Tourists—McCormick Field

Since 1924, Asheville teams have played their home games at McCormick Field. The stadium, which is shown in Fig. 3–1 ASH, is named to honor a prominent resident of Asheville and well-known biologist, Dr. Lewis McCormick. Even though it is considered a downtown stadium, the field is built into the

Figure 3–1 ASH. McCormick Field, Asheville, NC.

side of a hill and the diamond opens to a tree-lined mountain setting over the outfield fence. The ballpark offers a pleasant, relaxing environment to enjoy a baseball game. During 1946, 1947, and 1949, both the Asheville Tourists and Asheville Blues, a member of the Independent Negro League, shared the local stadium—McCormick Field—to play their home games.

Historic McCormick Field is the oldest of the current SAL stadiums. The field dates back to 1924. Since 1924, a team called the Asheville Tourists, but playing in various different leagues, has played its home games at this stadium during seventy-nine of the ninety-one baseball seasons.

McCormick Field was renovated in 1959 and then the grandstand was extensively renovated and modernized in the early 1990s. Today its seating capacity is 4000 fans. Right field has a very high wall—almost as tall as the Green Monster at Fenway Park in Boston. Seating is very close to the field for a good view, but there is high netting down the foul lines to the end of the infield diamond to protect fans from hard hit foul balls.

The stadium's grandstand seating area rings the infield from approximately the infield edge of the left field outfield grass to the starting point of the right field grass. A walkway divides the field level box seats from the general admission seating that rises up from the far side of the walkway. Box seats are the traditional individual style plastic seats found at most baseball stadiums, while the upper general admission sections are outfitted with plastic bench seats with a backrest. There is also a concrete bleacher area toward the far end of the general admission seating area on both the first base and third base sides of the diamond. A roof that is aligned with the infield grass part of the field covers the upper general admission seats. Sitting in this area offers protection from the sun or rain.

Concessions are housed on a concourse located on the entry side of the ballpark. For this reason, the game cannot be viewed while getting refreshments or visiting the team store. There is a large party pavilion in the left field corner and a group picnic area in the right field corner. Arrive early for the game. Parking is very limited in the stadium lots. One hour before game time is my recommendation.

In the movie *Bull Durham*, the character Crash Davis was a catcher who had played a short stint in the major leagues—21 days. He was continuing his minor league career playing for the Durham Bulls baseball club with the goal of breaking the current minor league career home run record, which was stated as 246. Towards the end of the movie, Crash, playing in an Asheville Tourists uniform and batting lefty, crushes a pitch over the left field wall at McCormick Field to break the minor league career home run mark. In the movie, he retires after hitting his record setting homer. The real home run record for minor leaguers who played their full career with teams located in the United States is actually 432. Russell "Buzz" Arlett, who played 19 seasons of minor league ball, holds that record. Arlett played 1 season in the majors—1931—for the Philadelphia Phillies and homered 18 times. He retired from baseball after the 1936 season.

An interesting novelty of McCormick Field is that it has a modern scoreboard, but the scoreboard does not permit the actual names of the individual teams to be displayed with lights. Instead, Tourists is permanently displayed on the scoreboard with large white letters in the position for the home team and the visiting team identified as Visitor. Therefore, at McCormick Field the Tourists are always playing the Visitors.

The South Atlantic League Years

The Asheville Tourists have played in today's South Atlantic League since 1976—4 seasons in the Western Carolinas League (1976–79) and 35 in

Name	Name	MLB Affiliate	Years
South Atlantic League	Asheville Tourists	Colorado Rockies	1994-today
South Atlantic League	Asheville Tourists	Houston Astros	1982-93
South Atlantic League	Asheville Tourists	Texas Rangers	1980-81
Western Carolinas League	Asheville Tourists	Texas Rangers	1976-79

Level	Team	Stadium	League
Rk	Grand Junction Rockies	Sam Suplizio Field Grand Junction, CO	Pioneer League
A-	Boise Hawks	Memorial Stadium Boise, ID	Northwest League
A	Asheville Tourists	McCormick Field Asheville, NC	South Atlantic League
A+	Modesto Nuts	John Thurman Field Modesto, CA	California League
AA	New Britain Rock Cats	New Britain Stadium New Britain, CT	Eastern League
AAA	Albuquerque Isotopes	Isotopes Park Albuquerque, NM	Pacific Coast League

Top: Table 3–2(a) ASH. Asheville Tourists SAL major league affiliations. *Above:* Table 3–2(b) ASH. Colorado Rockies minor league organization.

the SAL (1980–2014). The Asheville team has been called the Tourists every year since it joined the Western Carolinas League. As shown in Table 3–2(a) ASH, the Tourists have been the A-level affiliate of the Colorado Rockies since 1994. Prior to that they were a member of the Houston Astros (1982–93) and Texas Rangers (1976–81) minor league organizations. Table 3–2(b) ASH lists the Rockies' other minor league teams.

During their inaugural 1976 season the Tourists, under manager Wayne Terwilliger—major league second baseman from 1949 to 1960—won first place for the regular season with a 76W:62L record. However, they lost the Western Carolinas League Championship Series to the second place team, the Greenwood Braves. The Tourists were a member of the Northern Division of the Sally League from 1980 to 1995, Central Division from 1996 to 1999, and Southern Division from 2000 to the present. They also made playoff appearances during the 1984, 1986, 1987, 1996, 2001, 2008, 2009, and 2012 seasons.

The Tourists won the Northern Division title in 1984, 1986, and 1987, Central Division title in 1996, and Southern Division title in 2001 and 2012. However, they went on to win the South Atlantic League Championship in only two of those seasons—1984 and 2012.

In the first round of the 1984 playoffs, Asheville faced the Greensboro Hornets (New York Yankees), who led the Northern Division for the season with a 75W:69L record. The Tourists beat the Hornets to win the Northern Division title and advance to play the Southern Division champion Charleston Royals (Kansas City Royals) in the League Championship Series. Asheville beat the Royals in the best-of-five championship series 3 games to 2 to take home the team's first South Atlantic League title.

During the 1984 season, the Tourists' offense was led by power hitting first baseman Jim O'Dell. A summary of O'Dell's 1984 batting stats is given in Table 3–3 ASH. O'Dell led all regular players on the team in runs scored (76), doubles (21), home runs (19), runs batted in (78), total bases (190), and slugging percentage (.422). These stats ranked him in the top 10 in the South Atlantic League for the season in HR, RBI, TB, SLG, and OPS. The Asheville starting rotation was headed by right hander Anthony Kelley. Kelley won a team high 14 games and led all starters on the pitching staff with a .258 ERA and 1.237 WHIP. His stats ranked in the top 5 among all qualifying pitchers in the league in wins, earned run average, and walks plus hits per innings pitched. In fact, his 121 strikeouts, which ranked him second on the team in that pitching statistic, tied him for the third highest total in the league for the season. Neither O'Dell nor Kelley advanced to the majors during their professional baseball careers.

In 2012 manager Joe Mikulik led the Tourists to a first half season 47W:23L record that was the best in the division and an 88W:52L overall season record that was the best in the league. During the regular season, the Tourists' offense was powered by all-star first baseman Harold Riggins. Riggins led all regular players on the team in five batting stat categories: 19 HR,

G	AB	R	H	2B	3B	HR	RBI
136	450	76	110	21	1	19	78

TB	BB	SO	AVE	OBP	SLG	OPS
190	70	45	.244	.343	.422	.766

Table 3–3 ASH. Jim O'Dell 1984 batting stats.

76 RBI, .302 AVE, .546 SLG, and .934 OPS. He ranked in the top 10 among all players in the league in home runs, runs batted in, slugging percentage, and on-base plus slugging percentage. While Riggins supplied the power, shortstop Trevor Story drove the offense. He led the team in almost every other batting category—96 R, 132 H, 43 2B, 6 3B, 60 BB, and 241 TB. His 43 double ranked number 1 in the South Atlantic League for the season. The Tourists pitching rotation was led by left hander Tyler Anderson and righty Ben Alsup. Anderson was 12W:3L in 20 starts and had the lowest ERA (.247) and WHIP (1.08) among the team's regular starters. Alsup chipped in 14 wins in 24 starts while losing just 5 games.

During the 2012 postseason, Asheville beat the Rome Braves 2–1 in a best-of-three Southern Division playoff series and then took on the Northern Division winner—the Greensboro Grasshoppers—in the championship round. After dropping the first game, the Tourists went on to take the series 3 games to 1 and win their second South Atlantic League Championship title. Tyler Anderson went 2W:0L in the postseason. Over two games, Anderson pitched 13 innings and gave up just 1 run and 4 hits in each game. He did not walk a batter and struck out 12. The offense was spread up and down the lineup. However, Taylor Featherston, who led the team with a .393 on-base percentage during the regular season, stood out. He batted .333 with 2 home runs and drove in a team leading 9 runs. Leadoff batter Trevor Story hit .310 and led the team in runs scored with 7. Finally, right fielder Jared Simon had 11 hits and batted a team high .407. He scored 5 runs and knocked in 5.

At the end of the 2012 season, Joe Mikulik was the longest tenured manager of the Asheville Tourists—thirteen seasons from 2000 to 2012. He led all other former managers of the team with 938 wins. Mikulik received the South Atlantic League's 2012 Manager of the Year Award. After the season, he moved on to be an advisor for the Colorado Rockies. Alsup, Anderson, Riggins, Featherston, and Simon were all promoted to Colorado's A+ affiliate, the Modesto Nuts, for the 2013 season.

Successful Major Leaguers Who Played in Asheville

The Asheville Tourists' history is rich with former roster members who went on to be successful baseball players with a major league club. Table 3–4 ASH lists many of the players who played their A-level ball on McCormick Field during the modern South Atlantic League years and went on to have a successful career in the big leagues as defined by the following criteria:

• Players prior to 2000 must have appeared in major league games during at least 10 seasons.

• Players from 2000 through 2009 must have appeared in major league games during at least 10 seasons or each of the five seasons from 2010 through 2014 and still be active.

• A plus sign in the Seasons in MLB column means the player is still active and accumulating more years.

Looking at the table you see that most of these players joined the team for either their 1st or 2nd season of professional baseball. Players that were drafted directly after high school were typically 18 through 20 years old. For example, the table shows that Dave Righetti, who was drafted out of Pioneer High School, San Jose, California, by the Texas Rangers, joined the Tourists at 18 years of age. He played his first season of professional ball—1977—as a member of their starting rotation.

Those that played for a college were drafted at a little older age—typically 20, 21, or 22. For instance, Paul Mirabella was drafted at the age of 22 after playing baseball at Montclair State University in Montclair, New Jersey. He pitched one season for Asheville before being promoted to the Rangers' AA affiliate—at that point the Tulsa Drillers in the Texas League.

Season	Player	Age at ASH	MiLB Season	Position	MLB Debut	Age at Debut	MLB Team	Seasons in MLB
1976	Danny Darwin	20	1	RHP	9/8/78	22	TEX	21
	Paul Mirabella	22	1	LHP	7/28/78	24	TEX	13
1977	Dave Righetti	18	1	LHP	9/16/79	20	NYY	16
1978	Wayne Tolleson	22	1	SS	9/1/81	25	TEX	10
1979	Gene Nelson	18	2	RHP	5/4/81	20	NYY	13
1980	Pete O'Brien	22	2	1B	9/3/82	24	TEX	12
	Tony Fossas	22	2	LHP	5/15/88	30	TEX	12
	Tom Henke	22	1	RHP	9/10/82	24	TEX	14
	Dave Schmidt	23	2	RHP	5/1/81	24	TEX	12
	Walt Terrell	22	2	RHP	9/18/82	24	NYM	11
1981	Curt Wilkerson	20	2	SS	9/10/83	22	TEX	11
	Dwayne Henry	19	2	RHP	9/7/84	22	TEX	11
1982	x							
1983	x							
1984	x							
1985	x							
1986	x							
1987	Craig Biggio	21	1	2B	6/26/88	22	HOU	20
	Trent Hubbard	22	2	LF	7/7/94	30	COL	10

Above and opposite: Table 3–4 ASH. Asheville SAL players that went on to have long major league careers.

Season	Player	Age at ASH	MiLB Season	Position	MLB Debut	Age at Debut	MLB Team	Seasons in MLB
1988	Luis Gonzalez	20	1	LF	9/4/90	23	HOU	19
1989	Kenny Lofton	22	2	CF	9/14/91	24	HOU	17
	Shane Reynolds	21	1	RHP	7/20/92	24	HOU	13
1990	Brian Hunter	19	2	CF	6/27/94	23	HOU	10
1991	x							
1992	Bobby Abreu	18	2	RF	9/1/96	22	HOU	17
	Raúl Chávez	19	3	C	8/30/96	23	MON	11
	Hector Carrasco	22	5	RHP	4/4/94	24	CIN	12
1993	Melvin Mora	21	2	3B	5/30/99	27	NYM	13
1994	John Thomson	20	2	RHP	5/11/97	23	COL	10
	Jamey Wright	19	2	RHP	7/3/96	21	COL	18
1995	Todd Helton	21	1	1B	8/2/97	23	COL	17
1996	x							
1997	Jake Westbrook	19	2	RHP	6/17/00	22	NYY	13
1998	x							
1999	Matt Holliday	19	2	LF	4/16/04	24	COL	11+
	Juan Pierre	21	2	CF	8/7/00	22	COL	14
	Juan Uribe	19	2	SS	4/8/01	21	COL	14+
	Aaron Cook	20	3	RHP	8/10/02	23	COL	11
2000	Clint Barmes	21	1	SS	9/5/03	24	COL	12+
2001	x							
2002	Jayson Nix	19	2	3B	4/1/08	25	COL	7+
	Jeff Francis	21	1	RHP	8/25/04	23	COL	10+
2003	Jeff Baker	22	1	2B	4/4/05	23	COL	10+
	Ubaldo Jimenez	19	2	RHP	9/26/06	22	COL	9+
2004	Chris Iannetta	21	1	C	8/27/06	23	COL	9+
2005	Franklin Morales	19	2	LHP	8/18/07	21	COL	8+
	Pedro Strop	21	1	RHP	8/28/09	24	TEX	6+
	Chris Nelson	19	2	3B	6/19/10	24	COL	5+
2006	Dexter Fowler	20	2	CF	9/2/08	22	COL	7+
	Eric Young Jr.	21	3	LF	8/25/09	24	COL	6+
2007	Michael McKenry	22	2	C	9/8/10	25	COL	5+
	Esmil Rogers	21	2	RHP	9/12/09	24	COL	6+
2008	Everth Cabrera	21	3	SS	4/8/09	22	SDP	6+
	Jhoulys Chacin	20	3	RHP	7/25/09	21	COL	6+
2009	x							

Many players played a season of ball for a short-season rookie or A-level team prior to joining Asheville. That is why they joined the team for their second season in the minors. Gene Nelson did that. After being signed by Texas, he played the 1978 season at the rookie level for the Rangers in the Gulf Coast League. Nelson was promoted to the Tourists and played his second season in Asheville.

The table also includes the date that each player made his debut in a major league game. It typically takes a player two to five years to progress through their team's minor league system to the AAA level and then be called up to play his first game with the parent major league club. Again looking at Paul Mirabella in Table 3–4 ASH, you see that he played his first major league game for the Texas Rangers on July 28, 1978—a little more than two years after joining the Asheville team. Sometimes injuries extend this process.

Many players get the call to the majors, but few succeed and stay for many years. In the selection of players for the list in Table 3–4 ASH, I used 10 seasons at the major league level as the metric for anyone who played for the Asheville Tourists prior to 2000. For those that played on the team during the seasons of 2000 through 2009, I changed the metric so that the player needed to either have played 10 seasons in the major leagues or during the 2014 season and each of the prior 4 consecutive years. That is, he had to appear in games during each season of the five-year period from 2010 through 2014.

Players after 2009 were not considered, because they could not have yet played in games at the major league level for 5 consecutive seasons. The chart of Table 3–4 ASH includes all of the players that were drafted by the Rangers, Astros, or Rockies between 1976 and 2009 that made it to the big leagues and eventually satisfied these criteria.

The number in the right-most column in Table 3–4 ASH identifies the total number of seasons in which a player appeared in a major league game. Note that it shows that Paul Mirabella played in the majors during part or all of 13 seasons and Dave Righetti pitched in the majors during 16 seasons. If the number in this column includes a + sign to its right, that means that the player is still currently on the roster of a major league club and should accrue more seasons.

Most of the players listed in Table 3–4 ASH went on to make their major league debut with the then parent club of the Asheville Tourists. However, there are some exceptions. An example is Dave Righetti. Even though Righetti was drafted by the Texas Rangers, he was traded along with Paul Mirabella to the New York Yankees in a deal during the 1978 offseason for the Yankees closer Sparky Lyle. This is why it shows that Righetti made his pitching debut for the New York Yankees in September 1979 instead of with Texas.

Another interesting deviation from the norms that I have just outlined is Tony Fossas. He was signed by the Texas Rangers in June 1979 after playing baseball at the University of South Florida in Tampa. Fossas pitched the 1979 season at the rookie level for the Rangers affiliate in the Gulf Coast League and then advanced to the Asheville Tourists to begin the 1980 season. During that season, the 22-year-old Fossas was a key member of the Tourists' starting rotation and pitched an all-time team record of 197 innings. For many years, two hundred innings has been thought of as the goal for a very successful major league starting pitcher. Today a pitcher at the lower level of the minors, such as single A, often does not pitch much more than the 112 innings needed to qualify as a league leader.

Fossas lingered around in the minors for nine full seasons working on his craft before being called up to the majors in May 1988. Fossas pitched in his first major league game for the Rangers on May 15, 1988, at the age of 30. While in the minors Fossas had worked at perfecting his skill as both a starter and reliever.

After the 1988 season, Texas granted him free agency and he signed with the Milwaukee Brewers for the 1989 season. Fossas went on to become an excellent reliever and lefty specialist; he pitched in the majors until he was 41 years old and appeared in 567 games for seven different ball clubs. The most interesting fact is that he appeared as a reliever in all 567 games. Fossas never started a major league game.

Craig Biggio is another exception to the norm. He was drafted after playing baseball for Seton Hall University in South Orange, New Jersey, and signed with the Houston Astros on June 8, 1987, at the age of 21. Biggio played the 1987 season with the Tourists and batted .375 while appearing in just 64 games. He was promoted directly to the AAA level to start the 1988 season and as shown in Table 3–4 ASH made his major league debut with the Astros on June 26, 1988—less than one year and one month after being signed by Houston. After the 1988 season, Biggio never returned to the minors for another game. The second baseman and catcher went on to play 2850 games in the Astros uniform before retiring at the age of 41—and as we know he contributed 3060 hits for the Houston offense.

Juan Pierre, who played left field for the Tourists during the 1999 season, holds the Tourists' all-time single season hits record. That season he led both the Tourists and the South Atlantic League with 187 hits. This was a sign of things to come for Pierre. He made his major league debut in the Colorado Rockies uniform the next season. On August 7, 2000, at Coors Field he replaced Todd Helton in the bottom of the ninth inning as a pinch runner—the first game in what proved to be a fourteen season major league career.

He quickly settled in as Colorado's center fielder and leadoff batter. Pierre led all players in the National League in hits during the 2004 and 2006 seasons with 221 and 204 hits, respectively. Moreover, he ranked first in the National League in stolen bases during three seasons: 2001 (46), 2003 (65), and 2010

(68). Over the next thirteen seasons, Pierre played for seven major league clubs. He compiled 2217 hits, stole 614 bases, and had a .295 lifetime batting average.

Table 3–4 ASH lists 41 players who played their A-level ball for the Asheville Tourists between 1976 and 2009, who were called up by Texas, Houston, Colorado or another major league club, and then went on to have an extended career in the big leagues. Check them out to see which ones you remember.

A few members of the current Colorado Rockies roster played their A-level ball in recent years for the Asheville Tourists. For example, two of their key pitchers, closer Rex Brothers and starter Juan Nicasio, were both members of the Tourists' pitching staff during the 2009 season. Brothers evolved to become a key member of the Rockies' relief corps over the last few seasons. He made over 70 pitching appearances in both 2012 and 2013. Brothers took over as Colorado's primary closer about midway through the 2013 season and compiled 19 saves by the end of the year. To start the 2014 season he was back in the bullpen pitching in a late innings setup role. During the last four seasons, Nicasio moved up to become a member of Colorado's starting rotation. In 2013 he went 9W:9L in 31 starts. But during the 2014 season, he pitched both as a starter and reliever for the Rockies.

Another former Asheville Tourists player, Nolan Arenado, took over as the Rockies' regular third baseman during the 2013 season. Arenado, who prior to the 2013 season was ranked by Major League Baseball as the number 62 top prospect in all of Minor League Baseball, played for the Asheville Tourists during the 2010 season. Even though he played only 92 games for the Tourists in that season, he led the team with 41 doubles and ranked number 2 on the team in the other power related batting stats: home runs, runs batted in, and slugging percentage. Arenado made his major league debut with the Rockies on April 28, 2013, and went on to play third base in 130 games during his rookie season. He received the Gold Glove award for National League third baseman for his play in the field during both the 2013 and 2014 seasons.

Attractions in or Near Asheville

- **Downtown Asheville Shops and Restaurants**, 1 North Pack Square, Asheville, NC 28801
- **Grove Arcade**, 1 Page Ave., Asheville, NC 28801 (828) 252–7799

- **Historic Biltmore Village,** 7 Kitchen Pl., Asheville, NC 28803
- **Gray Line Asheville Historic Hop On Hop Off Trolley Tour,** 36 Montford Ave., Asheville, NC 28801 (828) 251–8687
- **Thomas Wolfe Memorial State Historic Site,** 52 N. Market St., Asheville, NC 28801 (828) 253–8304
- **Biltmore Estate and Antler Hill Village & Winery,** 1 Lodge St., Asheville, NC 28803 (800) 411–3812
- **Blue Ridge Parkway Scenic Ride,** 199 Hemphill Knob Rd., Asheville, NC 28803 (828) 271–4779

Dining in Asheville

BREWPUBS AND BREWERIES

- **Asheville Pizza and Brewing Company,** 77 Coxe Ave., Asheville, NC 28801 (828) 255–4077
- **Oyster House Brewing Company,** 625 Haywood Rd., Asheville, NC 28806 (828) 575–9370
- **Lexington Avenue Brewery (LAB),** 39 N. Lexington Ave., Asheville, NC 28801 (828) 252–0212

DOWNTOWN RESTAURANTS

- **The Bier Garden,** 46 Haywood St., Asheville, NC 28801 (828) 285–0002
- **The Southern Kitchen and Bar,** 41 N. Lexington Ave., Asheville, NC 28801 (828) 251–1777
- **Early Girl Eatery,** 8 Wall St., Asheville, NC 28801 (828) 259–9292
- **Luella's Bar-B-Que,** 501 Merrimon Ave., Asheville, NC 28804 (828) 505–7427
- **The Lobster Trap,** 35 Patton Ave., Asheville, NC 28801 (828) 350–0505
- **Carmel's Kitchen and Bar,** 1 Page Ave., Asheville, NC 28801 (828) 252–8730
- **Cafe 64,** 64 Haywood St., Asheville, NC 28801 828–252-8333
- **Double D's Coffee & Desserts (Coffee & Desserts only),** 41 Biltmore Ave., Asheville, NC 28801 (828) 505–2439
- **Kilwin's Ice Cream, Fudge, and Chocolates,** 26 Battery Park Ave., Asheville, NC 28801 (828) 252–2639

Augusta GreenJackets

Lake Olmstead Stadium
78 Milledge Rd., Augusta, GA 30904
www.milb.com/index.jsp?sid=t478

A number of the cities of the current South Atlantic League teams hosted professional baseball in the late 1800s. But Augusta, Georgia, and neighboring city Savannah were both hometowns of a baseball team in 1884. This is the earliest recorded date of baseball being played in any of the current fourteen SAL cities. In fact during the 1884 season Augusta fielded two teams—the Augusta Browns and Augusta Clinches—in the Georgia State League. This league had just six teams, all located in the state of Georgia.

As shown in Table 3–1 AUG, the early days of baseball in Augusta were quite turbulent. The city hosted a number of different named teams that played in several different leagues, but for just one season at a time. When the Georgia State League did not operate in 1885, the Augusta Clinches disbanded, while the Augusta Browns joined the Southern League—a multi-

Team Name	1st Year	Years	Leagues
Augusta Browns	1884	1	Georgia State League
Augusta Clinches	1884	1	Georgia State League
Augusta Browns	1885	1	Southern League
Augusta Browns	1886	1	Southern Association
Augusta	1886	1	Georgia State League
Augusta Electricians	1893	1	Southern Association
Augusta	1898	1	Southern League
Augusta Tourist	1904	12	South Atlantic League
Augusta Dollies	1919	1	South Atlantic League
Augusta Georgians	1920	2	South Atlantic League
Augusta Tygers	1922	8	South Atlantic League
Augusta Wolves	1930	1	South Atlantic League
Augusta Wolves	1931	1	Palmetto League
Augusta Tigers	1936	14	South Atlantic League
Augusta Rams	1953	2	South Atlantic League
Augusta Tigers	1955	4	South Atlantic League
Augusta Yankees	1962	2	South Atlantic League
Augusta Pirates	1988	6	South Atlantic League
Augusta GreenJackets	1994	21	South Atlantic League

Table 3–1 AUG. Teams that have played in Augusta, GA (source: www.baseball-reference.com).

state league with teams in Georgia, Tennessee, and Alabama—for its inaugural season. But the Southern League did not operate for the 1886 season and the Browns were again forced to find a new league in which to play. They joined a number of teams from other towns of the Southern League and engaged with another new baseball league—the Southern Association—for its inaugural season. At the same time, the Georgia State League was reformed for the 1986 season and the city of Augusta again fielded a second team that played in that league for just one season.

In the 1890s baseball was played in the city during only two seasons— the Augusta Electricians were a member of the Southern Association in 1893 and another Augusta team played in the Southern League in 1898. The 19th century closed without a baseball team playing in the city.

Professional baseball returned to Augusta early in the 20th century. In 1904, the South Atlantic League was formed as a C-class minor league and the city hosted a team called the Augusta Tourists in that league. This league, the original South Atlantic League, had baseball clubs located in Georgia, South Carolina, and Florida. Baseball was back, and this time it took hold.

Baseball great Ty Cobb played for the Augusta Tourists during the 1904 and 1905 seasons and led the club during 1905 with 134 hits and a .326 batting average. Cobb's contract was purchased by the Detroit Tigers of the American League on August 24, 1905, and he made his major league debut on August 30 of that year at the age of 18. Cobb went on to play 22 seasons in the Tigers uniform. Over his 24-year major league career, Cobb compiled 4,189 hits and had a lifetime batting average of .366. He was elected to the Baseball Hall of Fame in 1936.

The Tourists played in Augusta as a member of the South Atlantic League during twelve of the next fifteen seasons. This was the beginning of a long term engagement between the original South Atlantic League and the city of Augusta. Between 1904 and 1963 eight different named Augusta teams—the Tourists, Dollies, Georgians, Tygers, Wolves, Tigers, Rams, and Yankees— played in the league during 46 of the 59 seasons. But the Sally League did not operate during nine of the 13 seasons in which there was no team in Augusta. Therefore, the city was home to a team in 46 of the 50 seasons that the South Atlantic League did operate.

Note in Table 3–1 AUG that during the Sally era of baseball in Augusta there was just one short break with the league. For the 1931 season the Augusta Wolves played in the Palmetto League, but that was one of the years that the South Atlantic League did not operate.

Over those years, the teams of the original South Atlantic League were affiliated with Major League Baseball and played at a number of different levels of its minor league organization—A, B, C, and even AA for just 1 season. However, after the 1963 baseball season, the South Atlantic League disbanded and professional baseball ceased to be played again in Augusta for over two decades.

During the 1987 offseason, the Pittsburgh Pirates, who had their single A affiliate, the Macon Pirates, in the modern South Atlantic League, relocated that team to Augusta for the 1988 season as the Augusta Pirates. This was the first participation in the modern South Atlantic League by a team located in the city of Augusta. While still an affiliate of the Pittsburgh Pirates in 1994, the team was renamed the Augusta GreenJackets. This moniker was chosen to honor the green jacket that is given to the winner of The Masters golf tournament that is held at the nearby Augusta National Golf Club. Two thousand and fourteen was the twenty-first consecutive season that the Augusta Green-Jackets have played their games in the city.

The Home of the GreenJackets—Lake Olmstead Stadium

The GreenJackets' ballpark—Lake Olmstead Stadium—is not a downtown ball field. Instead, it is located a short distance outside the city center on land that was originally part of an attractive treed park—Lake Olmstead Park.

Lake Olmstead Stadium, which is shown in Fig. 3–1 AUG, is quite a nice venue for attending and viewing a baseball game. Most seating is in the grandstand area that ranges from around third base to first base. There is a walkway that separates the field level box seats behind home plate and the rows of seats that extend down the first and third base lines from the reserved grandstand seating. The rows of grandstand seats, where I sat, rise up from the walkway toward the outside wall of the stadium. These seats are benches similar to those of a bleacher, but with a back rest. All of the seats that range up from the walkway are protected from sun and inclement weather by the grandstand roof. Also there are large fans under the roof to circulate air on those hot southern days or evenings. Looking out across the field of play from a seat in the grandstand area behind home plate you see a dark green treed backdrop over the outfield walls.

The main concourse with the concessions is located behind the grandstand and runs down the third base side to a kids' play area known as the Fun Zone, which is toward the left field corner. On the first base side the concourse ends at a picnic and party deck near the right field corner. One

Figure 3–1 AUG. Lake Olmstead Stadium, Augusta, GA.

unique amenity of the ballpark is a walk-through misting area for cooling off on those hot summer days.

The entrance side of the stadium's grandstand is quite attractive. The lower section has brick facing. One section of the lower brick wall is dedicated as the Wall of Champions and has a plaque in the shape of a home plate to commemorate each of the team's league or division championship seasons. The upper level of the outside grandstand wall, which starts above the top row of the grandstand seats, is open to the air. However, it is lined with a protective ornate green iron framework. Parts of this upper area of the grandstand are decorated with large banners honoring Augusta's South Atlantic League teams of the past, such as the Augusta Yankees, and a number of those teams' players that went on to become stars in the majors. Some of the players recognized are Dustin Pedroia, Jon Lester, Brian Wilson, and Hanley Ramirez.

The team's mascot, Auggie, appears to be an oversized, very yellow bee. Could Auggie be a yellow jacket that wears a green jacket? But then again if Auggie is a yellow jacket he is really a wasp, not a bee. Right or wrong he is locally identified as a bee. Auggie attended his first GreenJackets home game on Opening Day 2006 and has been entertaining fans ever since.

Also, one can just walk across the street from the stadium, enter Lake Olmstead Park at any point, and walk just a short distance to the edge of the lake. There is a paved trail along the waterfront that can be used for a relaxing stroll. Also, the park has a disc golf course. Arrive early, bring a Frisbee, and play a round before the game. This park is a nice added attraction to the stadium. Since the game I planned to attend had been rained out even though the rain had stopped, I spent some enjoyable time walking through the park.

Plans are in the works for a new downtown riverfront stadium on the banks of the Savannah River. A lawsuit is seriously threatening those plans, however.

The South Atlantic League Years

Since joining the modern South Atlantic League in 1988 the city of Augusta has hosted teams of three different major league clubs. Table 3–2(a) AUG shows that they are the Pittsburgh Pirates, Boston Red Sox, and San Francisco Giants. Two thousand and fourteen was the Giants' tenth season as the major league affiliate of the Augusta GreenJackets. Over this twenty-six year period, an Augusta based team made eleven postseason appearances and won the South Atlantic League championship four times.

When the Pittsburgh Pirates relocated their Macon Pirates team to the city for the 1988 season, they named the team the Augusta Pirates. In their second season in the city, the Pirates' 77W:67L record put them at the top of the Southern Division. They went on to beat the Gastonia Rangers (Texas Rangers) to win the 1989 South Atlantic League title.

That season Augusta was not stocked with future big name players. The team's offense was quite diversified, but was powered by first baseman Keith

Name	MLB Affiliate	Years
Augusta GreenJackets	San Francisco Giants	2005-today
Augusta GreenJackets	Boston Red Sox	1999-2004
Augusta GreenJackets	Pittsburgh Pirates	1994-1998
Augusta Pirates	Pittsburgh Pirates	1988-1993

Above: Table 3–2(a) AUG. Augusta SAL teams' major league affiliations. *Opposite:* Table 3–2(b) AUG. San Francisco Giants minor league organization.

Level	Team	Stadium	League
Rk	AZL Giants	Scottsdale Stadium Scottsdale, AZ	Arizona League
A-	Salem-Keizer Volcanoes	Volcanoes Stadium Keizer, OR	Northwest League
A	Augusta GreenJackets	Lake Olmstead Stadium Augusta, GA	South Atlantic League
A+	San Jose Giants	San Jose Municipal Stadium San Jose, CA	California League
AA	Richmond Flying Squirrels	The Diamond Richmond, VA	Eastern League
AAA	Sacramento River Cats	Raley Field Sacramento, CA	Pacific Coast League

Raisanen. He led all regular players on the team in home runs with 15, runs batted in with 92, total bases with 183, slugging percentage with .419, and on-base plus slugging percentage with .786. Raisanen's HR total ranked him tied for sixth among all players in the South Atlantic League and he ranked fourth in the league in RBI. Outfielder Greg Sims gave the Pirates on-base percentage and speed on the base paths. He stole a team leading 46 bases and also led the team with 91 walks and a .418 on-base percentage. Sims ranked fifth in the league in SB, third in BB, and fourth in OBP.

Right-handed starter Pete Blohm led the team with a 13W:4L record. His 2.32 earned run average and 1.165 walks plus hits per inning pitched led the team. Blohm's 13 wins ranked him fifth among all starters in the league for the season and both his ERA and WHIP ranked him in the top ten. Out of the bullpen, Jeff Neely was the team's top reliever and closer. He made 54 relief appearances and had 19 saves. Neely's 19 saves ranked him tied for sixth in the league in that pitching stat for the season. Interestingly, none of these four team leaders ever advanced to play at the major league level.

During the Pittsburgh eleven season reign the Augusta team, which was renamed the GreenJackets for the 1994 season, went to the postseason two more times. The GreenJackets moved into their new ballpark, Lake Olmstead Stadium, for Opening Day of the 1995 season and proceeded to win the city's second SAL championship that year. They posted a 76W:62L record, which was the second best in the Southern Division. In the first round of the playoffs, Augusta beat the Columbus Red Stixx (Cleveland Indians) to win the Southern Division title and move on to face the Northern Division champion Piedmont Phillies (Philadelphia Phillies) in the best-of-five League Championship Series.

This season's team was a little like the 1989 team in that it had no big name players. However, a number of the team leaders, including outfielder Adrian Brown, catcher Wiki Gonzalez, and right-handed pitcher Kane Davis, went on to play at the major league level in five or more seasons. The Green-Jackets beat the Phillies 3 games to 2 to take home the league championship.

Augusta remained the host city of the Pittsburgh Pirates' A-level minor league club through the 1998 season. After that season, Pittsburgh moved their single A team to another South Atlantic League city—Hickory, North Carolina. The Boston Red Sox had positioned themselves to fill the void in Augusta. They relocated their A-level team—the Michigan Battle Cats of the Midwest League—to Augusta and the South Atlantic League for the 1999 season.

During the 1999 season, the South Atlantic League was organized into three divisions—the Northern, Central, and Southern. The postseason playoff was a tournament between the teams with the top eight regular season records. Augusta posted a 69W:70L regular season record, which ranked them eighth among all teams in the league and gained them a playoff berth. Infielder Angel Santos led the GreenJackets' offense in almost every batting statistic category. He ranked number 1 among regular players on the team in ten specific stats: R (83), 2B (30), HR (15), SB (25-tied), BB (62), AVE (.270), OBP (.360), SLG (.440), OPS (.800), and TB (205). However, Santos ranked in the top 10 in the South Atlantic League for the season in just doubles and in that stat he ranked tenth.

Left hander Greg Miller led the starting rotation with a team high 10 wins. Another pitcher, right hander Jason Norton, who pitched in 30 games, 17 as a starter, led all frequent starters in both ERA (2.32) and WHIP (0.985). He also struck out a team high 150 batters, but this was just 4 more than Miller who had 146 Ks. Both Norton and Miller ranked in the top 10 in the South Atlantic League in strikeouts for the season. Mark Cisar was the Green-Jackets' closer and he saved 27 games. This tied him for first in the league for saves by a closer during the 1999 season.

Starting from the bottom, the GreenJackets worked their way through the rungs of the ladder of the round robin tournament and met the Cape Fear Crocs (Montreal Expos) in the 1999 Sally League Championship Series. Augusta took the series 2 games to 1 to win their third South Atlantic League title.

Boston remained in Augusta for five seasons, but with plans in place for a new stadium in Greenville, South Carolina, the Red Sox relocated their A-level team there for the 2005 season. This opened the door for the San Francisco Giants to move their current South Atlantic League team from

Hagerstown to Augusta for the 2005 season. Two thousand and fourteen was the tenth season that the Augusta GreenJackets were the Giants' single A affiliate. A lists of the other teams in the San Francisco Giants' minor league organization is given in Table 3–2(b) AUG.

Since becoming the single A affiliate of the Giants, the GreenJackets have also won the South Atlantic League title. This took place in the 2008 season. Augusta won the 2nd half of the regular season with a 47W:22L record to gain a spot in the postseason. During the regular season, second baseman Nick Noonan and first baseman–designated hitter Thomas Neal supplied Augusta's offensive punch. Noonan led the regular players on the GreenJackets in five offensive categories: runs scored (79), hits (139), triples (7-tied), batting average (.279), and total bases (207). His 7 triples tied him for third in that offensive stat among all players in the South Atlantic League. Noonan made his major league debut with the Giants as a pinch hitter on April 3, 2013. He went on to play in 62 games as a utility infielder for San Francisco during that season.

Neal was the team leader in on-base percentage (.359), but also ranked number 1 in three power related batting stats: RBI (81), SLG (.444), and OPS (.803). Neal made his major league debut with the Cleveland Indians on September 2, 2012, at the age of 25 and played in a limited number of games for the New York Yankees and Chicago Cubs during the 2013 season.

The pitching staff was led by left-handed starter Madison Bumgarner. A summary of his pitching stats for the season is given in Table 3–3 AUG. Note that Bumgarner went 15W:3L in 24 starts for the GreenJackets. His 15 wins led the GreenJackets for the season and also tied him for the most wins in the South Atlantic League. He also led all pitchers in the league for the season in ERA (1.46), SO (164), and WHIP (0.932). Bumgarner pitched with great command and control as shown by his walking just 21 batters. In fact, his 1.46 ERA set the GreenJackets' all-time single season record for lowest ERA. Bumgarner still holds the team's ERA record today.

GP	GS	W	L	IP	H	R	ER
24	24	15	3	141.2	111	28	23

SO	BB	ERA	WHIP	H/9	BB/9	SO/9
164	21	1.46	0.932	7.1	1.3	10.4

Table 3–3 AUG. Madison Bumgarner 2008 pitching stats summary.

Bumgarner played a key role in Augusta's postseason run for the city's fourth South Atlantic League championship. In the first round of the playoffs Augusta faced the Asheville Tourists (Colorado Rockies) in the best-of-three Southern Division Championship Series. The GreenJackets swept the Tourists 2 games to 0 to win the Southern Division title. Next, Augusta faced the Northern Division winner West Virginia Power (Milwaukee Brewers) in the South Atlantic League Championship Series. Again they swept their opponent and won the series 3 games to 0 to take home the team's fourth South Atlantic League title. Nick Noonan led the GreenJackets' offense during the postseason. He batted .333 with 6 hits in 18 trips to the plate. Noonan also knocked in a team high 5 runs. Bumgarner went 2W:0L in two postseason starts. He pitched 14 innings between the two games and did not give up a run for a .000 postseason ERA. Bumgarner struck out 16 while walking just 2 batters. Another lefty hurler, Scott Barnes, also went 2–0 during Augusta's playoff run.

Successful Major Leaguers Who Played in Augusta

As in all of the other cities of the current South Atlantic League, fans of the local team have had the opportunity to see many players who became very successful major league ballplayers and in some cases even famous stars. Table 3–4 AUG shows that during the Pittsburgh Pirates years (1988–1998) a number of young players who tuned their batting, fielding, or pitching skills as a member of either the Augusta Pirates or Augusta GreenJackets went on to have a 10 or more year career at the major league level. For example, the followers of the Augusta Pirates got to see a 21-year-old Moises Alou, 22-year-old Tim Wakefield, and 22-year-old Tony Womack play during the developmental parts of their professional baseball careers. Each of these players went on to play many years at the major league level.

As explained earlier, my criterion for a long, successful career is that players who made their major league debuts prior to 2000 must have appeared in games at the major league level during at least ten seasons, and those that made their debut in 2000 or later must have played in major league games either during 10 seasons or each of the last five seasons, 2010–2014.

The Pittsburgh Pirates signed Tim Wakefield out of college in June 1988 and he played his second season of professional ball with the Augusta Pirates. Wakefield made his major league debut approximately four years later at Three Rivers Stadium on July 31, 1992, against the St. Louis Cardinals. Wakefield went the distance for the first win of his major league career. He limited

Season	Player	Age at AUG	MiLB Season	Position	MLB Debut	Age at Debut	MLB Team	Seasons in MLB
1988	Moises Alou	21	3	LF	7/26/90	24	PIT	17
	Carlos García	20	2	2B	9/20/90	22	PIT	10
	Orlando Merced	21	4	RF	6/27/90	23	PIT	13
1989	Tim Wakefield	22	1	RHP	7/31/92	25	PIT	19
1990	x							
1991	Brian Shouse	22	2	LHP	7/31/93	24	PIT	10
	Rick White	22	2	RHP	4/6/94	25	PIT	12
1992	Tony Womack	22	2	2B	9/10/93	23	PIT	13
1993	Jason Christiansen	22	2	LHP	4/26/95	25	PIT	11
	Esteban Loaiza	20	2	RHP	4/29/95	23	PIT	14
1994	Jason Johnson	20	3	RHP	8/27/97	23	PIT	11
1995	Jose Guillen	19	2	RF	4/1/97	20	PIT	14
1996	Aramis Ramirez	18	1	3B	5/28/98	19	PIT	17+
	Bronson Arroyo	19	2	RHP	6/12/00	23	PIT	15+
1997	Mike González	19	1	LHP	8/11/03	25	PIT	11
1998	x							
1999	x							
2000	Freddy Sánchez	22	1	2B	9/10/02	24	BOS	10
2001	Kevin Youkilis	22	1	1B	5/15/04	25	BOS	10
	Frank Francisco	21	3	RHP	5/14/04	24	TEX	10+
2002	x							
2003	Hanley Ramirez	19	2	SS	9/20/05	21	BOS	10+
	Jon Lester	19	2	LHP	6/10/06	22	BOS	9+
2004	Brandon Moss	20	3	1B	8/6/07	23	BOS	7+
	Dustin Pedroia	20	1	2B	8/22/06	23	BOS	8+
2005	Brian Wilson	23	2	RHP	4/23/06	24	SFG	9+
2006	Pablo Sandoval	19	3	3B	8/14/08	22	SFG	7+
	Sergio Romo	23	2	RHP	6/26/08	25	SFG	7+
2007	x							
2008	Madison Bumgarner	18	1	LHP	9/8/09	20	SFG	6+
2009	x							

Table 3–4 AUG. Augusta SAL players that went on to have long major league careers.

the Cardinals to 2 unearned runs, while striking out 10, as the Bucs went on to win 3 runs to 2. In April 1995 he was released by Pittsburgh, but signed by Boston six days later. Wakefield went on to pitch seventeen seasons in the Red Sox uniform. He pitched his nineteenth and final major league season in 2011 at the age of 44.

Tim Wakefield's road to the majors is quite interesting. What is Wakefield fondly remembered for by Red Sox fans? It was his one pitch, an exceptional floater—the knuckleball. He is one of the pitchers on a very short list that primarily threw the knuckleball and won 200 or more games during their careers. In fact his lifetime record, which is 200W:180L, puts him in the top 10 in terms of wins among all knuckleballers in the history of major league baseball.

But a more interesting question is, "Who was the Tim Wakefield that fans saw when attending a home game of the 1989 Augusta Pirates?" The answer is quite unexpected. First, Tim was promoted from the A- level to the Pirates late in the 1989 season, so he did not appear in many games. But when he did he was seen fielding first base or third base, not on the mound. During his first two seasons of professional baseball, Wakefield primarily played infield and most frequently first base. It was not until 1990, when playing for the Salem Buccaneers (Carolina League, A+ level), that he exclusively turned his focus to pitching. Also interesting is the fact that once Wakefield became a pitcher in 1990, he was the starter in every one of his minor league pitching appearances. Wakefield never threw one pitch in the minors as a reliever. On the other hand, during his major league career Wakefield was primarily a starting pitcher, but he did make 164 relief appearances.

During the Boston years (1998–2004) the fans of the GreenJackets had the opportunity to see a number of today's Red Sox stars. As mentioned earlier, Jon Lester took the mound at Lake Olmstead Stadium in Augusta at the age of 19. That was 2003—his second season of professional ball. Lester made 21 starts and 3 relief appearances for the GreenJackets on his way to a lackluster 6W:9L record. Lester's showing at the minor league level was not as impressive as his success at the major league level. Two thousand and eight was his first season as a full-time member of the Boston starting rotation. He advanced to quickly become the ace of the Red Sox pitching staff. However, Lester was traded to the Oakland Athletics for outfielder Yoenis Céspedes at the 2014 trading deadline. During the 2014 offseason, he signed a six year contract to pitch for the Chicago Cubs.

In 2004, an Arizona State University college ballplayer—Dustin Pedroia—was signed by the Red Sox in July and began his professional baseball career that month at the A level of the minors with the Augusta GreenJackets. In his first twelve games Pedroia went 20 for 50 and was batting .400. He was quickly promoted to the Sarasota Red Sox (Florida State League, A+ level). Pedroia was on the fast track to the majors. By the end of the 2005 season he was playing at the AAA level and made his major league debut as the shortstop of the Red Sox on August 22, 2006, at the age of 23. Pedroia was Boston's 2007 season Opening Day second baseman; he was voted the

2007 American League Rookie of the Year and took over the starting role for the Red Sox at second base. He won the American League Most Valuable Player award for his play during the 2008 season and is a four time American League All-Star.

In recent years, the fans of the GreenJackets have seen a number of former and current San Francisco Giants players pass through Lake Olmstead Stadium on their way to The Show. In 2005, a 23-year-old Brian Wilson was Augusta's closer. Wilson stood out as the closer for the Giants during the 2008 through 2011 seasons and had 6 saves and 1 win during the 2010 postseason as San Francisco went on to win the World Series that season.

Another pitcher listed in Table 3–4 AUG is left-handed starter Madison Bumgarner. As mentioned earlier, he had an exceptional 2008 season as a member of Augusta's starting rotation. Bumgarner got the call from the Giants when the rosters were expanded in September 2009. He had pitched in just 43 games—all as a starter—at the minor league level. Bumgarner made his major league debut on the mound at AT&T Park on September 8, 2009, at the young age of 20. In his first outing in the majors, Bumgarner started, went 5.1 innings, and gave up 2 runs on 5 hits while striking out 4 and walking just 1. He left the game with San Francisco on top of the San Diego Padres 3 runs to 2. However, the Giants relief corps gave up the lead after Bumgarner left and he got a no decision.

Since being recalled in 2010, Bumgarner has been a regular member of the San Francisco starting rotation. He posted double digit victories in 2011, 2012, 2013, and 2014. As the head of the Giants rotation in 2014, he had an 18W:10 loss record to lead the pitching staff in victories. Bumgarner represented San Francisco on both the 2013 and 2014 National League All-Star teams.

Bumgarner was a key contributor in San Francisco's 2010, 2012, and 2014 World Series victories. Over that period, his record in fourteen postseason games was 7W:3L and he went 4W:0L in five World Series appearances. During the 2014 playoffs, Madison was 4W:1L in six starts and one relief appearance and pitched 52.2 innings. In fact, Bumgarner received the Most Valuable Player Award for his play in both the 2014 National League Division Series and 2014 World Series. His 52.2 innings pitched during the 2014 postseason set a new record for the most innings thrown by a pitcher in a single postseason.

Bumgarner dominated the Kansas City Royals batting order in the 2014 World Series. As the starter in game one of the World Series in Kansas City, he notched a victory by throwing 7 innings of 3 hit 1 run ball as the Giants won the series opener 7–1. He returned to the mound in game 5 with the series tied 2 games all and threw a 4 hit complete game shutout to put San Francisco up 3 games to 2. Finally, in the series deciding game seven, Bumgarner came in the bottom of the 5th inning with the Giants up 3 runs to 2 and threw five innings of shutout ball for a save that clinched San Francisco's third World Series championship in five seasons. During the series, Bumgarner pitched to an outstanding .430 ERA over 21 innings.

San Francisco Giants third baseman Pablo Sandoval and closer Sergio Romo were members of the 2006 Augusta GreenJackets team. These two players played critical roles in the Giants' 2012 World Series–winning postseason. Sandoval batted .500 in the World Series and received the World Series MVP Award. But the Giants would not have won without their closer, Romo, who got the save in three of their four World Series wins.

Sandoval, who has been recognized for his exceptional postseason play, was a key offensive contributor in the Giants' 2014 championship run. He also set a record with his play during the 2014 postseason. His 26 hits broke the prior record of 25 for the most hits by a player in a single postseason. After the Giants' 2014 win, his all time postseason batting average sat at .344. However, Sandoval became a free agent after the season and signed a five year contract to play for the Boston Red Sox.

These are just a few of the interesting baseball players that came up through the minor league organization of the Pirates, Red Sox, and Giants and played their formative years in the city of Augusta. Check out the names of others in the listing of Table 3–4 AUG. There are sure to be others that will bring back fond baseball memories.

Attractions in Augusta

- **Broad Street Historic District,** Broad St. between 5th St. and 13th St., Augusta, GA 30901
- **Augusta Riverwalk—Savannah River,** 10 9th St., Augusta, GA 30901 (706) 821–1754
- **Augusta Canal Interpretive Center and Petersburg Boat Canal Tour,** 1450 Greene St., Augusta, GA 30901 (706) 823–0440 Ext. 4
- **Savannah River Boat Tour (Patriot Riverboat Tours),** 2 10th St., Augusta, GA 30901 (803) 730–9739
- **Historic Trolley Tour of Augusta (Downtown Visitors Center),** 560 Reynolds St., Augusta, GA 30901 (706) 724–4067
- **Boyhood Home of President Woodrow Wilson Tour,** 419 7th St., Augusta, GA 30901 (706) 722–9828
- **Augusta National Golf Club,** 2604 Washington Rd., Augusta, GA 30904 (706) 667–6000

Dining in Augusta

DOWNTOWN RESTAURANTS

- **Beamie's at the River**, 865 Reynolds St., Augusta, GA 30901 (706) 724–6593
- **Frog Hollow Tavern**, 1282 Broad St., Augusta, GA 30901 (706) 364–6906
- **The Cotton Patch**, 816 Cotton Ln., Augusta, GA 30901 (706) 724–4511
- **Mellow Mushroom**, 1167 Broad St., Augusta, GA 30901 (706) 828–5578
- **The Boar's Head Public House**, 1135 Broad St., Augusta, GA 30901 (706) 723–5177
- **Boll Weevil Café and Sweetery**, 10 Ninth St., Augusta, GA 30901 (706) 722–7772

OTHER RESTAURANTS
NEAR THE STADIUM

- **5 O'Clock Bistro,** 2111 Kings Way, Augusta, GA 30904 (706) 922–9560
- **French Market Grill**, 425 Highland Ave., Augusta, GA 30909 (706) 737–4865
- **Carolina Ale House**, 203 Robert C. Daniel Jr. Pkwy., Augusta, GA 30909 (762) 333–0019
- **Sconyers Bar-B-Que**, 2250 Sconyers Way, Augusta, GA 30906 (706) 790–5411

Charleston RiverDogs

Joseph P. Riley, Jr. Park
360 Fishburne St., Charleston, SC 29403
www.milb.com/index.jsp?sid=t233

Today I'm driving on a highway that is taking me down a peninsula that is bounded by the Cooper River to the east and the Ashley River to the west. Where am I going? I'm en route to one of the attractive historic destinations of the South Atlantic League—Charleston, South Carolina. This historic southern city is the home of the Charleston RiverDogs Baseball Club—the single-A affiliate of the New York Yankees. Charleston is nestled at the tip of this peninsula where the two rivers join to form Charleston Harbor in an area known as the Neck. Charleston Harbor is a gateway to the Atlantic Ocean.

Charleston is another of the current South Atlantic League cities that has a long and rich history of hosting professional baseball teams. Table 3–1 CSC traces the history of the baseball teams that played on the ball fields of Charleston, South Carolina. The first season in which it is documented that professional baseball was played in Charleston is 1886. That year the city fielded two teams—the Charleston Fultons in the Southern League of Colored Base Ballists and the Charleston Seagulls in the Southern Association. But both teams played just one year and were replaced by a new team—the Charleston Quakers—in a new league—the Southern League—for the 1887 season.

But the Seagulls returned for the 1888 season, nested in Charleston, and fielded a team during nineteen of the next thirty-three baseball seasons. The team's moniker evolved from the Seagulls to the Sea Gulls and eventually just

Team Name	1st Year	Years	Leagues
Charleston Fultons	1886	1	Southern League of Colored Base Ballists
Charleston Seagulls	1886	1	Southern Association
Charleston Quakers	1887	1	Southern League
Charleston SeaGulls	1888	1	Southern League
Charleston/Atlanta	1889	1	Southern League
Charleston Sea Gulls	1892	1	South Atlantic League
Charleston Seagulls	1893	2	Southern Association
Charleston Seagulls	1898	1	Southern League
Charleston Sea Gulls	1904	12	South Atlantic League
Charleston Gulls	1919	1	South Atlantic League
Charleston Palmettos	1920	1	South Atlantic League
Charleston Pals	1921	3	South Atlantic League
Charleston Rebels	1940	11	South Atlantic League
Charleston ChaSox	1959	1	South Atlantic League
Charleston White Sox	1960	2	South Atlantic League
Charleston Pirates	1973	3	Western Carolinas League
Charleston Patriots	1976	2	Western Carolinas League
Charleston Pirates	1978	1	Western Carolinas League
Charleston Royals	1980	5	South Atlantic League
Charleston Rainbows	1985	9	South Atlantic League
Charleston RiverDogs	1994	21	South Atlantic League

Table 3–1 CSC. Teams that have played in Charleston, SC (source: www.baseball-reference.com).

the Gulls in their final season, 1919. The Seagulls had settled down to stay in Charleston, but as Table 3–1 CSC shows they initially flew from league to league. After starting in the Southern Association in 1886, they migrated to the Southern League in 1888, South Atlantic League for the 1892 season, then back to the Southern Association in 1893, and eventually the Southern League again in 1898. These teams of the 1800s era of baseball in Charleston all played at the B level of minor league baseball.

After a six-season lapse during which there was no team in Charleston, a team now called the Sea Gulls emerged in 1904 and settled down to play in the original South Atlantic League. During that season three of the six teams of the Sally League were in cities that host modern South Atlantic League teams today. In addition to Charleston, teams played in Augusta and Savannah, Georgia. Things stabilized and the Sea Gulls or Gulls fielded a Sally League team in the city of Charleston during thirteen of the seasons between 1904 and 1919. The Sea Gulls of those years played at the C level of the minor leagues. This ended another era of professional baseball in the city of Charleston, which I have named the Gulls era and have decided that it was for the birds.

Well the truth is that was not really the end of an era of baseball in Charleston. The teams changed names but remained members of the Sally League. So I think a better name for this part of the history of professional baseball in Charleston would be the South Atlantic League era. Not only did the Sea Gulls play fourteen seasons in that league (remember that the Sea Gulls also played the 1892 season in the South Atlantic League), but over the next forty-two seasons (1920 through 1961) Charleston was home to five differently named Sally teams: the Charleston Palmettos, Charleston Pals, Charleston Rebels, Charleston ChaSox, and Charleston White Sox. The relationship between professional baseball and Charleston was on and off. Teams called the city home for just eighteen of those forty-two seasons, but during eight of them the South Atlantic League did not operate. So Charleston actually hosted a team in eighteen of the next thirty-four seasons that the league was active.

Table 3–1 CSC shows that the Charleston Rebels was the team that had the longest stay—eleven seasons between 1940 and 1953. During the later four years of this period, the team was affiliated with the Pittsburgh Pirates as their A-level minor league affiliate. In 1950 future Pittsburgh Pirates slugger Frank Thomas played for the Charleston Rebels. The next season he was promoted to the major leagues and made his debut on August 17, 1951, versus the Chicago Cubs at Forbes Field in Pittsburgh. That day Thomas was the Pirates' center fielder and batted third in their batting order—one slot above

Hall of Famer and Pirates great Ralph Kiner. He went 1 for 4 on the day with a double and 1 RBI. Thomas went on to play in the majors during sixteen seasons and the first eight of them with Pittsburgh. But 1953 was the last season for the Rebels, and professional baseball did not return to Charleston until 1959.

As shown in Table 3–1 CSC, it was the Chicago White Sox that brought baseball back to the city—first as the Charleston ChaSox in 1959. Then in 1960 they renamed the team the Charleston White Sox. Both of these teams played in the South Atlantic League. During the 1961 season, future major leaguers infielder-outfielder Don Buford (ten seasons White Sox and Orioles) and left-handed reliever and closer Joe Hoerner (fourteen seasons for six teams) were regulars for the Charleston White Sox team. But after this three-year stint with the Chicago White Sox, organized baseball left the city for more than a decade.

The Pittsburgh Pirates ushered in Charleston's modern South Atlantic League era of baseball in 1973 with the entry of the Charleston Pirates into the Western Carolinas League. Since then the city has fielded a team in forty-one of the forty-two baseball seasons. The one year missed was 1979. After the 1978 season, the Pirates relocated their team to Shelby, North Carolina, but then there was a one-year gap before the Kansas City Royals engaged with today's South Atlantic League with their Charleston Royals ball club.

The Home of the RiverDogs—Joseph P. Riley, Jr., Park

From the 1940s through 1996, professional baseball in Charleston was played at College Park. That baseball stadium, which is owned today by The Citadel, the Military College of South Carolina, is still used as the practice facility by their baseball team. College Park served as the home stadium of the Charleston RiverDogs from 1994 through the 1996 season. During the spring of 1996, the City of Charleston began construction of a new ballpark, located on the east bank of the Ashley River. The new stadium was named Joseph P. Riley Jr. Park after the then-mayor of the city. The ballpark is located approximately two and a half miles from the historic downtown section of Charleston.

The RiverDogs played their inaugural season at the new stadium in 1997 and it remains their home ballpark today. Figure 3–1 CSC shows a current day photo of the stadium. The ballpark, which has been nicknamed "The Joe" by locals, opens to a treed park-like setting over the outfield walls. Stairs lead from the main entrance by the ticket booth to the main concourse. This

Figure 3–1 CSC. Joseph P. Riley, Jr. Park, Charleston, SC.

concourse, which is located behind the third base stands, left field foul line stands, and left field wall, contains concessions with traditional ballpark food and drink, a team store, and some children's attractions. From the higher first base side seats and the first base side concourse, you can get a scenic view of the Ashley River off in the distance.

On the stands side of the third base concourse there is an alcove dedicated as the Charleston Baseball Hall of Fame. Candidates are selected by a Hall of Fame advisory committee. The nominees are then voted on and elected by the fans of the team. To date there are over 30 inductees and their names are proudly displayed on wall plaques in the Hall of Fame area. These Hall of Famers include second basemen Willie Randolph and Roberto Alomar and pitchers David Cone and John Candelaria, who all played minor league ball for a Charleston team. Randolph was also born in South Carolina. Another inductee is outfielder Gorman Thomas, who did not play for a Charleston team; instead, he was born and grew up in the city.

The South Atlantic League Years

The city of Charleston is the second of the three cities that have regularly hosted a South Atlantic League Minor League Baseball franchise since the days of the Western Carolinas League. As mentioned earlier, a Sally League team has called the city home in forty of the last forty-one baseball seasons. Note in Table 3–2(a) CSC that the Charleston Pirates were the first team to play their home games in Charleston. However, since then there have been four other South Atlantic League teams in the city: the Patriots, Royals, Rainbows, and today's RiverDogs. Those teams have been affiliated with six different major league clubs: Pittsburgh Pirates, Kansas City Royals, San Diego Padres, Texas Rangers, Tampa Bay Devil Rays, and New York Yankees. A Charleston team has gone to the postseason in just four of those forty-one seasons. These teams won the Southern Division title in three of those years— 1980, 1984, and 1988. However, none of the teams won the South Atlantic League title.

The Charleston Pirates played in the Western Carolinas League from 1973 through 1975. Prior to the start of the 1976 season, the team's name was

League	Name	MLB Affiliate	Years
South Atlantic League	Charleston RiverDogs	New York Yankees	2005-today
South Atlantic League	Charleston RiverDogs	Tampa Bay Devil Rays	1997-2004
South Atlantic League	Charleston RiverDogs	Texas Rangers	1994-1996
South Atlantic League	Charleston Rainbows	Texas Rangers	1993
South Atlantic League	Charleston Rainbows	San Diego Padres	1985-1992
South Atlantic League	Charleston Royals	Kansas City Royals	1980-1984
Western Carolinas League	Charelston Pirates	Pittsburgh Pirates	1978
Western Carolinas League	Charleston Patriots	Pittsburgh Pirates	1976-1977
Western Carolinas League	Charelston Pirates	Pittsburgh Pirates	1973-1975

Above: Table 3–2(a) CSC. Charleston SAL teams' major league affiliations. *Opposite:* Table 3–2(b) CSC. New York Yankees minor league organization.

Level	Team	Stadium	League
Rk	GCL Yankees	George M. Steinbrenner Field Tampa, FL	Gulf Coast League
Rk	Pulaski Yankees	Calfee Park Pulaski, VA	Appalachian League
A-	Staten Island Yankees	Richmond County Bank Ballpark Staten Island, NY	New York-Penn League
A	Charleston RiverDogs	Joseph P. Riley Jr. Park Charleston, SC	South Atlantic League
A+	Tampa Yankees	George M. Steinbrenner Field Tampa, FL	Florida State League
AA	Trenton Thunder	Arm & Hammer Park Trenton, NJ	Eastern League
AAA	Scranton/Wilkes-Barre Railriders	PNC Field Moosic, PA	International League

changed to the Charleston Patriots, but the Pirates remained their major league affiliate. The team retained the Patriots moniker through the 1977 season, but then in 1978 they reverted to their original name of Charleston Pirates.

Note from Table 3–2(a) CSC that, after the 1978 season, the Pirates terminated their affiliation with Charleston. But Pittsburgh remained affiliated with the Western Carolinas League by relocating its A-level team to the North Carolina city of Shelby as the Shelby Pirates. This resulted in a vacuum in Charleston and the city did not field a team for the 1979 season.

But in 1980 the Kansas City Royals engaged with the city and located a new A-level affiliate—the Charleston Royals—in College Park for the inaugural season of the South Atlantic League. That season the Charleston Royals won the Southern Division title and advanced to the postseason but lost in the South Atlantic Championship Series to the Greensboro Hornets (New York Yankees).

The offense of the 1980 Southern Division champions was led by future major leaguer Marvell Wynne. The Royals outfielder led the team in eight batting categories: runs scored (106), hits (152), triples (15), home runs (18), runs batted in (98), stolen bases (29), slugging percentage (.468), and total bases (256). Wynne ranked in the top 10 among all players in the South Atlantic League in each of these eight offensive stats. In fact he led the league in both triples and total bases and ranked second in runs scored and hits.

Wynne went on to play in the majors for 8 seasons with the Pirates, Padres, and Cubs. The Royals won the Southern Division title for a second time in 1984 but again lost in the league championship finals. But this time they lost to the Asheville Tourists (Houston Astros).

During the five seasons they were engaged with Charleston and the South Atlantic League, the Royals had a second A-level affiliate, the Fort Myers Royals in the Florida State League. Kansas City dropped the Charleston Royals in favor of their Fort Myers team during the 1984 offseason.

As shown in Table 3–2(a) CSC, the San Diego Padres filled the vacancy by adding a second A-level team to their minor league organization—the Charleston Rainbows—to start the 1985 season. The Rainbows were the Southern Division champions in 1988. The roster of this season's team also had a number of players that went on to have successful major league careers. Their shortstop was 18-year-old Jose Valentin, who played his first eight seasons at shortstop for the Milwaukee Brewers and then went on to play in another eight seasons for the White Sox, Dodgers, and Mets.

The pitching staff included right handers Doug Brocail and Omar Olivares. In 1988, both players were pitching a second season with the Rainbows. Brocail and Olivares pitched most frequently for the Rainbows as starters. On the other hand, in the major leagues, Brocail was primarily used as a reliever. He appeared in 626 games over a fifteen-season major league career during which he played for the Padres, Astros, Tigers and Rangers. Olivares pitched primarily as a starter during his twelve seasons in the majors. He pitched for eight different major league teams and his longest stint was five seasons with the St. Louis Cardinals—1990 through 1994. The Charleston Rainbows faced the Spartanburg Phillies in the 1988 South Atlantic League Championship Series but lost.

The Padres remained the affiliate of the Rainbows for seven seasons, but after the 1992 season they decided to cut back to a single A-level club and kept their other team, the Waterloo Diamonds in the Midwest League. They severed their relationship with Charleston and its Rainbows. But the Texas Rangers were there to step in and fill the void by sponsoring the Charleston Rainbows for the 1993 season.

The Texas Rangers arrived at a time when the Charleston Rainbows had just experienced their third consecutive losing season. During their first season representing the Rangers, 1993, the Rainbows went 65W:77L and finished in fifth place in the Southern Division of the SAL—29 games behind the division leader. In an effort to shed their losing image, the team's nickname was changed to the RiverDogs for the 1994 season and the Charleston RiverDogs of today were born. Along with the change in name, the team fielded a new mascot, named Charlie T. Riverdog, who is still a faithful supporter of the team today.

On the day that Joseph P. Riley Jr. Park opened, April 6, 1997, the Charleston RiverDogs also had a new major league affiliate—the Tampa Bay Devil Rays. But the RiverDogs did not post a winning season until 2000. During that season, the team had current major leaguers Carl Crawford and Josh Hamilton in the outfield. They batted .301 and .302, respectively. Crawford led the South Atlantic League in hits with 170, tied with one other player for second in triples (11), ranked third in stolen bases (55), and fourth in runs scored (99). Their starting rotation included current major league RHP Jose Veras (8W:8L) and former major league LHP Joe Kennedy (11W:6L). But a career minor leaguer, right hander Jim Magrane, led the pitching rotation with 12 wins and 5 losses. The RiverDogs ended the season with a 77W:66L record but did not make the postseason.

To start the 2005 season, the New York Yankees took over the reins of the Charleston RiverDogs and they remain the affiliate of the Charleston team in the South Atlantic League today. The other current New York Yankees minor league affiliates are listed in Table 3–2(b) CSC. In their first season, the Yankees' version of the RiverDogs won the first half season to gain a berth in the playoffs and finished the season with the best overall record in the Southern Division—80W:58L. Current major league pitchers Phil Coke (8W:11L) and Phillip Hughes (7W:1L) pitched for that team. After getting off to an excellent start, Hughes was promoted in July to the Yankees A+ team in the Florida State League—the Tampa Yankees. That season the RiverDogs lost in the Southern Division title round to the Kannapolis Intimidators (Chicago White Sox), who went on to win the 2005 South Atlantic League Championship title.

The Charleston RiverDogs hit the 80 win plateau in just one other baseball season. During 2008, they went 80W:59L but did not win the Southern Division in either the first half or second half of the season. Therefore, they did not make the playoffs. Jesus Montero split time between catching and designated hitter for the RiverDogs that season. Montero had an excellent offensive year. He led the South Atlantic League with 171 hits and his .326 batting average ranked him second in the league in that batting statistic category. However, he also ranked in the top 10 among all players in the league in six other offensive stats: number 2 in total bases (258), number 4 in doubles (34), tied for number 6 in RBI (87), tied for number 6 in runs scored (86), seventh in on-base plus slugging percentage (.868), and tied for eighth in slugging percentage (.411). Today his 171 hits and .326 batting average remain the River-Dogs' all-time team records for those two important offensive statistics.

Successful Major Leaguers Who Played in Charleston

Similar to the other cities with a long history of hosting franchises of today's South Atlantic League, the fans of Charleston's team had the opportunity to see many players who went on to have very successful major leagues careers. Table 3–3 CSC lists over forty ballplayers who made a stop to play A-level ball in Charleston on their road to the majors. All of these players spent all or part of their first, second, or in a few cases third year of professional baseball on the field of either College Park or Joseph P. Riley Jr. Park.

This list includes many memorable players—eleven of them played in the major leagues during fifteen or more seasons. Among this elite group are two brothers, Roberto Alomar and Sandy Alomar, who both played in the majors for 20 baseball seasons, and John Candelaria (19 seasons), Willie Randolph (18 seasons), Tony Pena (18 seasons), and David Cone (17 seasons). Candelaria, Randolph, and Pena all made their major league debut for the Pittsburgh Pirates. As well as having lengthy successful years as players, three of these six—Randolph, Pena, and Sandy Alomar—have managed at the major league level.

Candelaria was signed out of high school and quickly jumped to the majors. After pitching at the A level for the 1973 season and much of the next, he was promoted directly to AAA late in the 1974 season. Candelaria never pitched at the AA level and made only 10 starts in AAA before being called up to Pittsburgh in early June 1975. Candelaria was a starter for most of his career, but then adapted to the role of a reliever and lefty specialist for his final four seasons in the majors. Over his 19-year career he pitched in 600 games and made 356 starts. He retired having won 177 games while losing 122.

Among these six journeymen players, Willie Randoph played the most consecutive seasons for the same major league team—12 with the New York Yankees. Randolph's road to the majors and stay at that level is a little unique. First he progressed cleanly one year at a time through the Rk, A, AA, and AAA levels. He was called up by the Pirates in late July 1975 but played in only 30 games by the end of the season. During the 1975 off-season, he was traded to the New York Yankees along with pitchers Ken Brett and Doc Ellis for Yankees starter Doc Medich. Medich played one season for the Pirates and then was traded. Randolph became the Yankees' starting second baseman for more than a decade. At the major league level he played the field in 2152 games. Randolph played second base in 2151 of them and 1 game at third base

Season	Player	Age at CHS	MiLB Season	Position	MLB Debut	Age at Debut	MLB Team	Seasons in MLB
1973	John Candelaria	19	1	LHP	6/8/75	21	PIT	19
	Miguel Dilone	18	2	LF	9/2/74	19	PIT	12
	Willie Randolph	18	2	2B	7/29/75	21	PIT	18
1974	x							
1975	Ed Whitson	20	2	RHP	9/4/77	22	PIT	15
1976	Dale Berra	19	2	SS	8/22/77	20	PIT	11
	Tony Pena	19	1	C	9/1/80	23	PIT	18
	Don Robinson	19	2	RHP	4/10/78	20	PIT	15
1977	Junior Ortiz	17	1	C	9/20/82	22	PIT	13
	Pascual Perez	20	2	RHP	5/7/80	22	PIT	11
1978	Steve Farr	21	2	RHP	5/16/84	27	CLE	10
1979	No team							
1980	x							
1981	Mike Kingery	20	2	CF	7/7/86	25	KCR	10
1982	David Cone	19	2	RHP	6/8/86	23	KCR	17
	Danny Jackson	20	1	LHP	9/11/83	21	KCR	15
1983	x							
1984	Kevin Seitzer	22	2	3B	9/3/86	24	KCR	12
1985	Roberto Alomar	17	1	2B	4/22/88	20	SDP	20
	Sandy Alomar	19	2	C	9/30/88	22	SDP	20
1986	Carlos Baerga	17	1	2B	4/14/90	21	CLE	14
1987	Ricky Bones	18	2	RHP	8/11/91	22	SDP	11
	Doug Brocail	20	2	RHP	9/8/92	25	SDP	15
	Omar Olivares	19	1	RHP	8/18/90	23	STL	12
1988	Jose Valentin	18	2	SS	9/17/92	22	MIL	16
1989	Luis Lopez	18	2	SS	9/7/93	23	SDP	11
1990	Tim Worrell	22	1	RHP	6/25/93	25	SDP	14
1991	x							
1992	Joey Hamilton	21	1	RHP	5/24/94	23	SDP	10
1993	Scott Eyre	21	2	LHP	8/1/97	25	CHW	13
1994	x							
1995	Fernando Tatis	20	2	3B	7/26/97	22	TEX	11
1996	Ryan Dempster	19	2	RHP	5/23/98	21	FLA	16
1997	x							
1998	Aubrey Huff	21	1	1B	8/2/00	23	TBR	12
	Dan Wheeler	20	2	RHP	9/1/99	21	TBR	13
1999	x							

Table 3-3 CSC. Charleston SAL players that went on to have long major league careers.

in his first season at Pittsburgh. During his 18-year career, Randolph never returned to the minors to play another game.

Unlike Willie Randolph, Tony Pena did not take a focused, streamlined route to the majors. During his first season in the minors, 1976, Pena played

Season	Player	Age at CHS	MiLB Season	Position	MLB Debut	Age at Debut	MLB Team	Seasons in MLB
2000	Carl Crawford	18	2	LF	7/20/02	20	TBR	13+
	Josh Hamilton	19	2	CF	4/2/07	25	CIN	8+
	Jose Veras	19	3	RHP	8/5/06	25	NYY	9+
2001	James Shields	19	1	RHP	5/31/06	24	TBR	9+
2002	x							
2003	Jason Hammel	20	2	RHP	4/11/06	23	TBR	9+
2004	Reid Brignac	18	1	SS	7/4/08	22	TBR	7+
	Delmon Young	18	1	LF	8/29/06	20	TBR	9+
2005	Tyler Clippard	20	3	RHP	5/20/07	22	NYY	8+
	Phil Coke	22	3	LHP	9/1/08	26	NYY	7+
	Phil Hughes	19	2	RHP	4/26/07	20	NYY	8+
2006	Mike Dunn	22	2	LHP	9/4/09	24	NYY	6+
	Austin Jackson	19	2	CF	4/5/10	23	DET	5+
	Eduardo Nunez	19	2	SS	8/19/10	23	NYY	5+
	José Tabata	17	2	LF	6/9/10	21	PIT	5+
2007	John Axford	24	1	RHP	9/15/09	26	MIL	6+
	Ivan Nova	20	2	RHP	5/13/10	23	NYY	5+
	David Robertson	22	1	RHP	6/29/08	23	NYY	7+
2008	x							
2009	x							

Table 3–3 CSC (continued). Charleston SAL players that went on to have long major league careers.

33 games at the rookie level and 14 for the Charleston Patriots in the Western Carolinas League. However, in those games he played four different positions: catcher, first base, third base, and outfield. Pena did not settle in to just play catcher until the 1977 season, which was spent at the A level. The transition to full-time catcher delayed his progress. He developed a unique catching style in which he placed one knee on the ground and extended the other leg out to the side.

After playing five full seasons and with seven different teams in the minor leagues, Pena made his debut with the Pittsburgh Pirates on September 1, 2008. Interestingly, Pena caught 1950 games during his 18-year major league career; however, he also played a few at first base, third base, and in right field.

Ryan Dempster's path to the majors was also unusual. He spent his first three seasons of professional ball playing at the Rk, A-, A, and A+ levels. Dempster was promoted to AA for the start the 1998 season. After making just seven starts for the Portland Sea Dogs in the Eastern League, he was called up to the majors by the Florida Marlins. Dempster had never pitched in a game at the AAA level. However, he struggled and ended up at AAA later in that season. During the 1999 season, Dempster settled into the Marlins' starting rotation and by mid-season 2000 he was a National League All-Star. During the 2013 season, Dempster pitched for the Boston Red Sox and went 8W:9L in 29 starts. That was his sixteenth and final season in the majors.

Delmon Young, who played in Charleston during the Tampa Bay Rays years, has had an extended major league career and played for the Baltimore Orioles in 2014. At the age of 18 in 2004, Young played the outfield for the RiverDogs during his first season of professional baseball. He had an exceptional year with the bat. Table 3–4 CSC list a summary of his batting stats for that season. He led all regular players on the team in the power hitting offensive stats: hits (165), home runs (25), runs batted in (115), batting average (.322), slugging percentage (.538), on-base plus slugging percentage (.926), and total bases (276). Young ranked in the top 10 in the South Atlantic League for the season in each of these seven stat categories and also in runs scored and on-base percentage. His 165 H and 115 RBI ranked him number 1 in the league in those two batting stat categories. In fact, Young holds the Charleston RiverDogs' all-time single season record for four offensive statistics: most runs batted in, most total bases, highest slugging percentage and a tie for the lead in home runs.

Young made his major league debut in the Tampa Bay Rays uniform. He got the call to the majors in late August 2006. Young made his debut at U.S. Cellular Field in Chicago on August 29 as the Rays' right fielder and hitting eighth in their batting order. He was hit by a Freddy Garcia pitch in his first major league at-bat. But Young's major league career got off to a good start that day. Later in the game he took Garcia deep for his first home run at the major league level. Overall he went 2 for 3 on the day with 2 RBI. The next season Young took over as the Rays' starting right fielder. The year 2014 is the ninth consecutive season that Young has played games at the major league

G	AB	R	H	2B	3B	HR	RBI
131	513	95	165	26	5	25	115

TB	BB	SO	AVE	OBP	SLG	OPS
276	53	120	.322	.388	.538	.926

Table 3–4 CSC. Delmon Young 2004 batting stats summary.

level. During his career he has played for five different clubs: the Rays, Twins, Tigers, Phillies, and Orioles.

Since the New York Yankees have only been the affiliate of the RiverDogs since 2005, there is only a small list of currently active players who made their major league debuts with the Yankees. But reliever David Robertson, who took over the Yankees' closer role for the 2014 season, is among the five that qualify for this list. David Robertson played college ball at the University of Alabama before signing with the New York Yankees in 2006 at the age of 21. Table 3–3 CSC shows that he began his professional career in 2007 at the A level with the Charleston RiverDogs. Robertson was recruited with the intent of making him a reliever. During 2007 he made 24 relief appearances by the end of June. In his 47 innings of work, he pitched to an exceptional 0.77 ERA, 0.851 WHIP, and averaged 12.8 SO/9. He was promoted on June 30, 2007, to the T-Yanks (A+). By late August he had made 18 relief appearances for Tampa. Again his ERA, WHIP, and SO/9 ratio were excellent, 1.08, 0.990 and 10.0, respectively. Robertson was promoted to the Trenton Thunder (AA) in late August.

The following season, Robertson was a member of the Thunder's opening day roster, but after making just 9 relief appearances he was promoted to the Scranton/Wilkes-Barre Yankees on May 2, 2008. Less than 60 days later Robertson was at Shea Stadium making his major league debut versus the New York Mets. On June 29, 2008, he pitched the sixth and seventh innings in a 3–1 Yankees loss to the Mets. Robertson gave up 4 hits and 1 run in this brief appearance. Robertson's ride to the majors was fast—he made his major league debut less than 15 months after throwing his first pitch for the Charleston RiverDogs. He had a solid first season as the Yankees closer and notched 39 saves. However, Robertson became a free agent at the end of the season and signed a four year contract to pitch for the Chicago White Sox during the off-season.

Baseball Attractions in Charleston

- **College Park**, 714 Rutledge Ave., Charleston, SC 29403

Attractions in Charleston

- **French Quarter District (Visitors Center)**, 375 Meeting St., Charleston, SC 29403 (843) 724–7174

- **Historic Charleston City Market,** 188 Meeting St., Charleston, SC 29401 (843) 937–0920
- **South Carolina Aquarium**, 100 Aquarium Wharf, Charleston, SC 29401 (843) 577–3474
- **Fort Sumter National Monument and Fort Sumter Visitor Education Center at Liberty Square**, 340 Concord St., Charleston, SC 29401 (843) 577–0242
- **Battery & White Point Gardens**, 2 Murray Dr., Charleston, SC 29401
- **Patriots Point Naval & Maritime Museum**, 40 Patriots Point Rd., Mount Pleasant, SC 29464 (843) 884–2727
- **Magnolia Plantation & Gardens**, 3550 Ashley River Rd., Charleston, SC 29414 (800) 367–3517

Dining in Charleston

Brewpubs and Breweries

- **Southend Brewery & Smokehouse**, 161 E. Bay St., Charleston, SC 29401 (843) 853–4677

Downtown Restaurants

- **Poogan's Porch**, 72 Queen St., Charleston, SC 29401 (843) 577–2337
- **Hyman's Seafood**, 215 Meeting St., Charleston, SC 29401 (843) 723–6000
- **Gaulart & Maliclet Café Restaurant**, 98 Broad St., Charleston, SC 29401 (843) 577–9797
- **Charleston Beer Works**, 468 King St., Charleston, SC 29403 (843) 577–5885
- **Mellow Mushroom**, 309 King St., Charleston, SC 29401 (843) 723–7374
- **Dixie Supply Bakery & Café** (breakfast and lunch only), 62 State St., Charleston, SC 29401 (843) 722–5650
- **TBonz Gill & Grill**, 80 N. Market St. Charleston, SC 29401 (843) 577–2511
- **Kaminsky's Baking Co.**, 78 N. Market St., Charleston, SC 29401 (843) 853–8270
- **Kilwins Chocolate and Ice Cream**, 59 S. Market St., Charleston, SC 29401 (843) 722–6887

Delmarva Shorebirds

Arthur W. Perdue Stadium
6400 Hobbs Rd., Salisbury, MD 21804
www.milb.com/index.jsp?sid=t548

Today I'm en route to a baseball game at a stadium that is located on a peninsula that engulfs parts of the states of Delaware, Maryland, and Virginia—the Delmarva Peninsula. My destination is Salisbury—the largest city on the Eastern Shore of Maryland. I am traveling to attend a game of the Delmarva Shorebirds at their home ballpark, Arthur W. Perdue Stadium. Salisbury is located somewhat at the center of the Delmarva Peninsula. For this reason it is known as the Crossroads of Delmarva. The city has a number of interesting attractions and a historic downtown. Also, it is located approximately 30 miles from Maryland seashore destinations such as Ocean City.

Even though the Delmarva Peninsula is thought of as being attached to land at the north end, the creation of the Chesapeake and Delaware Canal has caused an artificial water barrier that makes the area effectively an island. Destinations on the peninsula can be reached only by bridge or tunnel from the mainland. There are several bridges that enable entrance to the peninsula from the north, but from mainland Maryland to the west there is only one option—the Bay Bridge from the Annapolis area and from mainland Virginia in the south the Chesapeake Bay Bridge-Tunnel.

Unlike many of the other towns and cities that are the home of a modern South Atlantic League team, the city of Salisbury does not have a long history of involvement with professional baseball. Table 3–1 DEL shows that prior to the arrival of a South Atlantic League team to the city in 1996, baseball had been played in the city during just 18 of the prior 74 years. The Delmarva Shorebirds have already played in the city for more than that many seasons.

Team Name	1st Year	Years	Leagues
Salisbury Indians	1922	9	Eastern Shore League
Salisbury Senators	1939	1	Eastern Shore League
Salisbury Cardinals	1940	6	Eastern Shore League
Salisbury A's	1951	1	Interstate League
Salisbury Reds	1952	1	Interstate League
Delmarva Shorebirds	1996	19	South Atlantic League

Table 3–1 DEL. Teams that have played in Salisbury, MD (source: www.baseball-reference.com).

The first professional baseball team that played in the city was the Salisbury Indians. The Eastern Shore League was founded prior to the 1922 season, and the Indians were one of its charter members. During its inaugural season, the league had six teams all located on the Delmarva Peninsula in Maryland, Delaware, or Virginia. All of those teams were located within 50 miles of Salisbury. The Salisbury Indians were a D-level minor league team and they played in that league for a total of nine seasons—1922 through 1928 and then again in 1937 and 1938. During the 1938 and 1939 seasons the Salisbury team was affiliated with the Washington Senators. Note in Table 3–1 DEL that prior to the 1939 season the team was renamed the Salisbury Senators and then the Salisbury Cardinals in 1940 while the team remained a D-class member of the Senators' minor league organization.

The Salisbury Cardinals became a St. Louis Cardinals' minor league affiliate in 1946. Right-handed pitcher Stu Miller played his first season of professional baseball as a member of the Salisbury Cardinals pitching staff in 1949 at the age of 21. Miller made his major league debut with the St. Louis Cardinals on August 12, 1952. He went on to pitch mostly as a reliever over the next sixteen seasons and retired in 1968 at the age of 40.

The runs of the Indians and Cardinals were not consecutive years. There were a number of baseball seasons during which the Eastern Shore League did not operate. As noted earlier, the Indians did not field a team for the eight seasons from 1929 to 1936. Similarly the Cardinals' six-season stretch had a four-year break during the World War II years—1942 through 1945. After the 1949 season, the Eastern Shore League disbanded.

Briefly during the 1950s—just the 1951 and 1952 seasons—baseball returned to Salisbury. In 1951 the Philadelphia Athletics (today the Oakland A's) operated a B-level minor league team in the city—the Salisbury A's—that was a member of the Interstate League and in 1952 it was represented by a team that was associated with the Cincinnati Reds and named the Salisbury Reds. But after the 1952 season this league folded and professional baseball ceased to be played in Salisbury for more than 40 years.

Professional baseball returned to the city of Salisbury on the Eastern Shore of Maryland for the 1996 season. That season the Montreal Expos moved their South Atlantic League team—the Albany Polecats of Albany, Georgia—over 800 miles north to Salisbury and named the team the Delmarva Shorebirds. But after that season, they relocated the team back south. The vacancy they left behind was filled prior to the 1997 season by the Baltimore Orioles. The prior season the O's had two advanced A-level affiliates, but no single-A team. They eliminated their California League A+ team, the High Desert Mavericks, placed an A-level affiliate in Salisbury as a member of the South Atlantic League, and kept the Delmarva Shorebirds team name. The Orioles remain the major league affiliate of the Shorebirds today.

The Home of the Shorebirds—Arthur W. Perdue Stadium

With the expectation that the Montreal Expos would be moving their South Atlantic League team from Georgia to Maryland for the start of the 1996 season, ground was broken on a new baseball stadium in Salisbury during August 1994. The new ballpark, called Arthur W. Perdue Stadium, was ready in time for the Delmarva Shorebirds' home opener on April 17, 1996. The ballpark is named after the founder of Perdue Farms, Inc., the parent company of the nationwide poultry and agricultural products producer whose home office is located in Salisbury. A photo of the stadium is shown in Fig. 3–1(a) DEL. It has been the home of the Shorebirds for each of the nineteen seasons that the team has been a member of the South Atlantic League.

Above: **Figure 3–1(a) DEL. Arthur W. Perdue Stadium, Salisbury, MD.** *Opposite:* **Figure 3–1(b) DEL. Eastern Shore Baseball Hall of Fame Museum.**

When walking into the stadium, you enter a wide concourse that runs behind the infield and down the outfield lines. The part of the concourse from approximately the start of the home team dugout to the end of the visitors' dugout is covered but is open to the field so that one may watch the game from any vantage point. Concessions are housed in this part of the stadium building on the far side of the concourse. The second floor of the covered section of the concourse is where the stadium's luxury suites are located. At the far left field end of the concourse is a children's play area that includes an interesting carousel.

Seats extend from the inner side of the concourse down to the field. The larger upper section of seating is general admission and is bench type seating, but with a back rest. At the bottom of the bowl there are field level reserved box seats that are individual plastic chairs. The seating capacity of the stadium is 5,200 fans.

The stadium features a Walk of Fame, which has posters to honor former Delmarva Shorebirds players who have gone on to the major leagues. A few of the players for whom plaques are included are Brian Roberts, Nick Markakis, Erik Bedard, and Willie Harris.

A number of rooms on the level below the first base side concourse house the Eastern Shore Baseball Hall of Fame Museum. This honors the rich history of amateur, semi-pro, and professional baseball on the Delmarva Peninsula. The museum has memorabilia, such as game tickets and programs, player and team photos, uniforms, and equipment for teams and players that have played on or hailed from the peninsula. Figure 3–1(b) DEL shows a view of the inside of the museum. The time I spent pregame and postgame exploring the museum was one of the highlights of my day.

The South Atlantic League Years

Delmarva is one of just a few teams in the South Atlantic League that has had long term, consistent support from a single major league club. As pointed out earlier and shown in Table 3–2(a) DEL, South Atlantic League baseball was first brought to Salisbury when the Montreal Expos moved their prior SAL team from Albany, Georgia to the city for the 1996 season. But

Name	MLB Affiliate	Years
Delmarva Shorebirds	Baltimore Orioles	1997-today
Delmarva Shorebirds	Montreal Expos	1996

Level	Team	Stadium	League
Rk	GCL Orioles	Ed Smith Stadium Sarasota, FL	Gulf Coast League
A-	Aberdeen IronBirds	Ripken Stadium Aberdeen, MD	New York-Penn League
A	Delmarva Shorebirds	Arthur W. Perdue Stadium Salisbury, MD	South Atlantic League
A+	Frederick Keys	Harry Grove Stadium Frederick, MD	Carolina League
AA	Bowie Baysox	Prince George's Stadium Bowie, MD	Eastern League
AAA	Norfolk Tides	Harbor Park Norfolk, VA	International League

Top: Table 3–2(a) DEL. Delmarva Shorebirds major league affiliations. *Above:* Table 3–2(b) DEL. Baltimore Orioles minor league organization.

when they relocated their team again prior to the next season, the Baltimore Orioles stepped in and took over as the new affiliate of the Delmarva Shorebirds. That relationship has been lasting. Two-thousand fourteen is the eighteenth consecutive season that the Shorebirds are the single-A affiliate of the Orioles. In spite of their late entry into the league, today the Shorebirds have the second longest continuous affiliation of any team in the Sally League with the same major league club. The Orioles' other minor league baseball clubs are listed in Table 3–2(b) DEL.

The Delmarva Shorebirds have always been a member of the Northern Division of the South Atlantic League; they have made six postseason appearances (1996, 1997, 1998, 2000, 2002 and 2005) and won the South Atlantic League championship twice—1997 and 2000. During their inaugural season—1996—as a member of the Montreal Expos minor league organization, the Shorebirds won a slot in the playoffs. They beat the Asheville Tourists (Colorado Rockies) 2 games to 1 in the first round of the playoffs to win their first Northern Division championship. That team was loaded with future major league talent. Catcher Michael Barrett, infielder Orlando Cabrera, and pitcher Javier Vazquez all played the full season in Salisbury. Cabrera led the team in runs scored (86), stolen bases (51), home runs (14), and total bases (207), and Vazquez, who made 27 starts, went 14W:3L to lead the team in wins. Vazquez's 14 wins in 1996 still stands as the all-time record for the most wins by a pitcher in the Shorebirds uniform. Delmarva faced the Savannah Sand Gnats (Los Angeles Dodgers) in the best-of-five South Atlantic League Championship Series, but they lost 3–1.

The Shorebirds went back to the postseason in 1997, but this time as an affiliate of the Baltimore Orioles. Figure 3–2 DEL is a photo of the players on that season's Delmarva Shorebirds roster. This team's offense featured third baseman Ryan Minor and first baseman Calvin Pickering. Both players had record setting seasons with the bat. A summary of their batting stats is given in Table 3–3 DEL. They finished number 1 or number 2 on the team in almost every batting statistic. For example, Minor led the team with 150 hits and Pickering came in second with 138, while Pickering led the team with 25 home runs and Minor was right behind him with 24. They were also number 1 and number 2 in RBI—Minor 97 and Pickering 79. Both Pickering and Minor ranked in the top 10 among all players in the South Atlantic League for the season in HR, RBI, AVE, OBP, SLG, OPS, and TB.

That season Minor set three all-time Shorebirds single season offensive statistic records that still stand today—150 hits, 42 doubles, and 266 total bases. Pickering is also a Shorebirds offensive record holder. His 25 home runs and .949 on-base plus slugging percentage make him the all-time leader

THE 1997 DELMARVA SHOREBIRDS

BACK ROW: GABE MOLINA, CRAIG DAEDELOW, MALEKE FOWLER, AMERICO PEGUERO, CAMERON FORBES, JOSHUA TOWERS, CARLOS CASIMIRO, ERIC CHAVEZ, RICHARD PAZ. **SECOND ROW:** LARRY JASTER, CURTIS CHARLES, IVANON COFFIE, TIM DECINCES, MATT ACHILLES, CHARLES ALLEY, ABRAHAM HACEN, RYAN KOHLMEIER, DARRELL DENT, ROBERTO RIVERA, MIKE MEYERS, JERRY BASS. **FRONT ROW:** BOBBY RODRIGUEZ, SCOTT EIBEY, BRIAN FALKENBORG, BOB MORSEMAN, CHAD PERONTO, CALVIN PICKERING, RYAN MINOR, TOMMY SHIELDS

CLASS A AFFILIATE OF THE BALTIMORE ORIOLES

Figure 3–2 DEL. Team photograph of the 1997 Delmarva Shorebirds (Courtesy Delmarva Shorebirds).

Player	AB	R	H	2B	3B	HR	RBI
Minor	488	83	150	42	1	24	97
Team Rank	#1	#2	#1	#1	T-#10	#2	#1
Pickering	444	88	138	31	1	25	79
Team Rank	#3	#1	#2	#2	T-#10	#1	#2

Player	TB	AVE	OBP	SLG	OPS
Minor	266	.307	.387	.545	.932
Team Rank	#1	#2	#3	#2	#2
Pickering	246	.311	.394	.554	.949
Team Rank	#2	#1	#2	#1	#1

Table 3–3 DEL. Summary of Ryan Minor and Calvin Pickering 1997 batting stats.

for a player in the Shorebirds uniform in those two power hitting stat categories. Both Minor and Pickering made their major league debuts in the Baltimore Orioles uniform but had short careers in the majors.

Starting pitcher Americo Peguero and closer Ryan Kohlmeier led the pitching staff. Peguero had 11 wins in 26 starts, and Kohlmeier had 24 saves. Kohlmeier had a brief stint as a reliever and closer with the Orioles and saved 19 games, but Peguero never got the call to the majors.

The 1997 South Atlantic League playoffs were structured as a round robin tournament between the teams with the eight best regular season records. There were three best-of-three postseason series: the first round, semifinals, and championship series. The Shorebirds swept the Hickory Crawdads (Chicago White Sox) 2–0 in round 1, edged by the Charleston AlleyCats (Cincinnati Reds) 2 games to 1 in the semifinal round, and then swept the Greensboro Bats (New York Yankees) to win the team's first South Atlantic League Championship title.

Led by future major league infielder Willie Harris and starter Erik Bedard during the 2000 season, the Delmarva Shorebirds won their second SAL championship. Harris, a speedster and key member of the Shorebirds lineup, led all regular players on the team in seven offensive stat categories: R (106), 2B (27), 3B (10), SB (38), SLG (.411), OPS (.807), and TB (195). Today his 106 runs scored still stands as the all-time single season record for a player in the Shorebirds uniform.

When the Piedmont Boll Weevils won the Northern Division during both the first and second halves of the 2000 season, the Shorebirds qualified for the postseason as a Northern Division wild card by having the second best full season record in the division. In the first round of the playoffs they defeated the Boll Weevils (Philadelphia Phillies) to become the Northern Division champions. In the finals round they swept the Columbus Red Stixx (Cleveland Indians) 3 games to 0 to bring home their second South Atlantic League title.

Successful Major Leaguers Who Played in Salisbury

Earlier I mentioned that just in the one season that the Delmarva Shorebirds played as a member of the Montreal Expos minor league organization, the local fans of the team had the opportunity to watch a number of players who went on to have very successful careers at the major league level. I identified three specific players: Michael Barrett, Orlando Cabrera, and Javier Vazquez. Table 3–4 DEL lists all of the players from both the Expos and Orioles eras who went on to play during 10 or more seasons in the majors or have played in the majors at least the last five consecutive years and are still accruing years. Note in the table that a fourth player—catcher Brian Schneider—was on the 1996 Shorebirds team. He did play for Delmarva but was promoted from the rookie level very late in the season. In fact, he appeared in just 5 games with the Shorebirds. The road taken to the major leagues by all of these players traveled through Salisbury where they made a brief stop to take the field in the Shorebirds uniform.

Right-handed pitcher Javier Vazquez was the ace of the 1996 Delmarva starting rotation and led the team in both wins and strikeouts. Nineteen ninety-six was the second season that he pitched at the A level. Vazquez pitched the entire 1995 season for the Albany Polecats—the Expos' prior affiliate in the South Atlantic League. His trip to the majors is interesting. During the 1996 season, Vasquez was just 19 years old but already playing his third season of professional baseball. He began the 1997 season in the starting rotation of the Palm Beach Expos (Florida State League, A+ level) but was promoted late in the season to Montreal's AA affiliate in the Eastern League—at that time the Harrisburg Senators. He made just 6 starts before the end of the season but went 4W:0L in those outings.

Season	Player	Age at DEL	MiLB Season	Position	MLB Debut	Age at Debut	MLB Team	Seasons in MLB
1996	Michael Barrett	19	2	C	9/19/98	21	MON	12
	Orlando Cabrera	21	3	SS	9/3/97	22	MON	15
	Brian Schneider	19	2	C	5/26/00	23	MON	13
	Javier Vazquez	19	3	RHP	4/3/98	21	MON	14
1997	x							
1998	Jayson Werth	19	2	RF	9/1/02	23	TOR	12+
1999	Willie Harris	21	1	LF	9/2/01	23	BAL	12
	Brian Roberts	21	1	2B	6/14/01	23	BAL	14+
2000	Erik Bedard	21	2	LHP	4/17/02	23	BAL	11+
2001	x							
2002	x							
2003	x							
2004	Nick Markakis	20	2	RF	4/3/06	22	BAL	9+
	Jim Johnson	21	4	RHP	7/29/06	23	BAL	9+
2005	x							
2006	David Hernández	21	2	RHP	5/28/09	24	BAL	5+
2007	x							
2008	x							
2009	x							

Table 3–4 DEL. Delmarva SAL players that went on to have long major league careers.

What is very interesting about Vazquez is that he made the jump to the majors at the start of the 1998 season without ever having pitched a game at the triple-A level and pitching in a total of just 88 games in the minors. He was a member of the Montreal Expos 1998 Opening Day roster and started the third game of the season, which was versus the Chicago Cubs at Wrigley Field. In his debut, Vazquez went five innings and gave up 3 runs on 6 hits and 2 walks. The Expos lost 6–2 and Vazquez took the loss. He went on to be a mainstay of the Montreal starting rotation for six seasons but was traded to the New York Yankees during the 2003 offseason. Overall Vazquez pitched for six teams during his 14 season major league career. Over those years he had only one brief stop back in the minors. Vazquez made 7 starts for the Ottawa Lynx in the International League (AAA) during the 1999 season.

Willie Harris' road to the majors was similar to that of Vazquez. Harris, shown in a Shorebirds uniform in Fig. 3-3 DEL, played in Delmarva during both the 1999 and 2000 seasons—the Baltimore Orioles era. Like Vazquez he played two seasons at the A level and was also promoted to the majors prior to having played a game at the AAA level. But there are a number of differences. Harris was drafted out of college and played his first professional game at the rookie level at the age of 21. His first season with Delmarva was a half season because he was drafted in June 1999, and he played in just nine games with the Baltimore Orioles before being traded to the Chicago White Sox during the 2001 offseason.

Table 3-4 DEL shows that Harris played in the majors during 12 seasons. His career may be best described as a journeyman utility player. Unlike many other role players, Harris could play in either the infield or outfield. The chart in Table 3-5 DEL shows that during his career Harris played six different positions—left, center, and right in the outfield and second, third, and short in the infield. His versatility enabled him to defend all

Figure 3-3 DEL. Willie Harris in the Shorebirds uniform (courtesy of Richard A. Passwater, Ph.D).

of those positions satisfactorily. Harris' lifetime fielding percentage was .985. Also, unlike many other utility players he often started the game at his position.

In addition to playing a variety of positions, Harris could hit with some power, bunt, take the extra base, and steal a base. Approximately 29 percent of the 508 hits during his career were for extra bases and 24 of them were triples. Moreover, he was successful in 104 of his 147 steal attempts. Harris also served as a pinch-hitter and designated hitter from time to time.

Field Position	Number of Games
Left Field	308
Center Field	237
Second Base	225
Right Field	51
Third Base	34
Shortstop	8

Table 3–5 DEL. Field positions played by Harris during his major league career.

Maybe Harris is best described as a super utility player. During his career he was frequently granted free agency but was then quickly re-signed by another major league club. He played for seven different teams: the Orioles, White Sox, Red Sox, Braves, Nationals, Mets, and Reds.

Another player who had an interesting journey to the major leagues is former Baltimore Orioles closer Jim Johnson. Johnson was signed by Baltimore out of high school and played his first season of professional ball in 2001 at the rookie level at the age of 18. However, he remained at the rookie level for the 2002 and 2003 seasons until he was promoted to the Delmarva Shorebirds prior to the 2004 season. During that season, he was primarily a starter—17 of his 20 appearances were starts—and he went 8W:7L. Very late in the 2004 season he was promoted to the A+ level and made one start for the Frederick Keys in the Carolina League.

Johnson pitched most of the 2005 season in the Keys' starting rotation and was again promoted very late in the season to the next level—AA with the Bowie Baysox in the Eastern League. He returned to the Baysox to start the 2006 season but was called up to the majors in late July. Johnson made his major league debut with Baltimore at Oriole Park at Camden Yards on July 29, 2006. He started the game, which was versus the Chicago White Sox, got knocked out after three innings, and took the loss.

That was the only game Johnson pitched before being sent back to the minors for the rest of the 2006 season and almost all of 2007. But, he was recalled to the majors by Baltimore on April 11, 2008. He settled into a regular reliever role and appeared in 54 games that season. In the next few years Johnson became a key member of the Orioles bullpen and got a shot at closing a few games. In 2012 he became Baltimore's full time closer and that is a job he did well. Johnson led all closers in the American League in both 2012 and 2013 in saves—51 in 2012 and 50 in 2013. He was selected to represent the American League in the 2012 All-Star Game. The O's traded Johnson to the Oakland Athletics during the 2013 offseason.

A few other players who were on the Delmarva Shorebirds roster in recent years are currently in the majors and contributing to the Baltimore Orioles' success. But these potentially up-and-coming stars do not meet the criteria for being included in Table 3–4 DEL. One such player is the current Orioles third baseman Manny Machado. Fans of the Shorebirds and Orioles got to see him play in Salisbury during the 2011 season at the age of 18. But Machado only played there for about one-third of the season before being promoted to the Frederick Keys (Carolina League, A+ level).

Machado was on the express track to the majors. He started the 2012 season at the AA level with the Bowie Baysox in the Eastern League. Machado was called up by Baltimore in early August and made his major league debut on August 9, 2012, at the age of 20. In that game he was the Orioles starting third baseman and hit in the number nine slot in their batting order. Machado hit a triple in his second major league at-bat and then came home on a sacrifice fly to score the first run of his major league career. He went 2–4 for the day with a triple, single, and 1 run scored. Machado was off to a great start. During 2013 he played 156 games at third base for the Orioles and was selected to represent the team on the American League All-Star Team. Machado has never played a minor league game at the AAA level and appeared in only 219 games before getting promoted to the majors. After getting off to a good start in the field and with the bat in 2014, he had a mid-season knee injury that required season ending surgery.

Baseball Attractions in or Near Salisbury

- **Eastern Shore Baseball Hall of Fame Museum**, 6400 Hobbs Rd., Salisbury, MD 21804 (410) 546–4444
- **Sports Legends Museum at Camden Yards**, 301 W. Camden St., Baltimore, MD 21201 (410) 727–1539
- **Babe Ruth Birthplace and Museum**, 216 Emory St., Baltimore, MD 21230 (410) 727–1539

- **Aberdeen IronBirds Home Game at Ripken Stadium,** 873 Long Dr., Aberdeen, MD 21001 (410) 297–9292
- **Potomac Nationals Home Game at Pfitzner Stadium,** 7 County Complex Ct., Woodbridge, VA 22192 (703) 590–2311
- **Bowie Baysox Home Game at Prince George's Stadium,** 4101 Crain Hwy. Bowie, MD 20716 (301) 464–4865

Attractions in or Near Salisbury

- **Salisbury Plaza and Downtown**, 109 W. Main St., Salisbury, MD 21801
- **Salisbury Zoo**, 755 S. Park Dr., Salisbury, MD 21802 (410) 548–3188
- **Ocean City Boardwalk (The Hugh T. Cropper Inlet Parking Lot)**, 809 S. Atlantic Ave., Ocean City, MD
- **Jolly Roger Amusement Park**, 2901 Philadelphia Ave., Ocean City, MD 21842 (410) 289–3477
- **Trimper's Rides and Amusements**, 700–730 S. Atlantic Ave., Ocean City, MD 21842 (410) 289–8617

Dining in or Near Salisbury

Brewpubs and Breweries

- **EVO Public House**, 201 E. Vine St., Salisbury, MD 21804 (443) 260–2337

Restaurants

- **Brew River Restaurant**, 502 W. Main St., Salisbury, MD 21801 (410) 677–6757
- **Roadie Joe's Bar and Grill,** 213 W. Main St., Salisbury, MD 21801 (443) 944-9156
- **Main Roots Coffee**, 111 W. Main St., Salisbury, MD 21801 (443) 944–9789
- **Market Street Inn and Pub**, 130 W. Market St., Salisbury, MD 21801 (410) 742–4145
- **The Irish Penny Pub and Grill**, 1014 S. Salisbury Blvd., Salisbury, MD 21801 (410) 742–0002
- **BLU Crabhouse and Raw Bar**, 2305 Philadelphia Ave., Ocean City, MD 21842 410-289-3322
- **Fish Tales**, 2207 Herring Way, Ocean City, MD 21842 (410) 289–0990

- **Conner's Beach Café**, 207 N. Atlantic Ave., Ocean City, MD 21842 (410) 289–4105
- **The Dough Roller (S. Division St. at Boardwalk Location)**, 606 S. Atlantic Ave., Ocean City, MD 21842 (410) 289–3501
- **Captain's Galley II**, 12817 Harbor Rd., West Ocean City, MD 21842 (410) 213–2525

Greensboro Grasshoppers

NewBridge Bank Park
408 Bellemeade St., Greensboro, NC 27401
www.milb.com/index.jsp?sid=t477

Greensboro, with a population of over 270,000 people, is the third largest city in North Carolina. Named after Revolutionary War hero Nathaniel Greene, today the city is a thriving urban and cultural center. The city is located in north-central North Carolina, approximately 70 miles directly west of Durham. This makes its South Atlantic League team, the Greensboro Grasshoppers, the closest team to the travel hub city of Durham, North Carolina. NewBridge Bank Park, the home of the Grasshoppers, is a downtown

Team Name	1st Year	Years	Leagues
Greensboro Farmers	1902	1	North Carolina League
Greensboro Farmers	1905	1	Virginia-North Carolina League
Greensboro Champs	1908	3	Carolina Association
Greensboro Patriots	1911	2	Carolina Association
Greensboro Patriots	1913	5	North Carolina State League
Greensboro Patriots	1920	14	Piedmont League
Greensboro Red Sox	1941	2	Piedmont League
Greensboro Patriots	1945	13	Carolina League
Greensboro Red Wings	1948	1	Independent Negro League
Greensboro Yankees	1958	10	Carolina League
Greensboro Patriots	1968	1	Carolina League
Greensboro Hornets	1979	1	Western Carolinas League
Greensboro Hornets	1980	14	South Atlantic League
Greensboro Bats	1994	11	South Atlantic League
Greensboro Grasshoppers	2005	10	South Atlantic League

Table 3–1 GBO. Teams that have played in Greensboro, NC (source: www.baseball-reference.com).

ballpark. The route to the stadium from Durham is an easy 67-mile run, mostly via Interstate 40, and typically takes a little more than an hour. So a home game of the Greensboro Grasshoppers can easily be attended with a day trip from Durham.

Like a number of other cities that host South Atlantic League teams, Greensboro has a long and dynamic history in support of professional baseball. Table 3–1 GBO shows that the first team to play ball in the city was named the Greensboro Farmers, and they played their first season, 1902, in the North Carolina League. However, that league lasted just that one season. A team named the Farmers again played in Greensboro during 1905, but as a member of the Virginia-North Carolina League. However, this league also disbanded after a single season of play and professional baseball ceased for the moment in Greensboro.

The next encounter between baseball and Greensboro began in 1908, when a Carolina Association team—the Greensboro Champs—set up in the town. That was the season that this D-level minor league was formed and it had six teams—three in North Carolina and three in South Carolina. Greensboro set the northeast corner of the league's footprint and was located approximately 200 miles from the furthest team, which was in Anderson, South Carolina. As shown in Table 3–1 GBO, this time baseball stuck—the city supported a team continuously for ten consecutive seasons. First, the Greensboro Champs for three seasons in the Carolina Association and then another team known as the Greensboro Patriots for two years. When the Carolina Association folded after the 1912 season, the Patriots and two other teams from the league joined a new league—the North Carolina State League—for its inaugural season, 1913. The Patriots remained a member of that league until it disbanded after the 1917 season. With the demise of the North Carolina State League, the string of ten consecutive years of professional baseball in Greensboro was broken.

After a lapse of two seasons, baseball and the Patriots returned to Greensboro. Now the Patriots and two other members of the 1917 North Carolina State League joined the Piedmont League for its 1920 inaugural season. For the first season, the league had six teams with five located in North Carolina and the sixth in Virginia. The Patriots had a good run in this league. They played fourteen seasons until the major league sponsor for their team— the St. Louis Cardinals—departed the city after the 1934 season. During the last three seasons, 1932–1934, the Patriots were a B-level minor league affiliate of the Cards.

The departure of the St. Louis Cardinals affiliate ushered in another period during which the city of Greensboro did not field a professional baseball team. But it was not the end of the city's connection to the Piedmont League or the Greensboro Patriots. Seven years later, in 1941, the Boston Red Sox fielded their Piedmont League team—the Greensboro Red Sox—in the city for two seasons. Then after a two year break without a baseball club, the Philadelphia Phillies engaged with the city. They fielded a C-level team with the Greensboro Patriots name, but now in the Carolina League for the 1945 season. From that point the city was the home of a Carolina League team for the next 24 seasons. There were thirteen seasons as the Greensboro Patriots during this stretch with three different major league clubs—first the Phillies, then the Cubs, and last the Red Sox.

But when the New York Yankees brought a team to town for the 1958 season the local Carolina League team was renamed the Greensboro Yankees. The Yankees called the city home though the 1967 season. During this 10 season stretch, a number of future New York Yankees starters took the field for the team. Fans in the city got to see pitchers Jim Bouton (1960), Mel Stottlemyre (1962), and Fritz Peterson (1965) take the mound. At bat and in the field, they saw shortstop Tommy Tresh (1959) and outfielders Roy White (1963) and Bobby Murcer (1965).

Through the 1962 season, the teams of Greensboro played at the B-, C-, or D-level classifications of minor league baseball. But then the MLB minor league system was restructured and began using the level designations that are in place today—rookie (Rk), single A (A), double A (AA), and triple A (AAA). Starting with the 1963 season, the Carolina League was ranked as an A-level league. From 1963 to today Greensboro has hosted a number of different named teams and in a few different leagues, but all of them have played at the A level of the modern MLB minor league system.

After the 1967 season, the New York Yankees moved their A-level team to another Carolina League city, Kinston, North Carolina, as the Kinston Eagles. However, the vacancy they left in Greensboro was immediately filled by the Houston Astros. The Astros turned back the clock and named their team the Greensboro Patriots. But this affiliation ended after one season and Greensboro was again without a baseball club. The departure of the Astros franchise marked the end of the pre–South Atlantic League era of baseball in Greensboro and professional baseball would not return to the city for a decade.

The Cincinnati Reds launched the modern era of baseball in Greensboro. In preparation for the 1979 season, the Reds moved their current Western Carolinas League team, the Shelby Reds, about 130 miles northeast to Greensboro and renamed them the Greensboro Hornets. The Western Carolinas League was in its seventeenth season of play. But that was its last. During the offseason, the league took on a new name, the South Atlantic League. Greensboro was now a host city of the modern South Atlantic League and as shown in Table 3–1 GBO the city has fielded a team in the league every year since 1980.

Table 3–1 GBO shows that Greensboro has had a long and relatively continuous involvement with professional baseball. A team played in the city in all but twenty-seven seasons over the one hundred thirteen-year period from 1902 through 2014. Moreover, the city has been represented by an A-level minor league team in the modern South Atlantic League each of the thirty-six seasons since engaging with the Cincinnati Reds and Western Carolinas League in 1979.

The Home of the Grasshoppers—NewBridge Bank Park

Since professional baseball has been played on a regular basis in Greensboro for 85 years, the teams have played in a number of different ballparks. The Greensboro Farmers, Champs, and Patriots played their home games at Cone Athletic Park. That ballpark was named after the Cone Mills Corporation, a Greensboro based textile manufacture that played a key role in the stadium's construction. Cone Athletic Park was the home field used by the teams that played in the city through 1930.

With Cone Athletic Park aging, a new baseball park, World War Memorial Stadium, was built in the mid–1920s and first used for professional baseball by the Greensboro Patriots in 1930. This stadium was used as one of the venues for an away game of the Durham Bulls in the popular sports movie *Bull Durham*. In the movie, the Bulls' team bus carrying the players to an away game pulls into the parking lot at the front of World War Memorial Stadium. The stadium is easily recognized by its distinctive front, which has three large arched entrance ways positioned between two extra-large piers. World War Memorial Stadium was named to honor local soldiers that died during World War I. There is a large bronze plaque on each of the piers with a list of names to honor local fallen war heroes.

World War Memorial Stadium remained the home for professional baseball in Greensboro for 75 years. With the infusion of modern ballparks in most of the South Atlantic League cities during the 1990, World War Memorial Stadium showed its age and no longer offered the modern facilities and amenities expected of a minor league baseball stadium. For this reason, the city of Greensboro set out on the path of constructing a new downtown stadium. Ground was broken for the new ball field in January 2004.

Figure 3–1 GBO. NewBridge Bank Park, Greensboro, NC.

Greensboro's 2005 baseball season opened with both an attractive new brick exterior stadium, initially called First Horizon Park, and a ball club with an interesting new name. The owners of the local South Atlantic League franchise, the Miami Marlins (then called the Florida Marlins) gave their team a new moniker—the Grasshoppers—to mark a new start for the team in the stadium's inaugural season. Figure 3–1 GBO shows that reminiscent of World War Memorial Stadium, the front of the new ballpark has three extra-large arches. They act as the entrance gateway to a wide, covered, elevated inner concourse behind home plate. The seats slope down from this concourse toward the field, which means that all seating is up close to the action. However, unlike most ballparks where the protective netting is typically limited to the area behind home plate, here the netting extends farther down the first and third baselines to better protect fans from injury. The second level of the front grandstand structure of the building houses luxury suites and an elevated party deck at the third base end.

The concourse extends to the left field corner but goes only partway down the right field line. Most of the concessions are located inside the building structure opposite the field side of the concourse and as kiosks on the concourse. Towards the left field corner are seating and table areas reserved for group picnics and parties. At the left field corner of the concourse is the Go Triad! Grandstand Bar, which offers additional seating for fans to view the game. The ballpark's seating capacity is 7,499.

Just past the start of the right field grass the concourse meets with a sloping grass berm that serves as a lawn seating area. There is another seating berm area behind the left field fence. In the right field corner, but away from the field, is a children's play area.

The part of the concourse that is located behind the infield is covered and offers some protection from the elements for seats at the top of the seating bowl. A large electronic scoreboard and graphic display is located beyond the right-center field wall, while over the outfield wall the city skyline provides an attractive backdrop while viewing the game from the first base side of home plate.

At games, fans are cheered on by Guilford, a furry, overstuffed grasshopper. He is named after the county of North Carolina in which Greensboro is located. Also, Guilford has two helpers—black Labrador dogs named Miss Babe Ruth and Master Yogi Berra—whose jobs include collecting bats left at home plate, retrieving loose balls during the game, carrying a bucket of replacement balls to the umpire, and running the bases at the end of the game.

The ballpark took on its current name—NewBridge Bank Park—prior to the 2008 season and is still the home of the Grasshoppers today. World War Memorial Stadium, which is located slightly over a mile to the east of NewBridge Bank Park, remains in use by a number of local college baseball teams.

The South Atlantic League Years

As mentioned earlier, the city of Greensboro first fielded a team associated with the modern South Atlantic League in 1979 when the league was still named the Western Carolinas League. Table 3–2(a) GBO shows that over the thirty-six seasons since then the team has gracefully transitioned between four different major league affiliates—Cincinnati Reds, New York Yankees, Boston Red Sox, and Miami (Florida) Marlins—without having lost a single season of play. In fact, two teams, the Reds and Yankees, played in the city during two separate periods.

From 1980 to 1984 the Greensboro Hornets were the A-level team of the Yankees in the South Atlantic League. During those same years, New York

League	Name	MLB Affiliate	Years
South Atlantic League	Greensboro Grasshoppers	Miami (Florida) Marlins	2005-today
South Atlantic League	Greensboro Bats	Florida Marlins	2003-2004
South Atlantic League	Greensboro Bats	New York Yankees	1994-2002
South Atlantic League	Greensboro Hornets	New York Yankees	1990-1993
South Atlantic League	Greensboro Hornets	Cincinnati Reds	1988-1989
South Atlantic League	Greensboro Hornets	Boston Red Sox	1985-1987
South Atlantic League	Greensboro Hornets	New York Yankees	1980-1984
Western Carolinas League	Greensboro Hornets	Cincinnati Reds	1979

Level	Team	Stadium	League
Rk	GCL Marlins	Roger Dean Stadium Jupiter, FL	Gulf Coast League
A-	Batavia Muckdogs	Dwyer Stadium Batavia, NY	New York-Penn League
A	Greensboro Grasshoppers	NewBridge Bank Park Greensboro, NC	South Atlantic League
A+	Jupiter Hammerheads	Roger Dean Stadium Jupiter, FL	Florida State League
AA	Jacksonville Suns	Bragan Field Jacksonville, FL	Southern League
AAA	New Orleans Zephyrs	Zephyr Field New Orleans, LA	Pacific Coast League

Top: Table 3–2(a) GBO. Greensboro teams' major league affiliations. *Above:* Table 3–2(b) GBO. Miami Marlins Minor League organization.

had a second single-A team—the Fort Lauderdale Yankees in the Florida State League. After the 1984 season, New York disengaged with Greensboro in favor of maintaining their team in the Florida State League. Over this five season stretch, the Hornets won the Northern Division title three times—1980, 1981, and 1982—and went on to win the South Atlantic League Championship in each of those seasons.

In 1980 the Hornets offense was driven by Don Mattingly and Otis Nixon. They both led the league in a number of batting statistics that season. As mentioned in Chapter 2, Mattingly ranked number 1 among all regular players in the South Atlantic League in hits (177), batting average (.358), and on-base percentage (.422). However, he also led the team in doubles (32), runs batted in (105), and total bases (246). Mattingly primarily played the outfield for the 1980 Hornets, but he then went on to become an exceptional fielding first baseman at the major league level.

Nixon was a table setter in the Hornets lineup. He led the league in runs scored (124), stolen bases (67) and walks (113). Interestingly, Nixon played shortstop and second base at that point in his career, but he played outfield positions at the major league level. Nixon appeared in over 1700 major league games and fielded an infield position during only one of them.

During the 1982 championship season, another future New York Yankees starter took the field for the Greensboro Hornets. Third baseman Mike Pagliarulo supplied an offensive punch for the Hornets. He led the team for the season with 22 home runs and was tied for the lead in total bases with 201. Pagliarulo took over as the New York Yankees' starting third baseman in 1985.

As the Yankees moved out the Red Sox moved in. Boston relocated their A-level team in the Carolina League, the Winston-Salem Spirits, to Greensboro as the Hornets for a seamless start to the 1985 season. The Hornets won the Northern Division in that season but lost in the championship series to the Southern Division winner Florence Blue Jays, Toronto's affiliate in Florence, South Carolina.

But after just three seasons Boston moved their single-A team back to the Carolina League by relocating the team to Lynchburg, Virginia. The Red Sox' departure ushered in a second period of affiliation between the Greensboro Hornets and the Cincinnati Reds. But this one was also short lived, and when the Reds left after just two seasons the door was opened for the New York Yankees to return.

Prior to the 1990 season, New York had two A-level teams—the Fort Lauderdale Yankees in the Florida State League and Prince William Yankees in the Carolina League. However, due to the creation of a new level in the MiLB structure that season, the Advanced A (A+) level, both of these leagues were designated by MLB as this new classification. With a vacancy at the A level of the New York Yankees minor league organization, they returned to the city of Greensboro and the Greensboro Hornets team.

The 1992 Greensboro Hornets were loaded with future Yankees stars. Andy Pettitte (10W:4 L) was a mainstay in their starting rotation; Jorge Posada (.277 batting average) was making the transition from infielder (2B/3B) to the catcher position, and Derek Jeter was promoted from rookie level ball very late in the season and played 11 games at shortstop.

Jeter remained in Greensboro to play shortstop for the complete 1993 season and hit .295 to lead the team in batting average. But at the same time, he struggled in the field. In 126 games as the Hornets' shortstop, he made 56 errors in 506 fielding chances for a very low .889 fielding percentage. Jeter was promoted to the Tampa Yankees in the Florida State League (A+) to start the 1994 season; working hard at his fielding, he evolved into a solid shortstop defender. Interestingly, at both the minor league and major league levels Jeter never took the field at any position other than shortstop. He played that position in 459 games in the minors and 2674 games during his 20 seasons in the majors. At the major league level, Jeter had an excellent .976 career fielding percentage at short.

During this second stint in Greensboro, the Yankees affiliate went to the playoffs four more time—1993, 1997, 1998, and 1999. In addition to Jeter, the 1993 team had future New York Yankees outfielder Shane Spencer and pitchers Ramiro Mendoza and Mariano Rivera. The Hornets won the Northern Division and went on to play the Savannah Cardinals (St. Louis Cardinals) in the championship round, but they lost the best-of-five series 3–2.

In 1997 the New York Yankees team in Greensboro, now called the Bats and a member of the Central Division, won the division title again. The offense of that season's team was powered by the bat of future New York Yankees first baseman Nick Johnson. He had an excellent season and led all regular players on the team in six batting stats: HR (16), RBI (75), BB (76), OBP (.398), SLG (.441), and OPS (.839). Future major league shortstop Cristian Guzman chipped in with 135 hits, the second highest total on the team. But the Bats did not return a winner. The Delmarva Shorebirds (Baltimore Orioles) took home the SAL Championship title.

After thirteen seasons with the Greensboro Hornets and Greensboro Bats, the New York Yankees made the decision to part ways with Greensboro and moved their single-A minor league franchise to the Midwest League for the 2003 season. The Florida Marlins jumped in to fill the vacancy. They relocated their prior A-level team—the Kane County Cougars (Midwest League) from Geneva, Illinois, to Greensboro as the Bats for the 2003 season and later renamed the team the Grasshoppers to coincide with the move to First Horizon Stadium in 2005. Under the leadership of today's Miami Marlins the Greensboro Grasshoppers went to the playoffs twice, won the Northern Division title in 2011 and 2012, and took home the South Atlantic League championship in 2011. The teams and locations of the Miami Marlins other minor league affiliates are listed in Table 3–2(b) GBO.

The Grasshoppers won the Northern Division during the 2nd half of the 2011 season to gain entry into the postseason and faced the Hickory Crawdads (Texas Rangers) for the Northern Division title. The 2011 best-of-three division series opened at NewBridge Bank Park and game 1 went 15 innings. The Grasshoppers went down by 1 run twice in extra innings but both times came back. In the top of the 15th, the Crawdads took a 4–3 lead on right fielder Josh Richmond's homer off reliever Mike Ojala. Hickory right hander Jose Monegro came in for the close, but he hit the leadoff batter, right fielder Marcell Ozuna, with a pitch. Then he served up a walk-off game winning home run to the Grasshoppers' number three batter, Christian Yelich. Greensboro had an exciting 5–4 opening game victory. Ozuna had an outstanding day with the bat. He went 4 for 6 in the game, scored 3 of the Grasshoppers' 5 runs, and knocked in 2 runners. The series moved to Hickory for game 2. The Grasshoppers, behind starter James Leverton, shut out the Crawdads 2 runs to 0 to sweep the series and clinch the Northern Division championship.

In the championship round of the 2011 playoffs, the Greensboro Grasshoppers met the Southern Division winner—the Savannah Sand Gnats (New York Mets). The Grasshoppers and Sand Gnats entered the deciding game five of the league championship series tied 2–2. The Grasshoppers' bats came to life. They broke out to a 7–2 lead with 5 runs in the top of the fourth and 2 more in the fifth. Then they cruised on to a 7–3 victory and won Greensboro's first South Atlantic League championship since 1982.

During the 2013 season, both Marcell Ozuna and Christian Yelich made their major league debut with the Miami Marlins. However, during that season both outfielders split time between the major league club and the Marlins' double-A affiliate, the Jacksonville Sun in the Southern League. Ozuna and Yelich were both in the Marlins' 2014 Opening Day lineup and have locked in the starting center field and left field jobs, respectively. Both had solid seasons with the bat and in the field. In fact, Yelich was one of three National League outfielders to receive the 2014 Gold Glove Award for his defensive play.

Successful Major Leaguers Who Played in Greensboro

Greensboro is a city whose baseball teams have a long history of participation in the South Atlantic League. For this reason, the team's fans have had an opportunity to see a large number of players who went on to have long and successful major league careers. The list in Table 3-3 GBO includes more than 40 players who performed on the baseball field at World War Memorial Stadium or NewBridge Bank Park (First Horizon Park) before going on to play many years for a major league club.

The New York Yankees had the single-A affiliate during 18 of the 35 years that a South Atlantic League team played in the city. In an earlier section I mentioned a number of Yankees stars who played for either the Greensboro

Season	Player	Age at GBO	MiLB Season	Position	MLB Debut	Age at Debut	MLB Team	Seasons in MLB
1979	Gary Redus	22	2	LF	9/7/82	25	CIN	13
1980	Greg Gagne	18	2	SS	6/5/83	21	MIN	15
	Rex Hudler	19	3	2B	9/9/84	24	NYY	13
	Don Mattingly	19	2	1B	9/8/82	21	NYY	14
	Otis Nixon	21	2	CF	9/9/83	24	NYY	17
1981	x							
1982	Mike Pagliarulo	22	2	3B	7/7/84	24	NYY	11
1983	Fredi González	19	2	C/Manager	4/2/07	43	FLA	8+
1983	Stan Javier	18	3	CF	4/15/84	20	NYY	17
	Roberto Kelly	18	2	CF	7/29/87	22	NYY	14
	Jim Corsi	21	2	RHP	6/28/88	26	OAK	10
1984	x							
1985	Josias Manzanillo	17	3	RHP	10/5/91	23	BOS	11
1986	Todd Pratt	19	2	C	7/29/92	25	PHI	14
1987	Curt Schilling	20	2	RHP	9/7/88	21	BAL	20
1988	Ed Taubensee	19	3	C	5/18/91	22	CLE	11
1989	Reggie Sanders	21	2	RF	8/22/91	23	CIN	17
1990	Russ Springer	21	2	RHP	4/17/92	23	NYY	18
1991	Carl Everett	20	2	CF	7/21/93	22	FLA	14
	Mariano Rivera	21	2	RHP	5/23/95	25	NYY	19
1992	Derek Jeter	18	1	SS	5/29/95	20	NYY	20
	Jorge Posada	20	2	C	9/4/95	24	NYY	17
	Andy Pettitte	20	2	LHP	4/29/95	22	NYY	18
1993	Mike DeJean	22	2	RHP	5/2/97	26	COL	10
	Ramiro Mendoza	21	1	RHP	5/25/96	23	NYY	10
1994	Ricky Ledee	21	5	LF	6/18/98	24	NYY	10
1995	x							
1996	Mike Lowell	22	2	3B	9/13/98	24	NYY	13
1997	Cristian Guzman	19	2	SS	4/6/99	21	MIN	11
	Nick Johnson	18	2	1B	8/21/01	22	NYY	10
	Marcus Thames	20	1	LF	6/10/02	25	NYY	10
	Tony Armas	19	3	RHP	8/16/99	21	MON	10
1998	Randy Choate	22	2	LHP	7/1/00	24	NYY	14+
1999	x							
2000	x							
2001	x							

Above and following: Table 3–3 GBO. Greensboro SAL players that went on to have long major league careers.

Season	Player	Age at GBO	MiLB Season	Position	MLB Debut	Age at Debut	MLB Team	Seasons in MLB
2002	Robinson Cano	19	1	2B	5/3/05	22	NYY	10+
	Dioner Navarro	18	2	C	9/7/04	20	NYY	11+
2003	Josh Johnson	19	2	RHP	9/10/05	21	FLA	9+
2004	Jason Vargas	21	1	LHP	7/14/05	22	FLA	9+
2005	x							
2006	Brett Hayes	22	2	C	5/22/09	25	FLA	6+
	Gaby Sánchez	22	2	1B	9/17/08	25	FLA	7+
	Chris Leroux	22	1	RHP	5/26/09	25	PIT	6+
2007	Chris Coghlan	22	2	LF	5/8/09	23	FLA	6+
	Logan Morrison	19	2	LF	7/27/10	22	FLA	5+
2008	Giancarlo Stanton	18	2	RF	6/8/10	20	FLA	5+
	Steve Cishek	22	2	RHP	9/26/10	24	FLA	5+
2009	x							

Hornets or Greensboro Bats, including Don Mattingly, Derek Jeter, Jorge Posada, and Andy Pettitte.

Another New York Yankees superstar and future Hall of Famer who made a stop in Greensboro was Mariano Rivera. In 1991, the second year of his pro ball career, a 20-year-old Rivera took the mound for the Greensboro Hornets and made 15 starts and 14 relief appearances. He returned for a second stint with the Hornets in 1993, but this time he was exclusively featured as a starter. What is interesting about Rivera's minor league career is that after the 1991 season he was never again used in a relief role. Overall he made 68 starts at the minor league level but pitched in relief only 35 times. Also, he had only 1 save in the minors and that was at the rookie level during his first season.

When Rivera made his major league debut with the Yankees on May 23, 1995, he was the starting pitcher. During his rookie season, he made 10 starts and 9 bullpen appearances. It was not until the next season, 1996, that he became the set-up man for closer John Wetteland. Then, in 1997 Rivera took over as the Yankees' full time closer. Rivera went on to play nineteen seasons in the Bronx, during which he had 652 saves, which set the new all-time major league saves record.

But the New York Yankees were not the only major league team that had future stars pass through the city of Greensboro on their way to the majors. For instance, in 1987, when the Hornets were affiliated with the Boston Red Sox, a 20-year-old Curt Schilling was a member of the team's starting rotation. Schilling went 8W:15L for the season but led the team and the South Atlantic League with 189 strikeouts. He made his major league debut with the Baltimore Orioles on Sept. 7, 1988, and went on to win 216 games during a 20 season career with five teams: Baltimore, Houston, Philadelphia, Arizona, and Boston. Schilling is one of just sixteen major league pitchers who have made over 3000 strikeouts during their careers. Maybe his most important pitching stat is that he went 11W:2L in 19 postseason starts, which includes a 4W:1L record in seven World Series appearances.

Another example is outfielder Reggie Sanders. When the Greensboro Hornets were the A-level team of the Cincinnati Reds in 1989, Sanders was their shortstop—yes, shortstop. He made 42 errors in 336 fielding chances. Needless to say the next season he played the outfield. Sanders made his major league debut as the center fielder and leadoff batter of the Cincinnati Reds on August 22, 1991, versus the Atlanta Braves. He played the next eight seasons in the Reds' outfield. Sanders was traded to the San Diego Padres during the 1998 offseason and went on to have a seventeen year career split between eight teams.

The current affiliate of the Greensboro team, the Miami (Florida) Marlins, is second to the Yankees in terms of longest engagement with a Greensboro team. The Bats and Grasshoppers have been the single-A minor league club of the Marlins since 2003—a total of twelve consecutive seasons. Even though this is quite recent baseball history, a number of former Marlins prospects who played on the diamond at NewBridge Bank Park in Greensboro have appeared in major league games during at least the last five seasons. Two that play a regular role for the Miami Marlins today are right fielder Giancarlo Stanton and closer Steve Cishek.

During the 2008 season, Giancarlo Stanton was a regular fixture in the Grasshoppers' outfield. As mentioned in Chapter 2, he led the league in home runs for that season with 39. The 6'6" power hitting right fielder had a big season at the plate. A summary of Stanton's batting stats appears in Table 3–4 GBO. He led all regular players on the Greensboro team in every one of these offensive stats except stolen bases and batting average. Moreover, in

G	AB	R	H	2B	3B	HR	RBI
125	468	89	137	26	3	39	97

TB	BB	SO	SB	AVE	OBP	SLG	OPS
286	58	153	4	.293	.381	.611	.993

Table 3–4 GBO. Giancarlo Stanton 2008 batting stat summary.

addition to leading the South Atlantic League in home runs, he ranked number 1 in the league in TB, SLG, and OPS. In fact, his 39 home runs, 286 total bases, .611 slugging percentage, and .993 on-base plus slugging percentage set the Grasshoppers' single season all-time record in each of those offensive statistic categories. Stanton remains the team record holder in those four power hitting stats today.

Table 3–3 GBO shows that 2014 was Stanton's fifth season playing with the Marlins. Stanton made his major league debut as the right fielder of the Florida Marlins on June 8, 2010, versus the Phillies at Citizens Bank Park in Philadelphia. He singled in his first major league at-bat and then went on to have a 3 for 5 day, while scoring 2 runs. Stanton has been the Miami Marlins' starting right fielder since 2011 and represented the team on both the 2012 and 2014 National League All-Star teams.

Stanton had another exceptional offensive season in 2014. He led the National League with 37 home runs and with a .555 slugging percentage. Moreover, he also finished the season ranked number 2 in the league in four other batting stat categories: RBI (105), BB (95), OBP (.395), and OPS (.950). However, his 2014 was cut short when he was hit in the face by a fastball on September 11th and hospitalized with severe facial injuries. In spite of the need to recover from this injury, the Miami Marlins signed the 25 year old Stanton during the 2014 off season to a thirteen year contract worth $325 million.

Baseball Attractions in Greensboro

• **World War Memorial Stadium**, 510 Yanceyville St., Greensboro, NC 27405 (336) 373–2955
• **Atlantic Coast Conference (ACC) Hall of Champions**, 1921 W. Lee St., Greensboro, NC 27403 (336) 315–8411

Attractions in Greensboro

• **Greensboro Science Center: Aquarium, Museum, and Zoo**, 4301 Lawndale Dr., Greensboro, NC 27455 (336) 288–3769
• **Bog Garden at Benjamin Park**, 1101 Hobbs Rd., Greensboro, NC 27410 (336) 373–2199

Dining in Greensboro

BREWPUBS AND BREWERIES

• **Natty Greene's Pub & Brewing Company**, 345 S. Elm St., Greensboro, NC 27401 (336) 274–1373

DOWNTOWN RESTAURANTS

• **Liberty Oak Restaurant and Bar**, 100-D W. Washington St., Greensboro, NC 27401 (336) 273–7057
• **Ham's Restaurant**, 324 S. Elm St., Greensboro, NC 27401 (336) 907–7753
• **M'Coul's Public House**, 110 W. McGee St., Greensboro, NC 27401 (336) 378–0204
• **Grey's Tavern**, 343 S. Elm Street., Greensboro, NC 27401 (336) 617–5341
• **Mellow Mushroom**, 609 S. Elm St., Greensboro, NC 27406 (336) 235–2840
• **Cheesecakes by Alex**, 315 S. Elm St., Greensboro, NC 27401 (336) 273–0970

Greenville Drive

Fluor Field at the West End
945 S Main St., Greenville, SC 29601
www.milb.com/index.jsp?sid=t428

My next South Atlantic League stop is for a home game of the Greenville Drive. Greenville, South Carolina, is located in the northwest corner of the state in the foothills of the Appalachian Mountains. I found the city very interesting. It has a very attractive downtown area that is built on the banks of the Reedy River.

Baseball has been an attraction in Greenville since the early 1900s. As shown in Table 3–1 GVL, eight different named teams have played in the city and have participated in a number of different leagues. Even though Greenville has a long engagement with professional baseball, the relationship has been a rocky road. The first team, the Greenville Mountaineers, who played in the city as a member of the South Carolina League in 1907, lasted for just one season. The team was rated as D level—a minor league baseball team classification that no longer exists.

Team Name	1st Year	Years	Leagues
Greenville Mountaineers	1907	1	South Carolina League
Greenville Spinners	1908	5	Carolina Association
Greenville Spinners	1919	12	South Atlantic League
Greenville Spinners	1931	1	Palmetto League
Greenville Spinners	1938	10	South Atlantic League
Greenville Spinners	1951	4	Tri-State League
Greenville Spinners	1961	2	South Atlantic League
Greenville Braves	1963	2	Western Carolinas League
Greenville Mets	1965	2	Western Carolinas League
Greenville Red Sox	1967	5	Western Carolinas League
Greenville Rangers	1972	1	Western Carolinas League
Greenville Braves	1984	21	Southern League
Greenville Bombers	2005	1	South Atlantic League
Greenville Drive	2006	9	South Atlantic League

Table 3–1 GVL. Teams that have played in Greenville, SC (source: www.baseball-reference.com).

The next season, the Greenville team and two others from the South Carolina League, the Anderson Electricians and Spartanburg Spartans, joined a new league, the Carolina Association, and took a new name—the Greenville Spinners. The league's other three teams—the Charlotte Hornets, Greensboro Champs, and Winston-Salem Twins—were in North Carolina. The Spinners played in Greenville as a member of the Carolina Association for five baseball seasons—1908–1912. This stint ended when the Carolina Association shut down operation after the 1912 season.

Professional baseball was not played again in Greenville until 1919. In that year, another Greenville Spinners team was formed as a member of the original South Atlantic League. By then, the league was well established. It had operated in fourteen of the previous fifteen baseball seasons. Between 1919 and 1962 the city of Greenville hosted a team nicknamed the Spinners for 24 of those 42 seasons as a member of the Sally League. But a number of those lapses were the result of the Sally League suspending operations. For example, the South Atlantic League temporarily shut down from 1931 through 1935.

Note in Table 3–1 GVL that the Spinners did engage to play in the Palmetto League for the 1931 season. That was the Palmetto League's inaugural season, but the league folded after its first season and professional baseball was not played again in Greenville until a Spinners team rejoined the South

Atlantic League in 1938. Table 3–1 GVL shows that the Spinners also broke from the Sally League to play in the Tri-State League for four seasons between 1951 and 1955.

Things changed in 1963. That was the inaugural season of the Western Carolinas League, and Greenville became the home of one of the teams of this new league. The then Milwaukee Braves formed a new single-A affiliate to play in the Western Carolinas League and named it the Greenville Braves. That team played their games at Meadowbrook Park in Greenville. Table 3–1 GVL shows that the Braves stayed just two seasons, but Greenville remained the home of a Western Carolinas League team through 1972. The team name and major league affiliation changed a number of times—Greenville Mets (New York Mets, 1965–1966), Greenville Red Sox (Boston Red Sox, 1967–1971), and Greenville Rangers (Texas Rangers, 1972).

After the Rangers moved their Western Carolinas League team to Gastonia, North Carolina, during the 1972 offseason, Greenville was again without a team, and professional baseball ceased in the city for another extended period of years. The city did not engage with another team until the 1984 season. Having built a new baseball stadium, Greenville Municipal Stadium, the city lured the Braves, but now the Atlanta Braves, back to the city. Atlanta relocated their double-A team in the Southern League from Savannah, Georgia, to Greenville. The AA-level Greenville Braves stayed in the city for 21 seasons. After the 2004 season, the Braves team was moved to play in another new stadium—Trustmark Park in Pearl, Mississippi. The reason for the move was that Greenville Municipal Stadium, now old, no longer offered the amenities to attract the fans of the day.

But the vacuum was quickly filled. The Boston Red Sox relocated their A-level affiliate, which was the Augusta GreenJackets in the South Atlantic League, to Greenville for the start of the 2005 season. Greenville built a new stadium, and this Red Sox Sally League team still calls the city home today. The city of Greenville, which hosted a charter member of the Western Carolinas League—the Greenville Braves—was now engaged with its successor, the modern South Atlantic League.

The Home of the Drive—Fluor Field at the West End

During the second half of the 20th century, the lack of a new or at least newly renovated stadium might have played a role in the transient nature of teams in Greenville. When the Greenville Braves of the Western Carolinas League moved into the city in 1963, they set up shop at Meadowbrook Park—

a ballpark that was built in 1938. As mentioned earlier, during the next few years, the 25-plus-year-old stadium was used by the Braves, Mets, and Red Sox.

The Texas Rangers SAL team was poised to move into the stadium for the 1972 baseball season. However, Meadowbrook Park was significantly damaged by fire prior to the start of the season. The stadium was temporarily retrofitted to enable the Greenville Rangers to play their games. But after the season, the stadium was demolished. Without a stadium available, the Rangers moved on to another city for the 1973 season.

Greenville did not replace Meadowbrook Park until the early 1980s, and without a stadium there was no opportunity to engage a new baseball team. However, with the commitment to build a new ballpark—Greenville Municipal Stadium—the Atlanta Braves moved their AA-level affiliate to Greenville to open the 1984 season. That stadium, which served as the home of the Greenville Braves of the Southern League, was located several miles outside the downtown area of the city. The Braves called the stadium home for over

Above: **Figure 3–1(a) GVL. Fluor Field at the West End, Greenville, SC.** *Opposite:* **Figure 3–1(b) GVL. The Green Monster at Fluor Field.**

20 baseball season. Though no longer in use for professional baseball, the stadium has been updated and today serves as the cornerstone of a local multi-field baseball complex.

Today's South Atlantic League team—the Greenville Drive—plays their games at Fluor Field at the West End. A commitment between the team and city officials to build this new stadium brought a new Boston Red Sox minor league franchise to the city for the 2005 season. Ground was not broken for the stadium until the spring of 2005 and the new team, called the Greenville Bombers this first season, had to play their games at the old Greenville Municipal Stadium.

The new stadium, originally named just West End Field, was ready for the home opener of the 2006 season. During the offseason the team's nickname was changed to the Drive. Greenville won their 2006 home opener 6–1 over the Columbus Catfish (Los Angeles Dodgers). The stadium was renamed Fluor Field at the West End after the Fluor Corporation, a global engineering construction company that contributes heavily to the local economy. The West End part of the name refers to the fact that the ball field was built in the historic West End District of the city, which is located on the west bank of the Reedy River.

Fluor Field at the West End is an attractive, modern downtown baseball facility. This ballpark, which is the newest of the current South Atlantic League stadiums, has a seating capacity of 5,700. Its main entrance and box office are located directly on South Main Street. The stadium has a wide concourse down the left field and right field lines, but it does not wrap around the outfield like in many of the other new ballparks. The concourse allows one to view the field and game activity while at the concessions area.

The ballpark was designed with Boston's Fenway Park in mind. Some of the distinguishing features of Fenway Park were incorporated into its design. As shown in Fig. 3–1(b) GVL, Fluor Field has a mini-Green Monster as its left field wall. Like at Fenway, scores are manually posted on the scoreboard. A Green Monster–like outfield field wall is a feature of a few of the other Red Sox minor league teams' ballparks. Also, the distance to the right field corner is identical to that at Fenway and a Pesky Pole marks the right field corner. Finally, a Boston Red Sox tradition is observed at each home game. During the middle of the 8th inning, fans join in to sing Neil Diamond's "Sweet Caroline" just like at Fenway Park in Boston. Like a number of the other South Atlantic League stadiums, the protective netting behind home plate is extended down the left field and right field lines to approximately the end of the dugouts.

At the rear entrance of the stadium, which is located to the first base side of home plate, the team has a Heritage Plaza that has plaques and banners recognizing some of the former players that spent their early playing days with a team in Greenville. They include Tommy Lasorda, who played with the Greenville Spinners when they were a Brooklyn Dodgers affiliate in 1949. He went on to have a very short major league career as a left-handed pitcher, but a 21-year Hall of Fame career as the manager of the Los Angeles Dodgers. Another Hall of Famer that is commemorated in the plaza is RHP Nolan Ryan. He played most of the 1966 season at Meadowbrook Park as a member of the Greenville Mets. Current Boston Red Sox pitcher Clay Buchholz, who played for the Greenville Drive during the 2006 season, is also remembered with a plaque. Finally, a plaque honors Boston Red Sox Hall of Fame right fielder Jim Rice. Rice did not play for a Greenville team, but instead grew up in Anderson, South Carolina, which is approximately 30 miles from Greenville.

Overall I found the stadium an interesting and friendly venue to view a ball game. Its attractive downtown location is ideal for convenient pre-game or post-game activities. The stadium is just steps from interesting local restaurants and other business establishments. For example, Mac's Speed Shop is located right across the street and Shoeless Joe Jackson Plaza a short walk down South Main Street. At the plaza there is a life-size bronze statue to honor the local baseball great. At this plaza there is also an interesting restaurant—Smoke on the Water.

Greenville was the hometown of legendary hitter Shoeless Joe Jackson. Jackson said that he got his nickname after one day playing a game in his socks because blisters on his feet hurt when he wore his baseball shoes. Shoeless Joe played his first season of minor league ball in 1908 for the Greenville Spinners and batted .346 for the season. Jackson made his major league debut with the Philadelphia Athletics on August 25, 1908, at the age of 21. In his first full season, 1911, he batted .408 for the Cleveland Naps. In 1912, his 226 hits for the Naps tied baseball legend Ty Cobb of the Detroit Tigers for the most hits in the American League for the season. The next season, 1913, Jackson again topped all batters in the AL in hits with 197.

During the later part of his major league career Jackson played for the Chicago White Sox. Due to his alleged involvement in the 1919 World Series scandal—the Black Sox Scandal—Jackson was one of a group of eight players that was banned for life from playing professional baseball prior to the 1921 season. Jackson played in the majors during 13 seasons and posted a lifetime batting average of .356. A Shoeless Joe Jackson Museum and Library is located right across the street from the rear entrance of Fluor Field.

The South Atlantic League Years

The review of the evolution of teams that played baseball in Greenville, South Carolina, identified that the city played a role in two distinct eras of the modern South Atlantic League's history. As shown in Table 3–2(a) GVL, the city was represented in the 1963 inaugural season of the Western Carolinas League by the Greenville Braves. Greenville remained a host of a Western Carolinas League team through the 1972 season, but the teams arrived and departed quickly: Milwaukee Braves (2 seasons), New York Mets (2 seasons), Texas Rangers (1 season) and the Boston Red Sox, who had the longest stay—5 seasons.

But then there was a long drought before a South Atlantic League team again played in the city. After the Atlanta Braves' AA team left in 2004, the Boston Red Sox made a return to the city. During the 2004 offseason, they dropped their affiliation with the Augusta GreenJackets in Augusta, Georgia, came to an agreement with the city of Greenville about the building of a new stadium, and engaged the Greenville Bombers as their new A-level team in the modern South Atlantic League for the 2005 season. With the new stadium

League	Name	MLB Affiliate	Years
South Atlantic League	Greenville Drive	Boston Red Sox	2006-today
South Atlantic League	Greenville Bombers	Boston Red Sox	2005
Western Carolinas League	Greenville Rangers	Texas Rangers	1972
Western Carolinas League	Greenville Red Sox	Boston Red Sox	1967-1971
Western Carolinas League	Greenville Mets	New York Mets	1965-1966
Western Carolinas League	Greenville Braves	Boston Braves	1963-1964

Level	Team	Stadium	League
Rk	GCL Red Sox	JetBlue Park Fort Myers, FL	Gulf Coast League
A-	Lowell Spinner	LeLacheur Park Lowell, MA	New York-Penn League
A	Greenville Drive	Fluor Field Greenville, SC	South Atlantic League
A+	Salem Red Sox	LewisGale Field Salem, VA	Carolina League
AA	Portland SeaDogs	Hadlock Field Portland, MA	Eastern League
AAA	Pawtucket Red Sox	McCoy Stadium Pawtucket, RI	International League

Top: Table 3–2(a) GVL. Greenville teams' major league affiliation. *Above:* Table 3–2(b) GVL. Boston Red Sox minor league organization.

not yet complete, the Bombers played their first season at Greenville Municipal Stadium. To start the 2006 season, the Red Sox affiliate started with a new stadium—at that time called West End Field—and a new team nickname—the Drive. Table 3–2(b) GVL lists Boston's other minor league affiliates.

The year 2014 was the Greenville Drive's ninth season playing in the city. Over this nine year period the Drive have won either the first half or second half of the season during just two years, were the Southern Division Champions in both of these seasons, but never succeeded in winning the South Atlantic League championship.

Greenville won the first half of the 2009 season with a 39W:29L record to lock in a ticket to the postseason. They opened the first round of the Southern Division playoffs versus the Asheville Tourists (Colorado Rockies). During the regular season, the Drive's offense was powered by catcher Ryan Lavarnway. He led all regular players on the team in ten batting categories: R (60), H (115), 2B (36), HR (21), RBI (87), AVE (.285), OBP (.367), SLG (.540), OPS (.907), and TB (218). Lavarnway ranked in the top 10 among all players in the league in seven of those stats: 2B, HR, RBI, AVE, SLG, OPS, and TB. In fact, his .540 slugging percentage ranked him number one in the league in that power hitting stat. Moreover, his 87 runs batted in remain the Drive's all-time single season RBI record today. Their starting rotation was led by right-handed pitchers Brock Huntzinger (10W:9L) and Stolmy Pimentel (10W:7L).

The Drive swept the Tourists by winning games 1 and 2 of the best-of-three Southern Division Championship Series. In game 1, Lavarnway and third baseman Will Middlebrooks homered in the top of the ninth inning to give the Drive a come from behind victory. Game 2 was also a come from behind win. In that game, Greenville's right fielder Mitch Denning hit a walk-off solo home run in the bottom of the ninth to win the game and close out the series. Greenville won both games by an identical score—3 runs to 2.

In the league championship round, the Drive faced the Northern Division champion Lakewood BlueClaws (Philadelphia Phillies). Lavarnway went 5 for 19 and Casey Kelly 5 for 15. But, the Greenville offense could not mount a consistent attack against the BlueClaws pitching. The Drive dropped the best-of-five championship series 3 games to 1. Pimentel had two quality starts in the postseason and the Drive won both of those games. However, he received a no decision in both outings.

During the second half of the 2010 season, Greenville posted a 41W:28L record to finish first in the Southern Division. That gave them a berth in the postseason. This time they faced the Savannah Sand Gnats (New York Mets) in the opening round of the Southern Division Championship Series. Again, the Drive swept the best-of-three series in 2 games to win the Southern Division title. In game 1 they got a strong outing from starter and winning pitcher Drake Britton. His pitching stats for the 5 inning outing were 2 R, 5 H, 1 BB, and 8 SO. The offense was led by first baseman Reynaldo Rodriguez, who went 3 for 5 on the day with 2 doubles and knocked in 3 runs. Catcher Christian Vazquez also contributed 3 hits, but in 4 trips to the plate. He knocked in 2 runs. The Drive won 8–3. Starter Chris Balcom-Miller went 5 innings in game 2 to lead Greenville to a 5–4 victory. Reynaldo Rodriguez had the key hit—a 2 run homer in the top of the sixth that put the Drive in front to stay. Balcom-Miller got the win for Greenville.

In the best-of-five South Atlantic League Championship Series, Greenville again faced off against the Lakewood BlueClaws. The Drive won game 1 by a score of 3 runs to 1 behind starter Drake Britton, his second win of the postseason. Britton threw 5 innings of 1 hit shutout ball. But that was Greenville's only win in the series. Lakewood won the next three games to clinch their second consecutive South Atlantic League title.

Successful Major Leaguers Who Played in Greenville

Even though there had been long droughts during which there was no professional baseball played in Greenville, the baseball fans in the city have had the opportunity to see many up and coming prospects. My theme has been to focus on prospects during their early formative years—those in which they played their A-level ball in the South Atlantic League. But, there was more than a thirty year lapse in modern South Atlantic League play since the Greenville Rangers departed after the 1972 season. For many years during that period the Atlanta Braves had their AA team playing in the city, and many of the players from that team went on to have success at the major league level.

Table 3–3 GVL lists all of the baseball players who played their A ball in Greenville as a member of either a Western Carolinas League team (1963–1972) or South Atlantic League team (2005–2009) and then went on to have a successful major league career. As pointed out earlier, my criteria for successful is that the player must have played at the major league level in at least ten seasons or that the player has played in the majors during the last five seasons—2010–2014—and is still accruing years.

Looking at Table 3–3 GVL you see that a good number of players from the teams of the Western Carolinas League went on to have extended stays in the major leagues. In fact the list includes two who played more than twenty seasons, pitcher Nolan Ryan and right fielder Dwight Evans, and four others, Jerry Koosman (LHP), Cecil Cooper (1B), John Curtis (LHP), and Ben Oglivie (LF), with fifteen or more years. In fact, Nolan Ryan's twenty-seven-year Hall of Fame baseball career is the longest of any player in the modern era of major league baseball—that is since 1900. Ryan made his major league debut with the New York Mets on September 11, 1966, at the age of 19 and pitched his last game on September 22, 1993, while playing for the Texas Rangers at the age of 46.

Season	Player	Age at GVL	MiLB Season	Position	MLB Debut	Age at Debut	MLB Team	Seasons in MLB
1963	x							
1964	Cito Gaston	20	1	CF	9/14/68	23	ATL	11
1965	Jerry Johnson	21	3	RHP	7/17/68	24	PHI	10
	Jerry Koosman	22	1	LHP	4/14/67	24	NYM	19
	Dick Selma	21	3	RHP	9/2/65	21	NYM	10
1966	Duffy Dyer	20	1	C	9/21/68	23	NYM	14
	Bob Heise	19	1	SS	9/12/67	20	NYM	11
	Nolan Ryan	19	2	RHP	9/11/66	19	NYM	27
1967	x							
1968	x							
1969	Cecil Cooper	19	2	1B	9/8/71	21	BOS	17
	John Curtis	21	2	LHP	8/13/70	22	BOS	15
	Ben Oglivie	20	2	LF	9/4/71	22	BOS	16
1970	Dwight Evans	18	2	RF	9/16/72	20	BOS	20
1971	Tim Blackwell	18	2	C	7/3/74	21	BOS	10
	Rick Burleson	20	2	SS	5/4/74	23	BOS	13
	Bo Díaz	18	1	C	9/6/77	24	BOS	13
1972	x							
1973-2004	No team							
2005	x							
2006	Clay Buchholz	21	2	RHP	8/17/07	23	BOS	8+
2007	Josh Reddick	20	1	RF	7/31/09	22	BOS	6+
	Félix Doubront	19	3	LHP	6/18/10	22	BOS	5+
2008	x							
2009	x							

Table 3-3 GVL. Greenville SAL players that went on to have long major league careers.

Even though a New York Mets single-A affiliate played just two seasons in Greenville, five players from those two teams went on to debut with the Mets and have long, successful baseball careers. In addition to Nolan Ryan, the list includes Mets great lefty Jerry Koosman and fan favorite Duffy Dyer.

Well, we all know how successful Nolan Ryan was in the majors, but how did he do at Greenville? In 1966, a 19-year-old Ryan pitched for the Greenville Mets during his second season of professional baseball. Ryan made 28 starts that season and posted an extraordinary 17W:2L record with an excellent ERA (2.51) and WHIP (1.290). To get 17 wins in the minor leagues and especially at the lower levels is very rare. Maybe it could happen back in Ryan's day, but today pitch counts are stringently enforced and young pitchers are often removed prior to the fifth inning of games in which they would probably receive the win. But by not completing five full innings, they end up with a no-decision.

But this leads to the big question. Did Nolan Ryan—the all-time leader in no-hitters at the major league level—pitch a no-no while a member of the Greenville Mets starting rotation? No, Ryan did not pitch a no-no. However, as mentioned in Chapter 2, Daniel Bard was the starting pitcher of a no-hitter that was thrown by him and reliever Ryan Phillips during the Greenville Drive's 2007 season.

Table 3–3 GVL also shows that after a slow start in 1967 and 1968, the Boston Red Sox had quite a few former Greenville Red Sox players go on to debut for their major league club and have long stays in The Show. The player in this list whose Red Sox career stands out is Dwight Evans—affectionately known as "Dewey" to Boston fans. Evans played 20 seasons in the majors—19 with the Red Sox. Over his career he played the outfield in 2146 games and was the starting right fielder in 1995 of them.

Evans played his second season of professional ball with the Greenville Red Sox in 1970 at the age of 18. Evans had a solid season with the bat and in the field. He hit .276 and with power. Thirty-two of his 98 hits (approximately 33 percent) were for extra bases. Also, his outfield play was excellent. Evans made just 6 errors in 145 chances in the field—a .959 fielding percentage. His 10 outfield assists and 2 double plays were a sign of things to come.

As a major leaguer, Dewey was recognized as a good power hitter and excellent right fielder with a strong throwing arm. Over his twenty-year career, he batted .272 and 941 of his 2446 hits were for extra bases—approximately 38 percent. These numbers are right in line with those of his Greenville season. In the outfield, his career FLD% average was .987 and he had 157 outfield assists that included 42 double plays, while making just 59 errors. These are exceptional fielding stats and even better than those he posted for the Greenville Red Sox.

In recent years, Greenville Drive fans had the opportunity to see some of today's Red Sox players as they played their early years at Fluor Field at the West End. The listing in Table 3–3 GVL shows that Boston's current right-handed pitching ace, Clay Buchholz, was a member of the Drive's 2006 roster. Buchholz was a key member of the Drive's starting rotation that season and went 9W:4L in 21 starts. His 9 wins tied him for the most wins on the team. Buchholz made his major league debut on the mound at Fenway Park on August 17, 2007. He started and went six complete innings while pitching the Red Sox to an 8-4 victory over the Angels. En route to his first win in the majors, Buchholz gave up 4 runs (3 earned) on 8 hits, while walking 3 and striking out 5. Two thousand fourteen was the two-time American League All-Star's eighth season as a member of the Boston Red Sox starting rotation.

A few of the Boston Red Sox' current up and coming players played a season for the Greenville Drive. Boston's end of 2013 number one prospect infielder, Xander Bogaerts, and number two top prospects outfielder, Jackie Bradley, both played for the Drive during the 2011 season. Bogaerts and Bradley made their major league debut with Boston during the 2013 season and were members of the Red Sox's 2014 Opening Day roster. Bogaerts was Boston's 2014 season opening day shortstop. He started at either short or third during 142 games in 2014—his first full season in the Majors. As the season progressed, Bradley settled in as the Red Sox regular center fielder and made 105 starts in that position by the end of the season.

Baseball Attractions in Greenville

- **Shoeless Joe Jackson Museum and Baseball Library**, 356 Field St., Greenville, SC 29601 (864) 346–4867
- **Shoeless Joe Jackson Statue**, 1 Augusta St., Greenville, SC 29601
- **Greenville Municipal Stadium at Conestee Park**, 840 Mauldin Rd., Greenville, SC 29607

Attractions in Greenville

- **Main Street Business District—Centrally Located Visitors Center**, 206 S. Main St., Greenville, SC 29601 (864) 233–0461
- **Falls Park on the Reedy River—Waterfalls and Liberty Bridge**, 601 S. Main St., Greenville, SC 29601 (864) 467–4355
- **Swamp Rabbit Trail—entering at Falls Park**, 601 S. Main St., Greenville, SC 29601
- **Greenville Zoo**, 150 Cleveland Park Dr., Greenville, SC 29601 (864) 467–4300

Dining in Greenville

BREWPUBS AND BREWERIES

- **Blue Ridge Brewing**, 217 N. Main St., Greenville, SC 29601 (864) 232–4677

Downtown Restaurants

- **Smoke on the Water Restaurant**, 1 Augusta St., Ste. 202, Greenville, SC 29601 (864) 232–9091
- **Mellow Mushroom**, 1 Augusta St., Ste. 201, Greenville, South Carolina 29601 (864) 233–9020
- **Carolina Ale House**, 113 S. Main St., Greenville, SC 29601 (864) 351–0521
- **Mac's Speed Shop**, 930 S. Main St., Greenville, SC 29601 (864) 271–8285
- **Sassafras Southern Bistro**, 103 N. Main St., Greenville, SC 29601 (864) 235–5670
- **Barley's Taproom & Pizzeria**, 25 W. Washington St., Greenville, SC 29601 (864) 232–3706
- **Addys Dutch Cafe & Restaurant**, 17 E. Coffee St., Greenville, SC 29601 (864) 232–2339

Hagerstown Suns

Municipal Stadium
274 Memorial Blvd., Hagerstown, MD 21740
www.milb.com/index.jsp?sid=t563

The city of Hagerstown, which is located in the Cumberland Valley section of the Appalachian Mountains, is the largest city in northwestern Maryland. Hagerstown is nicknamed the "Hub City" because of its rich history related to train transportation and shipping in the region. Today trains still play a role in the commerce of the city but relative to the shipping of freight. Like several other interesting historic cities that host baseball teams in the South Atlantic League, Hagerstown has a very attractive old-time downtown with interesting restaurants and other business establishments to visit.

Baseball is also a key part of the heritage of the city. Table 3–1 HAG shows that as in many of the other towns and cities that are home to a South Atlantic League team, professional baseball has been played in the city since the mid–1890s. Note that during the 1895 and 1896 baseball seasons the city hosted the Hagerstown Champions and Hagerstown Lions, respectively, in the Cumberland Valley League.

Hagerstown is just a short distance from the state lines of West Virginia and Pennsylvania and it was this tri-state region that was the home of the Cumberland Valley League. During the 1895 season, the league consisted of just four teams: the Hagerstown Champions in Maryland, two teams in Penn-

Team Name	1st Year	Years	Leagues
Hagerstown Champions	1895	1	Cumberland Valley League
Hagerstown Lions	1896	1	Cumberland Valley League
Hagerstown Blues	1915	1	Blue Ridge League
Hagerstown Terriers	1916	3	Blue Ridge League
Hagerstown Champs	1920	2	Blue Ridge League
Hagerstown Terriers	1922	2	Blue Ridge League
Hagerstown Hubs	1924	7	Blue Ridge League
Hagerstown Hubs	1931	1	Middle Atlantic League
Hagerstown Owls	1941	9	Interstate League
Hagerstown Braves	1950	3	Interstate League
Hagerstown Braves	1953	1	Piedmont League
Hagerstown Packets	1954	2	Piedmont League
Hagerstown Suns	1981	8	Carolina League
Hagerstown Suns	1989	4	Eastern League
Hagerstown Suns	1993	22	South Atlantic League

Table 3-1 HAG. Teams that have played in Hagerstown, MD (source: www.baseball-reference.com).

sylvania—the Chambersburg Maroons and Carlisle Colts—and another in West Virginia, the Martinsburg Patriots. Hagerstown was centrally located to the other towns, which were all within a 50 mile traveling distance for the Hagerstown Champions. But the Cumberland Valley League did not survive past these two seasons. The first era of professional baseball in Hagerstown had come to an end, and baseball would not be played again in the city for a couple of decades.

Baseball returned to Hagerstown in 1915, when the city hosted a team for the inaugural season of a new baseball league—the Blue Ridge League. The Hagerstown Blues represented the city in the league during the 1915 season. During its inaugural season, the Blue Ridge League fielded six teams, four in cities formerly associated with the Cumberland Valley League—Hagerstown, Maryland, Chambersburg and Hanover, Pennsylvania, and Martinsburg, Virginia—and added teams in Gettysburg, Pennsylvania, and Frederick, Maryland. Even with the addition of these extra teams, the radius of the footprint of the leagues as measured from Hagerstown remained a maximum of approximately 50 miles.

The Blue Ridge League prospered and fielded teams in fifteen of the next sixteen baseball seasons. Hagerstown was the host city of a team in the league during each of those seasons, but the moniker of the team continued to evolve. Note in Table 3–1 HAG that the Hagerstown Blues were followed by the Terriers (1916–1918 and 1922–1923), Champs (1920–1921), and the Hubs (1924–1930). The teams of the Blue Ridge League played their games at the D level of Major League Baseball's minor league system.

After the 1930 season, the Blue Ridge League ceased to play. For the following season the Hagerstown Hubs engaged with a C-level league—the Middle Atlantic League. But they participated just for that one season. The departure of the Hubs from this league ushered in another decade-long lapse before professional baseball would again be played in the city of Hagerstown.

Baseball returned to Hagerstown when the Detroit Tigers added a B-level team to participate in the Interstate League in 1941. This team, nicknamed the Owls, played there as a member of the Tigers' minor league organization for eight seasons. As its name suggests, this league spanned a much larger area than the prior leagues in which Hagerstown was the home of a team. Four of its teams were located in Pennsylvania, but there were also teams in New Jersey, Delaware, and Connecticut. The Hagerstown Owls set both the southernmost and westernmost boundary of the teams in the league.

The connection between Hagerstown and the Interstate League lasted twelve seasons. But during that period, the team name and major league affiliation changed a number of times. When the Detroit Tigers left the city after the 1948 season, the Owls became an affiliate of the Washington Senators for the 1949 season. Then, in 1950 the Boston Braves arrived and renamed the team the Hagerstown Braves.

After the 1952 season the Interstate League folded, so the Boston Braves engaged their B level affiliate in Hagerstown with the Piedmont League for the 1953 season. However, after that season the Braves restructured their minor league organization and as part of that eliminated a number of teams, including the Hagerstown Braves. Luckily the Washington Senators were poised to add a B-level team to their minor league system in 1954 and placed that team in the Piedmont League as the Hagerstown Packets. But the end of the 1955 season brought the demise of the Piedmont League and the end of a second era of professional baseball in Hagerstown. Professional baseball would not return to the city for more than twenty-five years.

During the Interstate League and Piedmont League years, baseball fans in Hagerstown got to see some players who went on to have extended major league careers play their minor league ball in the city. For example, power-hitting outfielder Bob Allison, who played for the Hagerstown Packets during the 1955 season, went on to debut with the Washington Senators on September 16, 1958, and played 13 seasons in Washington as a member of the Senators and then, after they relocated to Minnesota, as a Twin. Also, right-hander Pedro Ramos, who pitched in the majors during 15 seasons, pitched for the Hagerstown Packets during the 1954 season.

The most recent era of baseball in Hagerstown is all about the Hagerstown Suns. The Suns first showed up on the scene in 1981, when the Baltimore Orioles added a second A-level minor league affiliate in the Carolina League. The next year the Orioles eliminated their other A-level team, the Miami Orioles of the Florida State League, and baseball was back in business in Hagerstown. Between 1981 and 1988, future Orioles stars played their formative years in front of the Hagerstown Suns fans at Municipal Stadium. For example, right-handed pitchers John Habyan (1982, 1983, and 1984), infielder Billy Ripken (1984), right-handed pitcher Pete Harnisch (1987), and reliever Greg Olson (1988) all played during one or more seasons for the A-level Hagerstown Suns of the Carolina League and then went on to play in 10 or more seasons at the major league level.

For the start of the 1989 season, the Orioles realigned their minor league organization. They moved their AA-level team—the Charlotte Knights—in the Southern League to Hagerstown, named them the Suns, and affiliated them with the Eastern League. Interestingly, since the Hagerstown Suns moved from the A to AA level of the minor league structure, a number of ballplayers who played their A-level ball with the Suns in the late 1980 also played AA ball in the city when the team was a member of the Eastern League. One example is outfielder Steve Finley, who played his A-level ball for the Suns in 1987 and 1988 but remained there in 1989 to play AA ball. Finley debuted with Baltimore on April 3, 1989, at the age of 24 and then went on to play at the major league level during nineteen seasons. Similarly, first baseman David Segui played single-A ball during 1988 in Hagerstown and returned to play double-A in 1989. Segui made his major league debut with the Orioles on May 8, 1990, and played in the majors during fifteen seasons.

The Suns remained the Orioles' double-A team through the 1992 season. After that year, Baltimore disengaged with the city and moved their AA team to Bowie, Maryland. But when Baltimore departed, the vacancy they left behind was immediately filled by a single-A team of the Toronto Blue Jays for the 1993 season. That team—again called the Hagerstown Suns—was a member of the modern South Atlantic League. Even though the major league affiliation of the Hagerstown Suns has changed a number of times, the team's name remains the same today and 2014 was the twenty-second consecutive season that the team was affiliated with today's South Atlantic League.

The Home of the Suns—Municipal Stadium

Municipal Stadium in Hagerstown is one of the historic ballparks of the South Atlantic League. The stadium was built in 1930 and was ready for use by the Hagerstown Hubs of the Blue Ridge League on May 8, 1930. It is the third oldest professional baseball stadium that is currently in use in the United States. The original Municipal Stadium served as the home field for all of the teams that played in the city through 1955—the Hubs, Owls, Braves, and Packets. This field is known for being the place where Willie Mays played in his first professional baseball game as a member of the 1950 Trenton Giants of the Interstate League. The ballpark is located about one and a half miles from the historic downtown of the city.

As mentioned earlier, professional baseball was not played in Hagerstown between 1956 and 1980. In preparation for the return of baseball to the city in 1981 by the Baltimore Orioles' A-level affiliate in the Carolina League, the Hagerstown Suns, the stadium underwent extensive renovation and modernization of its facilities and expansion of the seating capacity. After the stadium became the home of the Blue Jays' single-A team in the South Atlantic League, another round of improvements was performed in 1995 to bring the stadium more in line with ballparks of the day. In 2011, additional enhance-

Figure 3–1 HAG. Municipal Stadium, Hagerstown, MD.

ments were made to the seating and the stadium was equipped with a modern electronic scoreboard.

Figure 3–1 HAG shows the box office and grandstand of Municipal Stadium as viewed from the parking lot near the main entrance. The current seating capacity is 4,600, but much of that is general admission seating. Ringing the infield area from close to first base to third base are a few rows of box seats that are identified as VIP seating by the team. The VIP sections have individual plastic folding seats. There is a narrow walkway that separates these VIP seats from the general admission seats that slope upward toward the back of the grandstand. The grandstand seating is also in individual seats with a back. These general admission seats in the grandstand area behind home plate are protected from sun and rain by the grandstand roof. There are additional uncovered general admission sections on both the first base and third base lines, but these general admission areas have unreserved bleacher-like benches for sitting.

There is a concourse area around the back side of the grandstand that continues down toward the left field corner. Food concessions, the team store, and restrooms are located in the back side of the grandstand structure at various locations along the concourse and in separate buildings on the far side of the concourse. Toward the left field end of the concourse there is an area with no paid seating that permits you to watch from the outfield fence. This is the location of the Yuengling Beer Garden, which is an interesting area set up with high tables and picnic tables. This is a nice area from which to casually view the game action. Moreover, there is a group party and picnic deck in the right field corner.

The Hagerstown Suns mascot is a tall overstuffed caterpillar called Woolie. You will find him at the game enthusiastically greeting children and cheering the fans on to root for a Suns victory. In general, I found Municipal Stadium a simple, interesting traditional-style ballpark in which to enjoy a baseball game.

The South Atlantic League Years

Hagerstown, Maryland, has been the home of a South Atlantic League team since 1993. As shown in Table 3–2(a) HAG the team has always been known as the Hagerstown Suns; however, over the years it has been affiliated with four different major league clubs: the Toronto Blue Jays, San Francisco Giants, New York Mets, and Washington Nationals. The years that the Suns transitioned between these four major league affiliates are identified in Table 3–2(a) HAG.

Name	MLB Affiliate	Years
Hagerstown Suns	Washington Nationals	2007-today
Hagerstown Suns	New York Mets	2005-2006
Hagerstown Suns	San Francisco Giants	2001-2004
Hagerstown Suns	Toronto Blue Jays	1993-2000

Level	Team	Stadium	League
Rk	GCL Nationals	Carl Barger Baseball Complex Viera, FL	Gulf Coast League
A-	Auburn Doubledays	Falcon Park Auburn, NY	New York-Penn League
A	Hagerstown Suns	Municipal Stadium Hagerstown, MD	South Atlantic League
A+	Potomac Nationals	Pfitzner Stadium Woodbridge, VA	Carolina League
AA	Harrisburg Senators	Metro Bank Park Harrisburg, PA	Eastern League
AAA	Syracuse Chiefs	NBT Bank Stadium Syracuse, NY	International League

Top: Table 3-2(a) HAG. Hagerstown Suns major league affiliations. *Above:* Table 3-2(b) HAG. Washington Nationals minor league organization.

The Suns have always been a member of the Northern Division of the Sally League. Having made seven postseason appearances over the past twenty-two seasons, they are one of the more successful teams in the league. Hagerstown won the Northern Division title in five of those seasons: 1994, 1998, 1999, 2005, and 2013. In spite of the fact that they made five trips to the league finals, the Hagerstown Suns have never won the South Atlantic League championship.

When the Orioles relocated their Eastern League team from the city after the 1992 season, the Blue Jays moved their current South Atlantic League affiliate, the Myrtle Beach Hurricanes, to the city for the 1993 season as the Hagerstown Suns. While the single-A member of the Toronto minor league organization, the Suns went to the league playoffs three times—1994, 1998, and 1999.

In 1994 the Suns offense was driven by catcher–designated hitter Joseph

Durso. He led all regular players on the team in runs scored (77), bases on balls (61), batting average (.304), on-base percentage (.400), slugging percentage (.471), and on-base plus slugging percentage (.872). For the season, Durso ranked in the top 10 among all players in the South Atlantic League in AVE, OBP, SLG, and OPS.

Edwin Hurtado led the starters with an 11W:2L record and 2.95 ERA, while closer David Sinnes had 37 saves and led the regular relievers with a 1.92 ERA and 1.082 WHIP. Sinnes' 37 saves tied him for the league lead in this pitching statistic category for the season. Hagerstown swept the Hickory Crawdads (Chicago White Sox) in the first round of the playoffs to win the team's first South Atlantic League Northern Division title. But the Suns lost in the league championship round to the Savannah Cardinals (St. Louis Cardinals).

During the 1998 and 1999 seasons, the South Atlantic League was organized as three divisions—Northern, Southern, and Central. The Hagerstown Suns won the Northern Division championship in both seasons. For those years, the division champion was determined by the full regular season record. But the postseason play for the South Atlantic League Championship was arranged as a round robin-like tournament between the eight teams with the best full season record. The Suns lost in an early round of the tournament in both seasons.

While a minor league franchise of the New York Mets in 2005, Hagerstown had the best record in the Northern Division for the first half of the season to clinch a slot in the postseason. Center fielder Carlos Gomez supplied the speed for the Suns' offense. He led the team in R (75), H (134), 3B (6), and SB (64). His 64 stolen bases led the South Atlantic League for the season and also ties him with Eury Perez (2010 Suns) as the all-time leader in that offensive stat category in the Hagerstown Suns uniform.

The team's power hitters were third baseman Grant Psomas and first baseman Mike Carp. They tied for the team lead with 19 home runs; Carp led the team with 63 RBI; and Psomas led all regular players with 62 BB, .300 AVE, .403 OBP, .551 SLG and .955 OPS. Carp was the runner up in both the slugging percentage and on-base plus slugging percentage stats. Psomas ranked in the top 10 in the league in OBP, SLG, and OPS. That season, the Suns beat the Delmarva Shorebirds (Baltimore Orioles) to win a fourth Northern Division championship but again lost in the league championship round—this time to the Kannapolis Intimidators (Chicago White Sox). Both Carp and Gomez made the jump to the majors. Two thousand fourteen was Gomez's eighth consecutive season in the majors. Gomez, who has an excellent .987 career fielding percentage in center field, took over as the starter in that position for the Milwaukee Brewers in 2012. Carp has played at the major league level during six seasons. He began the 2014 season playing first base and left field for the Boston Red Sox but was selected off waivers by the Texas Rangers in August.

Note from Table 3–2(a) HAG that the Washington Nationals took over as the major league affiliate of the Hagerstown Suns in 2007. The year 2014 was the eighth season that the Suns were the single-A affiliate of the Washington Nationals in the South Atlantic League. A list of the Nationals' other minor league clubs is shown in Table 3–2(b) HAG. Since the Suns have been the Washington Nationals affiliate in the South Atlantic League, they have appeared in the postseason playoffs twice—2012 and 2013.

During the 2013 playoffs, Hagerstown, who had won the first half of the season with a 38W:29L record, faced off in the Northern Division Championship Series against the second half winner—the West Virginia Power (Pittsburgh Pirates). The Suns beat the Power in the first round 2 games to 1 to win the team's fifth Northern Division title. During this series, the Suns' offense was led by center fielder Isaac Ballou, second baseman Tony Renda, and catcher Pedro Severino. Ballou had 6 hits in 11 at-bats for a .583 series batting average. Renda and Severino were close behind. Renda went 6 for 13 to hit .462, while Severino was 5 for 11 for a .456 average. Third baseman and number 3 batter Shawn Pleffner led the Suns with 6 RBI.

Hagerstown got excellent pitching performances out of their game 1 and 3 starters, right-hander Austin Voth and lefty Kylin Turnbull, respectively. Voth pitched 5 scoreless innings while giving up just 3 hits, walking 2, and striking out 5. Turnbull also went 5 innings and gave up 2 runs on 5 hits and 2 bases on balls. Both got the win for their strong outing and at that point were 1–0 in postseason play.

In the best-of-five South Atlantic League Championship Series, Hagerstown faced the Southern Division champion Savannah Sand Gnats (New York Mets). The Suns won game 1 at home by a score of 6–1 behind a strong 5 inning pitching performance by right-hander Jake Johansen. However, they dropped the next three games as the Sand Gnats went on to win the South Atlantic League title.

Successful Major Leaguers Who Played in Hagerstown

Over the years a number of young Blue Jays, Giants, Mets, and Nationals prospects played the early, formative parts of their baseball careers on the field of Municipal Stadium in Hagerstown. Fans of the Hagerstown Suns had

Season	Player	Age at HAG	MiLB Season	Position	MLB Debut	Age at Debut	MLB Team	Seasons in MLB
1993	x							
1994	Shannon Stewart	20	3	LF	9/2/95	21	TOR	14
1995	x							
1996	Casey Blake	22	1	3B	8/14/99	25	TOR	13
	Chris Woodward	20	2	SS	6/7/99	22	TOR	12
1997	x							
1998	César Izturis	18	2	SS	6/23/01	21	TOR	13
	Vernon Wells	19	2	CF	8/30/99	20	TOR	15
	Michael Young	21	2	SS	9/29/00	23	TEX	14
1999	Orlando Hudson	21	2	2B	5/20/98	24	TOR	11
	Felipe Lopez	19	2	SS	8/3/01	21	TOR	11
2000	Reed Johnson	23	2	LF	4/17/03	26	TOR	12+
	Guillermo Quiroz	18	2	CF	9/4/04	22	TOR	10+
	Álex Ríos	19	2	RF	5/27/04	23	TOR	11+
2001	x							
2002	Francisco Liriano	18	2	LHP	9/5/05	21	MIN	9+
2003	Matt Cain	18	2	RHP	8/29/05	20	SFG	10+
2004	Nate Schierholtz	20	2	RF	6/11/07	23	SFG	8+
	Brian Wilson	22	1	RHP	4/23/06	24	SFG	9+
2005	Mike Carp	19	2	1B	6/17/09	22	SEA	6+
	Carlos Gomez	19	2	CF	5/13/07	21	NYM	8+
2006	Drew Butera	22	2	CF	4/9/10	26	MIN	5+
	Jonathon Niese	19	2	LHP	9/2/08	21	NYM	7+
	Bobby Parnell	21	2	RHP	9/15/08	24	NYM	7+
2007	Marco Estrada	23	3	RHP	8/20/08	25	WSN	7+
2008	x							
2009	Drew Storen	21	1	RHP	5/17/10	22	WSN	5+

Table 3-3 HAG. Hagerstown SAL players that went on to have long major league careers.

the opportunity to see them play at the A-level of minor league baseball as they attempted to hone their baseball skills in preparation for hopefully one day reaching The Show. Table 3-3 HAG lists over twenty players who played for the Suns and went on to have successful careers as measured by either playing 10 seasons in the majors or having played at least the last five seasons and being still in the majors accumulating more years.

The table shows that the Toronto Blue Jays were quite successful at cultivating young talent through their minor league organization. Between 1993 and 2000, eleven players on the roster of the Hagerstown Suns went on to have long major league careers and all but one of them made their debut in the Blue Jays uniform. Note in Table 3-3 HAG that Vernon Wells, who was a member of the 1998 Hagerstown Suns team, made his debut with Toronto on August 30, 1999, at the age of 20. Wells played his fifteenth season at the major league level as a member of the 2013 New York Yankees. A second player from that season's Suns team, Michael Young, played his fourteenth season of major league ball with Philadelphia and Los Angeles in 2013. Young was traded by Toronto to the Texas Rangers during July 2000 while playing AA ball with the Tennessee Smokies in the Southern League. For that reason, he made his debut with the Rangers on September 29, 2000.

During the 1998 season, fans of the Suns got to see Wells as the team's center fielder and Young as its second baseman. Together they led the team's offense and one or the other of them led the regular players on the team in almost every batting statistic category. For example, Young led the team in hits (147), triples (5), total bases (238), and on-base percentage (.354), while Wells was number one in doubles (35) and batting average (.285). They were tied with 86 runs scored each. At the major league level Wells was a three time American League All-Star and Young a seven time American League All-Star. Two thousand thirteen was the last season that both Young and Wells played in the majors.

Note that during the Giants years (2001–2004) fans of the Suns got to see a number of their top prospects who went on to play in the majors. One of them is Matt Cain, who had been the ace right-hander of the San Francisco starting rotation for a number of years. Cain had made 30 or more starts for the Giants each season from 2006 through 2013. He was a member of the Giants' 2014 starting rotation, but his season was ended in July due to an elbow injury. Cain is a three time National League All-Star.

While the New York Mets were associated with the Hagerstown Suns, two of the current members of their pitching staff—Jonathon Niese and Bobby Parnell—played for the team. Both pitchers played in Hagerstown during the 2006 season and were members of the team's starting rotation. As shown in Table 3–3 HAG, both Niese and Parnell were September call-ups during the 2008 season. Since the 2010 season, Niese has been a fixture in the Mets' starting rotation. On the other hand, Parnell has been used as a late innings reliever—set-up man or closer—and as the team's primary closer in 2013 registered 22 saves. While throwing just 1 inning of relief on Opening Day of the 2014 season, Parnell injured his elbow and had season-ending Tommy John surgery.

Since the Washington Nationals took over the Hagerstown Suns in 2007, there have not been sufficient years for many players to have accumulated five consecutive years of play at the major league level. However, a few of today's key players on the Nationals roster played in front of an audience at Municipal Stadium in recent years. They include: left fielder Bryce Harper

G	AB	R	H	2B	3B	HR	RBI
72	258	49	82	17	1	14	46

TB	BB	SO	SB	AVE	OBP	SLG	OPS
143	44	61	19	.318	.423	.554	.977

Table 3–4 HAG. Bryce Harper 2011 batting stats.

and relief pitcher Drew Storen. The year 2014 was Storen's fifth as a regular member of the Nationals' relief corps. He has typically made over fifty appearances a season out of the bullpen.

Harper appears to be on the path to superstardom. He entered the minor leagues at the A level in 2011 at the age of eighteen and played about two-thirds of the season with the Hagerstown Suns. A summary of his 2011 batting stats with the Suns is given in Table 3–4 HAG. Harper was promoted on July 4, 2011, to the Harrisburg Senators—the Nationals' AA affiliate in the Eastern League. He began the 2012 season at the AAA level of Washington's minor league organization—the Syracuse Chiefs in the International League. However, Harper was promoted to the majors on April 28, 2012, after playing in just twenty-one AAA games. In his major league debut on April 28, Harper played left field, batted in the number 7 slot of the Nationals' batting order, and went 1 for 3 on the day with a double and an RBI. Harper is the recipient of the 2012 National League Rookie of the Year Award and has been selected to play for the National League All-Star team during both the 2012 and 2013 seasons.

Baseball Attractions Near Hagerstown

• **Fredrick Keys Home Game at Harry Grove Stadium**, 21 Stadium Dr., Frederick, Maryland 21703 (301) 815–9939

Attractions in Hagerstown

• **Historic Downtown Hagerstown**, 38 S. Potomac St., Hagerstown, MD 21740

- **Hagerstown Roundhouse Museum**, 296 S. Burhans Blvd., Hagerstown, MD 21741 (301) 739–4665
- **Discovery Station**, 101 W. Washington St., Hagerstown, MD 21740 (301) 790–0076

Dining in Hagerstown

BREWPUBS AND BREWERIES

- **Benny's Pub—Antietam Brewery**, 49 Eastern Blvd., Hagerstown, MD 21740 (301) 791–5915

DOWNTOWN RESTAURANTS

- **Schmankerl Stube Bavarian Restaurant**, 58 S. Potomac St., Hagerstown, MD 21740 (301) 797–3354
- **Bulls and Bears Restaurant & Pub**, 38 S. Potomac St., Hagerstown, MD 21740 (301) 791–0370
- **Rhubarb House**, 12 Public Square, Hagerstown, MD 21740 (301) 733–4399
- **The Gourmet Goat**, 41 N. Potomac St., Hagerstown, MD 21740 (301) 790–2343
- **28 South**, 28 S. Potomac St., Hagerstown, MD 21740 (240) 347–4932
- **Stadium Grill & Tavern**, 401 S. Cannon Ave., Hagerstown, MD 21740 (301) 714–0849
- **Greens n Grains Market Café**, 2 W. Washington St., Hagerstown, MD 21740 (240) 347–4985

Hickory Crawdads

L. P. Frans Stadium
2500 Clement Blvd. NW, Hickory, NC 28601
www.milb.com/index.jsp?sid=t448

This afternoon I am heading north en route to game two of a South Atlantic League two-city double header. I have already attended a late morning home game of the Greenville Drive in Greenville, South Carolina. Now I am making the approximately 108 mile run to L. P. Frans Stadium in Hickory, North Carolina, to see the Charleston RiverDogs play the Hickory Crawdads. Hickory, which is located on the banks of the Catawba River, is an interesting

Team Name	1st Year	Years	Leagues
Hickory Rebels	1936	3	Carolina Baseball League
Hickory Rebels	1939	2	Tar Heel League
Hickory Rebels	1942	8	North Carolina State League
Hickory Rebels	1952	1	Western Carolina League
Hickory Rebels	1953	2	Tar Heel League
Hickory Rebels	1960	1	Western Carolina League
Hickory Crawdads	1993	22	South Atlantic League

Table 3–1 HIC. Teams that have played in Hickory, NC (source: www.baseball-reference.com).

destination in the foothills of the Appalachian Mountains in northwestern North Carolina. The city has an industrial past and a long history as a center for the design and manufacturing of high quality furniture. Today the furniture industry still plays an important role in Hickory's economy.

In addition to its ties to the furniture industry, the city of Hickory has a long-term connection with professional baseball. Table 3–1 HIC shows that a team called the Hickory Rebels first played in the city in 1936 as a member of an independent baseball league—the Carolina Baseball League. Hickory on and off hosted a team with that name through the 1960 baseball season. Overall the Rebels played during seventeen seasons in four different named baseball leagues.

During the 1936 season, the Carolina Baseball League fielded eight teams, all located in western North Carolina. The town of Hickory sits toward the northern perimeter of the footprint set by the teams of the league. The travel distance for the Rebels to their farthest opponent, who played their games in Concord, North Carolina, was just over sixty miles to the southeast, and the nearest team in Valdese, North Carolina, was less than seventeen miles to the west. But the membership in the league dropped to six teams by the next season and it folded at the end of the 1938 season.

As shown in Table 3–1 HIC, the next season the Rebels and teams from three other towns of the Carolina Baseball League joined the newly formed Tar Heel League. This league was affiliated with the National Association of Professional Baseball Leagues, which was the organization that represented professional baseball teams at that time. During its inaugural season, the league had six teams. This time Hickory was more centrally located. The team farthest from Hickory, the Shelby Nationals, was less than forty miles away.

Teams of the Tar Heel League played at the D level of the Minor League Baseball system, and a number of them had ongoing business relationships with the major league clubs of the day. But the league lasted only two seasons before it was disbanded in 1940. This variant of the Tar Heel League has no connection to the Tar Heel League that later played a role in the formation of today's South Atlantic League. Instead, after the demise of this league, the name Tar Heel League lay dormant for more than a decade. This ended the short first era of professional baseball in Hickory.

The next era of Rebels baseball in Hickory was intertwined with leagues that eventually played key roles in the formation of the modern South Atlantic League—the North Carolina State League, Western Carolina League, and the new Tar Heel League of the early 1950s. Note in Table 3–1 HIC that after a one season lapse of baseball in Hickory the Rebels joined an ongoing league—the North Carolina State League—to start the 1942 season. The league was starting its fifth consecutive year of operation. However, the league did not field teams during the World War II years of 1943 and 1944, but it resumed regular play for the 1945 season. The Hickory Rebels returned to the league in 1945 and were now the D-level affiliate of the New York Giants baseball club. They remained an affiliate of the Giants through the 1949 season and a member of the North Carolina State League through 1951.

As shown in Table 3–1 HIC, the Hickory Rebels switched to the Western Carolina League for the start of the 1952 baseball season where they were the D-level representative of the Chicago Cubs. During that season both the Western Carolina League and North Carolina State League were struggling. They both operated with just six teams. At the end of the season, both leagues folded. The next season—1953—teams from the North Carolina State League and Western Carolina League combined to attempt a revival of the Tar Heel League. The Hickory Rebels were one of them and remained an affiliate of the Chicago Cubs through the transition. But that league folded after just two seasons of play, and that event ended the second era of professional baseball in Hickory.

Table 3–1 HIC shows that the Hickory Rebels played again, but just for the 1960 season, as an unaffiliated team in a new variant of the Western Carolina League. That was the last season in the history of Hickory Rebels baseball. The Rebels had completed their seventeenth season in Hickory as a member of either an independent or affiliated minor league. Professional baseball would not return to Hickory for more than thirty years.

The modern era of professional baseball in Hickory began in 1993. Prior to that season, the Chicago White Sox decided to field a second single-A minor league affiliate as a member of the South Atlantic League. They located the team in Hickory and named it the Crawdads. Since then the team has undergone a few changes in affiliation, but the team's name has remained the same.

Two thousand fourteen was the twenty-second season in which the Crawdads played in Hickory as a member of the modern South Atlantic League. They are currently the single-A affiliate of the Texas Rangers.

The Home of the Crawdads—L. P. Frans Stadium

With the opportunity to bring professional baseball back to Hickory, a new stadium had to be constructed. Ground was broken for the new ballpark in the fall of 1992 and the Hickory Crawdads played their first game there on April 16, 1993. The stadium was named after the L. P. Frans family, who played a key role in funding the stadium and bringing professional baseball back to Hickory.

L. P. Frans Stadium is modern but simple. You enter through an attractive brick arch to an open air concourse. On the field side of the concourse from first base to third base is a building that houses the luxury suites. Therefore, you cannot see the game while at concessions on the concourse behind the infield area. But as you walk along the concourse toward the outfield it opens to view the field. An interesting touch is that on the walls along the concourse

Figure 3–1 HIC. L. P. Frans Stadium, Hickory, NC.

are posters that list members of the South Atlantic League Hall of Fame, the names of Crawdads major league alumni, and the lineups for the day's game.

You enter the seating area of the stadium from the concourse at the very top of the seating bowl. The rows of seats cascade down toward the field level. There is a walkway that separates the lower field level box seats from the upper level reserved seats behind home plate and the bench seating that continues down the first base and third base lines. A grandstand roof covers the upper rows of the reserved seating area behind home plate and offers some protection from sun and rain. The stadium was designed to accommodate 5062 fans, but about one-third of that is with bleacher-like seating.

L. P. Frans Stadium has all the conveniences and amenities of other modern minor league ballparks. There is a children's play area down the left field line that includes a small merry-go-round. For adults there is the Crawdads Café toward the right field corner with a bar and a more interesting assortment of food. Finally there are Conrad and Candy, the team's Crawdad mascots, to keep fans amused and cheering them on to root for the home team.

The South Atlantic League Years

As mentioned earlier, Hickory had a brief encounter with the predecessor leagues of the modern South Atlantic League. The Hickory Rebels baseball team was a member of both the North Carolina State League and Western Carolina League during the early 1950s and again with the Western Carolina League for just the 1960 season. Nineteen-sixty was the last season that professional baseball was played in Hickory until the Crawdads joined the South Atlantic League in 1993.

Prior to the 1993 season, the Chicago White Sox already had an A-level team—the South Bend White Sox—in the Midwest League. Even though the White Sox introduced a new single-A affiliate in Hickory to start the 1993 season, they maintained their A-level team in the Midwest League. However, after the 1996 season the South Bend White Sox were phased out in favor of the Hickory Crawdads. As shown in Table 3–2(a) HIC, the Hickory Crawdads remained a

Name	MLB Affiliate	Years
Hickory Crawdads	Texas Rangers	2009-today
Hickory Crawdads	Pittsburgh Pirates	1999-2008
Hickory Crawdads	Chicago White Sox	1993-1998

Above: Table 3–2(a) HIC. Hickory teams' major league affiliations. *Opposite page:* Table 3–2(b) HIC. Texas Rangers minor league organization.

Level	Team	Stadium	League
Rk	AZL Rangers	Surprise Stadium Surprise, AZ	Arizona League
A-	Spokane Indians	Avista Stadium Spokane, WA	Northwest League
A	Hickory Crawdads	L. P. Frans Stadium Hickory, NC	South Atlantic League
A+	High Desert Mavericks	Mavericks Stadium Adelanto, CA	California League
AA	Frisco RoughRiders	Dr Pepper Ballpark Frisco, TX	Texas League
AAA	Round Rock Express	Dell Diamond Round Rock, TX	Pacific Coast League

member of the White Sox minor league organization for six seasons. Over this period, the Crawdads appeared twice in the South Atlantic League postseason; however, they lost both times in the first round.

During the 1998 offseason, Chicago reengaged with the Midwest League and placed their A-level team—now the Burlington Bees—in Burlington, Iowa. But Table 3–2(a) HIC shows that the Pittsburgh Pirates stepped in to fill the vacancy and enable minor league baseball to continue without interruption in Hickory. The Pirates relocated their single-A team from another South Atlantic League city, Augusta, Georgia, to Hickory as the Crawdads in time for Opening Day of the 1999 season.

While under the reign of the Pirates, the Crawdads had successes. They played in the South Atlantic League postseason five times but returned a winner just twice. During the 2002 season, Hickory won the division for the first half of the season with a 44W:26L record. The Crawdads beat the Delmarva Shorebirds (Baltimore Orioles) in the first round of the playoffs to take their first Northern Division Championship. They went on to face the Southern Division Champions—the Columbus Red Stixx (Cleveland Indians)—in the best-of-five game League Championship Series.

During the 2002 regular season the Crawdads offense was driven by first baseman Walter Young. He led all regular players on the team in six key batting statistic categories: runs (84), hits (164), doubles (34), home runs (25), runs batted in (103), and total bases (277). These stats ranked him number 1 in the South Atlantic League in a number of offensive categories—H, HR, and TB. Young got called up by the Baltimore Orioles in 2005, but he had a very brief stint in the majors.

There were other key contributors to the Hickory 2002 offense. Current Toronto Blue Jays star right fielder Jose Bautista was Hickory's third baseman, and two journeymen major leaguers—infielder Jeff Keppinger and catcher Ryan Doumit—were also in the Crawdads lineup. Bautista and Keppinger were right behind Young in many batting stats.

The team had five solid starters who all went double digits in wins and compiled winning records for the season. They included three right-handed pitchers, Chris Young, Ian Snell, and John Van Benschoten, who went on to play at the major league level. Of them, Chris Young had the longest stay in the majors—10 seasons and still counting.

During the 2002 Championship Series versus Columbus, Young started and won game 1. He was also on the hill for the championship-deciding game 5 and had a solid outing. After he departed, the Crawdads came from behind for a 3–2 victory and notched their first South Atlantic League Championship title.

Hickory also won the South Atlantic League Championship in 2004. That season the Crawdads won the Northern Division during the second half season to gain their third consecutive appearance in the postseason. Hickory swept the Charleston AlleyCats (Toronto Blue Jays) 2 games to 0 in the first round of the playoffs to win their second Northern Division title and advance to the South Atlantic League Championship Series. The Crawdads then swept the Capital City Bombers (New York Mets) in the best-of-five championship series to take home their second South Atlantic League title.

During the 2004 season the Hickory offense was powered by first baseman Jon Benick, and center fielder Nyjer Morgan supplied the speed on the base paths. Benick, who was in his fourth season in the minors and had already played games at the A+ and AA levels, had an outstanding offensive year. He had a team leading .328 batting average and led the Crawdads in each of these other batting stat categories: H (160), HR (32), RBI (104), AVE (.328), OBP (.396), SLG (.592), OPS (.988), and TB (289). Benick ranked in the top 5 in the South Atlantic League in each of these eight batting categories for the season. In fact, his 32 home runs ranked number 1 in the league. That season Benick set two of the Crawdads' all-time offensive stat records. His 104 runs batted in and 289 total bases still stand today as the highest total for each of those batting statistics reached by a player in the Hickory Crawdads uniform. On the other hand, from the leadoff spot in the batting order, Morgan created RBI opportunities for Benick. He had 131 hits, walked 53 times, was hit by 33 pitches, stole 55 bases, and scored 83 runs. Morgan's 55 stolen bases ranked him second in the league in that offensive stat.

The Crawdads' 2004 pitching rotation included future major leaguers lefty Tom Gorzelanny and right handers Juan Carlos Oviedo and Matt Capps. When Gorzelanny was promoted at midseason to the Lynchburg Hillcats (Carolina League, A+ level), he was 7W:2L in 15 starts. He led all regular starters with both a low 2.23 ERA and 1.043 WHIP.

After the 2008 season, Pittsburgh moved their A level-team to another South Atlantic League city, Charleston, West Virginia, as the West Virginia Power. But as shown in Table 3–2(a) HIC, the Texas Rangers came to the rescue. They relocated their Midwest League single-A affiliate, the Clinton LumberKings, from Clinton, Iowa, to Hickory, North Carolina, as the Crawdads. As a Texas affiliate, Hickory appeared twice in the South Atlantic League postseason. In 2010 the Crawdads were a wild card entry, but in 2011 they won the Northern Division during the first half season. However, the Crawdads lost in the first round of the playoffs both seasons.

During the 2011 season, Baseball America's 2013 number 1 prospect in all of minor league baseball—Jurickson Profar—played shortstop for the Hickory Crawdads. He led the team in doubles (37), triples (8), bases on balls (tied for first with 65), runs scored (86), and slugging percentage (.493). His 37 two-base hits set a new Crawdads all-time team record for that offensive statistic category. Profar made his major league debut with Texas on September 2, 2012, at the age of 19. He played second base and batted 9th in the Rangers order. Profar went 2 for 4 versus Cleveland Indians pitching that day and hit a home run in his first major league at-bat. Profar played much of the 2013 season for the Rangers and appeared in a total of 85 games. He most frequently played second base but also filled in at third, short, and in left field.

Two thousand and fourteen was the fifth season in which the Crawdads represented the Texas Rangers as their A-level minor league affiliate. The Rangers' other minor league franchises are listed in Table 3–2(b) HIC.

Successful Major Leaguers Who Played in Hickory

Over the years a number of former Hickory Crawdads players went on to have extended careers with the White Sox and Pirates or another major league club. Table 3–3 HIC lists all players who have either played in ten or more seasons for a major league baseball club or are currently playing in the major leagues and have appeared in games during at least the last five consecutive seasons. Note that there have not yet been a sufficient number of years for any prospect of the Texas Rangers to meet this minimum five major league season requirement.

Season	Player	Age at HIC	MiLB Season	Position	MLB Debut	Age at Debut	MLB Team	Seasons in MLB
1960	x							
1993	Greg Norton	20	1	1B	8/18/96	24	CHW	13
	Magglio Ordonez	19	2	RF	8/29/97	23	CHW	15
1994	x							
1995	Carlos Lee	19	2	LF	5/7/99	22	CHW	14
1996	Chad Bradford	21	1	RHP	8/1/98	23	CHW	12
1997	Joe Crede	19	2	3B	9/12/00	22	CHW	10
1998	Aaron Rowand	20	1	CF	6/16/01	23	CHW	11
	Jon Garland	18	2	RHP	7/4/00	20	CHW	13
1999	Joe Beimel	22	2	LHP	4/8/01	23	PIT	11
2000	x							
2001	Ryan Doumit	20	3	C	6/5/05	24	PIT	10+
	Nate McLouth	19	1	CF	6/29/05	23	PIT	10+
	Sean Burnett	18	2	LHP	5/30/04	21	PIT	8+
	Chris Young	22	1	RHP	8/24/04	25	TEX	10+
2002	Jose Bautista	21	2	RF	4/4/04	23	BAL	11+
	Rajai Davis	21	2	CF	8/14/06	25	PIT	9+
2003	Zach Duke	20	2	LHP	7/2/05	22	PIT	10+
2004	Tom Gorzelanny	21	2	LHP	9/25/05	23	PIT	10+
	Paul Maholm	22	2	LHP	8/30/05	23	PIT	10+
2005	Neil Walker	19	2	2B	9/1/09	23	PIT	6+
2006	Brad Lincoln	21	1	RHP	6/9/10	25	PIT	5+
	Andrew McCutchen	19	2	CF	6/4/09	22	PIT	6+
	Steve Pearce	23	2	1B	9/1/07	24	PIT	8+
2007	Alex Presley	21	2	LF	9/8/10	25	PIT	5+
2008	x							
2009	x							

Table 3–3 HIC. Hickory SAL players that went on to have long major league careers.

Between 1993 and 1998 fans of the Hickory Crawdads had the opportunity to see a continuous series of players who went on to contribute to the success of the Chicago White Sox. They included outfielders Magglio Ordonez, Carlos Lee, and Aaron Rowand; third baseman Joe Crede; first baseman Greg Norton; and pitchers Chad Bradford and Jon Garland. All of these players debuted with the White Sox between 1996 and 2001 and went on to play 10 or more seasons at the major league level.

Note in Table 3–3 HIC that Ordonez played the most seasons in the majors—fifteen. Of them, eight were with the Chicago White Sox. He debuted with the White Sox on August 29, 1997, in a game versus the Houston Astros. On that day he played right field, batted ninth in the White Sox lineup, and went 2 for 3 with the bat. Ordonez opened the 1998 season as Chicago's starting right fielder. After the 2004 season Ordonez became a free agent and signed to play with the Detroit Tigers for the 2005 season. Even though he retired from the Tigers at the age of 37, his career was potentially shortened by ankle injuries that he experienced during the 2010 and 2011 seasons. Over his career he compiled a lifetime batting average of .309 and hit 294 home runs. Moreover, he was a member of six American League All-Star teams.

But Joe Crede played one more year than Ordonez in the White Sox uniform. He debuted in Chicago on September 12, 2000, and played nine of his ten major league seasons for the team. Crede was a member of the Chicago White Sox 2005 World Series championship team.

Among the five White Sox field players listed in Table 3–3 HIC, Carlos Lee had the best offensive season while playing at Hickory. Lee was promoted from the Bristol White Sox (Appalachian League, Rk level) to the Crawdads at the middle of the 1995 season and returned to play there for the complete 1996 season. During 1996 he had an exceptional season with the bat. Table 3–4 HIC summarizes his batting statistics for that season. Lee led the regular field players on the team in almost every batting statistic category: hits, doubles, triples, runs batted in, batting average, slugging percentage, on-base plus slugging percentage, and total bases. His 150 hits and .313 batting average ranked him second best among all players in the South Atlantic League in those offensive stats for the year. Moreover, Lee's 209 total bases ranked eighth best in the league.

Table 3–3 HIC also shows that a number of Pittsburgh Pirates prospects that played for the Crawdads went on to have successful major league careers. Since Hickory became the Pirates' single-A franchise in 1999, many of these players are still active and working their way towards the target of playing during 10 seasons in the majors. Earlier I mentioned that Jose Bautista, Jeff Keppinger, and Tom Gorzelanny all played in Hickory during the Pittsburgh years. Gorzelanny debuted for the Pirates on September 25, 2005, and the

G	AB	R	H	2B	3B	HR	RBI
119	480	65	150	23	6	8	70

TB	BB	SO	SB	AVE	OBP	SLG	OPS
209	23	50	18	.313	.337	.435	.772

Table 3–4 HIC. Carlos Lee 1996 batting stats.

next season moved into their starting rotation. He pitched for the Pirates until he was traded to the Chicago Cubs in July 2009. In recent years, Gorzelanny has pitched both as a starter and reliever. During the 2013 season, he made 43 appearances for the Milwaukee Brewers, which included 10 starts. After a delayed start to the 2014 season due to an injury, Gorzelanny was back in the Brewers bullpen.

On the other hand, the Baltimore Orioles selected Jose Bautista from the Pirates in the 2003 Rule 5 draft. That is the reason he made his major league debut with Baltimore on April 4, 2004. Tampa Bay obtained Bautista off waivers on June 3, 2004, and traded him to Kansas City before the end of the month. On July 30, 2004, he was included in a three-way deal between the Royals, Mets, and Pirates that sent him to Pittsburgh. Bautista had played for three major league teams in less than 60 days. At that point, his career stabilized and he played four seasons with the Pirates. However, Bautista was traded again in August 2008, this time to the Toronto Blue Jays where he settled in to become the Blue Jays' starting right fielder and a key member of the team's offense.

This list of current Pittsburgh Pirates players that passed through Hickory on their way to the majors includes two of the team's current field players: second baseman Neil Walker and center fielder Andrew McCutchen. The 2014 season was the sixth for both players with the major league club. McCutchen has become a star player for Pittsburgh. He was selected to represent the Pirates in the All-Star game each season from 2011 through 2014, received the silver slugger award for an National League outfielder in 2012, 2013, and 2014, and received the National League Most Valuable Player Award for his outstanding play during the 2013 season.

Of the Pirates players listed in Table 3–3 HIC, the field players who had the best offensive performance while at Hickory were Neil Walker and Rajai Davis. For the 2005 season, Walker led the regular players on the Crawdads team in most batting statistic categories. His offensive stats for that

G	AB	R	H	2B	3B	HR	RBI
120	485	78	146	33	2	12	68

TB	BB	SO	SB	AVE	OBP	SLG	OPS
219	20	71	7	.301	.332	.452	.784

Table 3–5 HIC. Neil Walker 2005 batting stats.

season are summarized in Table 3–5 HIC. Walker ranked number 1 among the regular players on the team in runs, hits, doubles, runs batted in, batting average, slugging, on-base plus slugging percentage, and total bases. More-over, he was ranked in the top 10 among all players in the South Atlantic League in runs (tied for ninth), hits (tied for fourth), doubles (tied for sixth), and total bases (eight). Walker was just out of the league's top 10 in batting average (eleventh).

Davis's stats in 2003, which was his second season on the Hickory roster, stood out less on the team, but many ranked high in the overall league rank-ing. A summary of his batting stats appears in Table 3–6 HIC. Davis led the team in most offensive statistics that are associated with speed: runs scored, hits, triples, and stolen bases. Relative to all regular players in the South Atlantic League, he ranked in the top five in runs (number 3), hits (number 3), and stolen bases (number 3). Moreover, he was in the top ten in the league in triples (number 6), batting average (number 7), and on base percentage (number 8).

Even though no prospect of the Texas Rangers that passed through Hick-ory on his way to the majors has played at the major league level each of the last five seasons, fans of the Crawdads got to see a few players who played a key role for the Rangers' 2013 pitching staff. For example, left-handed reliever Robbie Ross served the role of a short reliever and lefty specialist and pitched in 65 of the Rangers' games that season. Ross was in the Crawdads' starting rotation during the first half of the 2010 season. In 2014, he pitched for the Rangers as both a starter and reliever, but was traded to Boston during the offseason. Also, right hander Martin Perez, who was recalled from AAA in late June 2013, took over a regular role in the Texas starting rotation and went 10W:6L in 20 starts. Perez pitched as both a starter and reliever for Hickory during the 2009 season. He began the 2014 season in Texas' starting rotation, but his season ended in May with an elbow injury that led to Tommy John surgery.

G	AB	R	H	2B	3B	HR	RBI
125	478	84	146	21	7	6	54

TB	BB	SO	SB	AVE	OBP	SLG	OPS
199	55	65	40	.305	.383	.416	.799

Table 3–6 HIC. Rajai Davis 2003 batting stats.

As mentioned earlier, Texas' top 2013 prospect—infielder Jurickson Profar, who played shortstop for the 2011 Crawdads—spent much of the 2013 season with the Rangers. Profar was poised to be the Texas Rangers' opening day second baseman. However, he injured a muscle in his throwing shoulder during spring training and opened the 2014 season on the disabled list. The torn muscle kept him out of action for the complete season.

Attractions in or Near Hickory

- **Union Square Restaurants and Shops**, 232 Union Square NW, Hickory NC 28601
- **Harper House–Hickory History Center**, 310 N. Center St., Hickory, NC 28601 (828) 324–7294
- **Catawba Science Center**, 243 3rd Ave. NE, Hickory, NC 28601 (828) 322–8169
- **Hickory Motor Speedway**, 3130 20th Ave. SE, Newton, NC 28658 (828) 464–3655

Dining in Hickory

BREWPUBS AND BREWERIES

- **Olde Hickory Tap Room**, 222 Union Square, Hickory, NC 28601 (828) 322–1965

DOWNTOWN RESTAURANTS

- **The Vintage House**, 271 3rd Ave. NW, Hickory NC 28601 (828) 324–1210
- **Josh's on Union Square**, 206 Union Square NW, Hickory, NC 28601 (828) 324–5674
- **Roasted 'Tater**, 2220 N. Center St., Hickory, NC 28601 (828) 855–3682
- **Hickory Tavern**, 2982 N. Center St., Hickory, NC 28601 (828) 322–2699
- **Taste Full Beans Coffeehouse**, 29 2nd St. NW, Hickory NC 28601 (828) 325–0108
- **Mellow Mushroom**, 1185 Lenoir Rhyne Blvd. SE, Hickory, NC 28602 (828) 322–8491

Kannapolis Intimidators

CMC-NorthEast Stadium
2888 Moose Rd., Kannapolis, NC 28083
www.milb.com/index.jsp?sid=t487

This morning I am racing southwest from Durham on route I-85. Why racing? A late start, rush hour traffic, and getting into the racing state of mind. Stock car racing is the official sport of North Carolina. I am traveling toward Charlotte, North Carolina, the heart of NASCAR racing and home of the NASCAR Hall of Fame. In fact, I'm heading to Kannapolis, North Carolina, the hometown of legendary auto racers—the Earnhardt family—for an early morning baseball game. It's Education Day at CMC-NorthEast Stadium, and because of that the Kannapolis Intimidators' home game versus the visiting West Virginia Power is scheduled to start at 10:05AM. That is not just an early start, that is a real early start, and my car looks lonely among all those big school buses.

But before getting back to Dale Earnhardt Sr. and his impact on baseball in Kannapolis, let's take a short cruise through the earlier history of baseball in the city. Table 3–1 KAN shows that unlike many of the other hometowns of the current South Atlantic League clubs, Kannapolis has a very limited baseball past. Moreover, much of its association with baseball teams has been with those of the modern South Atlantic League. The first baseball team to call the city home was the Kannapolis Towlers in the 1930s. The Towlers played in the independent Carolina Baseball League from 1935 through 1938. The league was initially formed with six teams and most of them were located in small towns to the northeast of Charlotte. In fact, from 1936 to 1938 a team from another city that today hosts a South Atlantic League team played in the league—the Rebels from Hickory, North Carolina. However, the league disbanded after just four seasons of play.

For the 1939 season Kannapolis hosted a D-level team, now called the

Team Name	1st Year	Years	Leagues
Kannapolis Towlers	1935	4	Carolina Baseball League
Kannapolis Towelers	1939	3	North Carolina State League
Piedmont Phillies	1995	1	South Atlantic League
Piedmont Boll Weevils	1996	5	South Atlantic League
Kannapolis Intimidators	2001	14	South Atlantic League

Table 3–1 KAN. Teams that have played in Kannapolis, NC (source: www.baseball-reference.com).

Kannapolis Towelers—slightly different spelling—in the North Carolina State League. The North Carolina State League was one of the early baseball leagues that played a role in the evolutionary path of today's South Atlantic League. The Towelers played through the 1941 season as a member of this league. But the end of that season brought to a close the early era of professional baseball in Kannapolis.

Professional baseball did not return to Kannapolis for over 55 years, not until the Philadelphia Phillies relocated their A-level affiliate in the South Atlantic League—the Spartanburg Phillies—to the city in 1995 and renamed the team the Piedmont Phillies. The next season the team's nickname was changed to the Boll Weevils in memory of the city's cotton and textile industry past. The Boll Weevils remained the Phillies' single-A affiliate through the 2000 season.

After the close of the 2000 season, the team was purchased by a group of investors that included legendary auto racer Dale Earnhardt Sr. Philadelphia had already made plans to establish a new South Atlantic League affiliate in Lakewood, New Jersey. The new ownership group engaged with the Chicago White Sox to field a team for the 2001 season. The team adopted the nickname of their new owner—Dale Earnhardt Sr., the "Intimidator"—and became the Kannapolis Intimidators. But Earnhardt never got to see the team play a game. He died in an accident while racing in the Daytona 500 in February 2001. However, Dale Earnhardt Inc. remained part of the team's ownership through the 2003 season. The Intimidators remain the A-level affiliate of the White Sox today.

The Home of the Intimidators—CMC-NorthEast Stadium

The decision by city and county officials to fund a new stadium played a key role in the return of professional baseball to Kannapolis. With the opportunity to play home games in a new stadium, the ownership of the Spartanburg Phillies moved their team to the 4,700 seat Fieldcrest Cannon Stadium prior to the 1995 baseball season. The team, which was renamed the Piedmont Phillies, resumed the role of A-level affiliate of the Philadelphia Phillies in the South Atlantic League. The stadium was finished during the winter and the Phillies won their 1995 season home opener by a score of 7–3 over the Hickory Crawdads on April 8.

During the 2011 postseason, a business agreement between Carolinas Medical Center-NorthEast was finalized and as shown in Fig. 3–1 KAN, the

Figure 3-1 KAN. CMC-NorthEast Stadium, Kannapolis, NC.

ballpark was renamed CMC-NorthEast Stadium. However, the stadium is still affectionately referred to by local fans as the "The Cannon." The ballpark is located approximately four miles from the central Kannapolis downtown area.

CMC-NorthEast Stadium employs a modern design, which does not have the usual covered grandstand behind the infield area. Instead, it has a wide, open concourse between the seats on the first base–right field and third base–left field lines and buildings that house the concessions, team shop, and luxury suites and other structures on the far side of the concourse. Due to this stadium design, all seating except that in the luxury suites is at the field level. Also, all seats, with the exception of those in the suites, have no covering to protect fans from the sun or rain.

On the other hand, this layout permits fans to view the game from almost any point in the ballpark. Well, almost any spot! A small building on the field side of the concourse backs up to the seats behind home plate and serves as the press box. Because of this structure, there is no concourse area to view the game from directly behind home plate.

Since this section of North Carolina has a rich auto racing history and Dale Earnhardt Sr. and Dale Earnhardt Inc. were part of the ownership group for a period of time, the stadium has taken on a bit of an auto racing and Dale Earnhardt theme. For example, the playground in the children's play area is called the Pit Stop Playground, the team merchandise store is named The Intimidation Station, and of course the current team moniker, Intimidators, is from Earnhardt's nickname. In memory of the former owner, uniform number 3 (the number on the race car of Dale Earnhardt Sr.) was retired in 2002. Also a black flag with that number flies on a flag pole adjacent to the American and North Carolina state flags behind the left field wall to honor his memory.

The South Atlantic League Years

Unlike many of the other current cities that are home to modern South Atlantic League teams, Kannapolis has had a short but quite stable presence in the league. With its new stadium, the city attracted the Philadelphia Phillies to relocate their single-A affiliate to Fieldcrest Cannon Stadium in 1995. As shown in Table 3–2(a) KAN, the team played their first season as the Piedmont Phillies, but were then renamed the Piedmont Boll Weevils. The Cannon remained the home of a Phillies single-A minor league team for six seasons.

Upon entry to the South Atlantic League in 1995, the team was assigned to the Northern Division. However, due to a realignment of the league to three divisions prior to the 1996 season, they became a member of the Central Division through the 1999 season. While a member of the Philadelphia Phillies minor league organization, the Piedmont team went to the South Atlantic League playoffs three times but came home with only one Northern Division championship. In 1995 the Piedmont Phillies beat the Asheville Tourists (Colorado Rockies) in the first round of the postseason to win their first Northern Division title. But they lost to the Southern Division champi-

Name	MLB Affiliate	Years
Kannapolis Intimidators	Chicago White Sox	2001-today
Piedmont Boll Weevils	Philadelphia Phillies	1996-2000
Piedmont Phillies	Philadelphia Phillies	1995

Above: Table 3–2(a) KAN. Kannapolis teams' major league affiliation. *Opposite:* Table 3–2(b) KAN. Chicago White Sox minor league organization.

Level	Team	Stadium	League
Rk	Great Falls Voyagers	Centene Stadium Great Falls, MT	Pioneer League
A	Kannapolis Intimidators	CMC-NorthEast Stadium Kannapolis, NC	South Atlantic League
A+	Winston-Salem Dash	BB&T Ballpark Winston-Salem, NC	Carolina League
AA	Birmingham Barons	Regions Field Birmingham, AL	Southern League
AAA	Charlotte Knights	BB&T Ballpark Charlotte, NC	International League

ons, the Augusta GreenJackets (Pittsburgh Pirates), in the league championship round.

During the Piedmont Boll Weevils years, a number of future Philadelphia Phillies players took the field at the Cannon. They include star shortstop Jimmy Rollins (1997), right-handed starting pitcher Brett Myers (2000), and righty reliever Ryan Madson (2000).

As pointed out earlier, a number of changes took place during the 2000 offseason. The team was purchased by Dale Earnhardt Sr.; the Philadelphia Phillies relocated their single-A team to Lakewood, New Jersey; and the vacuum created by the Phillies' departure was filled with a Chicago White Sox team. After the 2000 season, the White Sox disengaged with the Burlington Bees of the Midwest League and established their new A-level affiliate—the Kannapolis Intimidators—at Fieldcrest Cannon Stadium. Table 3–2(b) KAN lists the other teams of the Chicago White Sox minor league organization. Note that three of those teams are associated with cities in North Carolina. The other two are the Winston-Salem Dash (Carolina League, A+ level) and Charlotte Knights (International League, AAA).

Over the years the Intimidators have also moved back and forth between the divisions of the South Atlantic League. In 2001, they started in the Northern Division, but were switched to the Southern Division after the 2004 season. Prior to the 2009 season, Kannapolis returned to the Northern Division where it remains today. Since 2001, the Kannapolis Intimidators, also known as the K-Town Intimidators, have made two postseason appearances—2005 and 2009.

During the 2005 season, Kannapolis beat the Charleston RiverDogs (New York Yankees) 2 games to 0 to claim their first Southern Division title.

Outfielder David Cook and first baseman Josh Hansen led the Intimidators' regular season offense. They each had 24 home runs to top the team in that batting statistic category. Cook led all regular players on the team in six other offensive stats: R (75), 3B (3, tied with others), BB (72), OBP (.403), SLG (.552), and OPS (.954). Those stats ranked him in the top ten in the South Atlantic League in home runs, bases on balls, on-base percentage, slugging, and on-base plus slugging percentage for the season. In fact, his 72 BB, .403 OBP, .552 SLG, and .952 OPS set the Intimidators' all-time single-season offensive records that still stand today. Hanson led the team in most other batting categories: H (135), 2B (28), RBI (90), and TB (237). His home runs, runs batted in and total bases totals also ranked him in the top ten in the league.

Right-hander Jack Egbert, who pitched to a 10W:5L record, led the pitching staff in wins. Moreover, his 1.10 walks plus hits per inning pitched was the lowest among the regular starters. Egbert ranked in the top 10 among all pitchers in the South Atlantic League in W and WHIP pitching stats for the season.

The Intimidators went on to face the Hagerstown Suns (Baltimore Orioles) in the League Championship Series. K-Town won the best-of-five series 3 games to 1 to become the 2005 South Atlantic League champions. Egbert was the starter and winning pitcher for Kannapolis in the series-deciding game 4. He went 6 innings and gave up 0 runs on 4 hits, while walking 1 and striking out 5. The Intimidators won the game 3–0 to capture their only South Atlantic League title. Egbert made brief appearances in the majors during the 2009 and 2012 season.

In 2009 Kannapolis won the division for the second half season and made their second postseason appearance. During the regular season, left-handed pitcher Charles Leesman led the Kannapolis starting rotation. He went 13W:5L for the season and led all starters with a 3.08 ERA and 1.41 WHIP. His 13 wins led all pitchers in the South Atlantic League for the season. Leesman made his major league debut with the Chicago White Sox on August 9, 2013. Right-handed reliever Dan Remenowski had 24 saves, which ranked him third among all closers in the South Atlantic League. Relative to the team's offense, third baseman Jon Gilmore led the team in five offensive statistic categories: hits (138), doubles (27), runs batted in (67), bases on balls (34), and total bases (182). Kannapolis played the Lakewood BlueClaws (Philadelphia Phillies) in the Northern Division Championship Series, but got swept 2 games to 0 in the best-of-three series

Since the 2001 season, a number of future major leaguers took the field for the K-Town Intimidators. They include: left-handed starter Gio Gonzalez (2004), righty starter Brandon McCarthy (2004), center fielder Chris Young (2004), and second baseman Gordon Beckham (2008). The year 2014 was the Intimidators' fourteenth season as the Chicago White Sox affiliate in the league. This is tied with the Lakewood BlueClaws for the third longest association among current SAL teams with their current major league affiliate.

Successful Major Leaguers Who Played in Kannapolis

Over the last 20 seasons, fans of the Kannapolis South Atlantic League teams have had the opportunity to see many top prospects play their early ball on the field of Fieldcrest Cannon–CMC-NorthEast Stadium. Table 3–3 KAN lists a number of ballplayers who were members of either the Boll Weevils or Intimidators roster and went on to have successful careers at the major league level.

During the Phillies years, 18-year-old Jimmy Rollins was promoted from the rookie level to play shortstop for the Piedmont Boll Weevils. Rollins was the catalyst of the 1997 team's offense. He led the team in six offensive statistical categories—R (94), H (151), 3B (8), BB (52), SB (46), and TB (207). These stats were high enough to place him within the top 10 among all batting leaders in the South Atlantic League in runs, hits, triples, and stolen bases for the season.

At the age of 21 years old, Jimmy Rollins made his debut on September 17, 2000, as the Philadelphia Phillies shortstop. His major league career got off to a good start. Rollins, batting second in the Phillies order, went 2 for 4 on that day, scored 2 runs, hit his first triple, and stole his first base. He was the Phillies' 2001 season Opening Day shortstop and number 2 batter, took over as the full time shortstop, and started 156 games at that position. Rollins was the recipient of the National League Most Valuable Player award for his outstanding play during the 2007 season. Two thousand fourteen was the three time National League All-Star and four time Gold Glove Award winner's fourteenth season as the Phillies' shortstop. But Rollins' contract with Philadelphia was to end after the 2015 season and that would make him a free agent. With free agency looming in the near future, the Phillies traded Rollins to the Los Angeles Dodgers during the 2014 offseason.

A number of other current major leaguers played for the Kannapolis Intimidators during the Chicago White Sox years. Gio Gonzalez pitched for the K-Town Intimidators during both the 2004 and 2005 seasons. During his first season of professional ball, the 18-year-old Gonzalez was promoted mid-season from the rookie level to Kannapolis and went 1 win, 2 losses in 8 starts before the end of the 2004 season. Gonzalez returned to Kannapolis for the start of the 2005 season and was 5W:3L when promoted to the Winston-Salem Dash (Carolina League, A+).

Season	Player	Age at KAN	MiLB Season	Position	MLB Debut	Age at Debut	MLB Team	Seasons in MLB
1995	x							
1996	x							
1997	Jimmy Rollins	18	2	SS	9/17/00	21	PHI	15+
	Adam Eaton	19	1	RHP	5/30/00	22	SDP	10
1998	x							
1999	x							
2000	Marlon Byrd	22	2	CF	9/8/02	25	PHI	13+
	Brett Myers	19	2	RHP	7/24/02	21	PHI	12
2001	Humberto Quintero	21	3	C	9/3/03	24	SDP	12+
2002	Mike Morse	20	3	RF	5/31/05	23	SEA	10+
2003	x							
2004	Chris Young	20	3	CF	8/18/06	22	ARI	9+
	Gio González	18	1	LHP	8/6/08	22	OAK	7+
	Brandon McCarthy	20	3	RHP	5/22/05	21	CHW	9+
2005	Chris Getz	21	1	2B	4/28/08	24	CHW	7+
	Lucas Harrell	20	2	RHP	7/30/10	25	CHW	5+
2006	Chris Carter	19	2	1B	8/9/10	23	OAK	5+
2007	x							
2008	Gordon Beckham	21	1	2B	6/4/09	22	CHW	6+
	Brent Morel	21	1	3B	9/7/10	23	CHW	5+
2009	x							

Table 3-3 KAN. Kannapolis SAL players that went on to have long Major League careers.

In an unusual sequence of events, the White Sox traded Gonzalez to the Philadelphia Phillies after the 2005 season in a deal that brought Jim Thome to the White Sox, but the Phillies traded him back to the White Sox along with right-handed starter Gavin Floyd after the 2006 season for right-handed starter Freddy Garcia. This was the start to a series of trades that involved him. Gonzalez pitched the 2007 season at the AA level in the Chicago White Sox minor league organization, but they traded him again in January 2008. This time Gonzalez was sent to the Oakland Athletics in a trade that brought Nick Swisher to the White Sox.

Late in the 2008 season, Gonzalez made his major league debut with the A's and took a loss in his first outing. However, in his next start he pitched 5 innings of 5 hit, 1 run ball. The A's won 2-1 and Gonzalez posted his first major league win. Gonzalez went on to be a key member of the Oakland starting rotation from 2009 to 2011. But he was traded during the 2011 off-season to the Washington Nationals. Two thousand and twelve was a breakout season for Gonzalez. His 2012 regular season record for the Nationals was

21W:8L and his 21 victories led all pitchers in the National League. Gonzalez has twice been a member of his league's all-star team—2011 in the American League representing the Athletics and 2012 in the National League as a member of the Nationals. Gonzalez is under contract to play in Washington through the 2016 season and the Nats have team options that could keep him with the team through 2018.

Another player listed in Table 3–3 KAN is former Chicago White Sox second baseman Gordon Beckham. Unlike Rollins and Gonzalez, Beckham was signed on August 8, 2008, after playing college ball. Having experience with the University of Georgia baseball team, he entered the professional ranks directly at the A level with the Kannapolis Intimidators. Beckham played just 14 games at Kannapolis before the end of the 2008 season.

Beckham's road to The Show was exceptionally fast. He began the 2009 season with the Birmingham Barons (Southern League, AA). After playing in just 38 games at the AA level he was batting .299. Beckham was promoted on May 28 to the Charlotte Knights (International League, AAA). In his first six games with the Knights Beckham went 13 for 28 and was batting .464. He was called up on June 4, 2009, after playing just those six games and made his major league debut at third base for the White Sox.

Beckham played in just 59 minor league games before being promoted to the majors. At the minor league level, he normally played shortstop. However, during the balance of the 2009 season he was the starting third baseman for Chicago. Beckham made the transition to the second base position in 2010 and was the starter at that position for the White Sox. However, he was traded to the Los Angeles Angels of Anaheim in late August 2014, became a free agent after the season, and re-signed with the Chicago White Sox.

Baseball Attractions Near Kannapolis

- **Charlotte Knights Home Game at BB&T Ballpark**, 324 S. Mint St., Charlotte, NC 28202 (704) 357–8071
- **Enos Slaughter Exhibit at the Person County Museum**, 309 N. Main St., Roxboro, NC 27573 (336) 597–2884

Attractions in or Near Kannapolis

- **Dale Earnhardt Plaza**, 175 S. Main St., Kannapolis, NC 28081

- **Charlotte Motor Speedway Tour**, 5555 Concord Pkwy S., Concord, NC 28027 (704) 455–3223
- **NASCAR Hall of Fame**, 400 E. Martin Luther King Jr. Blvd., Charlotte, NC 28202 (704) 654–4400
- **Richard Petty Museum**, 309 Branson Mill Rd., Level Cross, NC (336) 495–1143

Dining in or Near Kannapolis

BREWPUBS AND BREWERIES

- **Rock Bottom Restaurant and Brewery**, 401 N. Tryon St., Charlotte, NC 28202 704–334–2739
- **The Olde Mecklenburg Brewery**, 215 Southside Dr., Charlotte, NC 28217 (704) 525–5644

RESTAURANTS

- **Restaurant Forty Six**, 101 West Ave., Kannapolis, NC 28081 (704) 250–4646
- **Brew Pub**, 515 S. Main St., Kannapolis, NC 28081 (704) 938–2337
- **McCabes Smokehouse Restaurant**, 316 Brookdale St., Kannapolis, NC 28083 (704) 298–4250
- **Queen City Q**, 225 E. 6th St., Charlotte, NC 28202 (704) 334–8437
- **Mellow Mushroom**, 255 W. Martin Luther King Jr. Blvd., Charlotte, NC 28202 (704) 371–4725
- **The Capital Grill**, 201 N. Tryon St., Charlotte, NC 28202 (704) 348–1400
- **Valhalla Pub & Eatery**, 317 S. Church St., Charlotte, NC 28202 (704) 332–3273

Lakewood BlueClaws

FirstEnergy Park
2 Stadium Way, Lakewood, NJ 08701
www.milb.com/index.jsp?sid=t427

The most northern team in the South Atlantic League is the Lakewood BlueClaws. They are located in Lakewood, New Jersey, a suburb of New York City that is approximately 70 miles south of the city along the New Jersey coast. The township is conveniently located near some of New Jersey's popular Atlantic Coast seashore destinations. For instance, the drive from FirstEnergy Park—the home ballpark of the BlueClaws—to Point Pleasant Beach, New Jersey, which is an interesting shore community with beaches, a boardwalk, amusements, and waterfront restaurants and bars, is approximately 11 miles. Even though Lakewood is considered a suburb of New York City, it is actually less than 60 miles from the heart of Philadelphia. A trip to see a Lakewood BlueClaws game offers one the opportunity to take in some of the sights of New York City or Philadelphia and have a New Jersey shore adventure at one of a number of beachside towns.

Unlike most of the other host locations of South Atlantic League teams, the township of Lakewood had no prior professional baseball history. Table 3-1 LWD shows that the Lakewood BlueClaws are the first and only baseball

Team Name	1st Year	Years	Leagues
Lakewood BlueClaws	2001	14	South Atlantic League

Table 3-1 LWD. Teams that have played in Lakewood, NJ.

team associated with a major league club to play in the township. The owners of the Piedmont Boll Weevils—the Philadelphia Phillies' A-level affiliate in the South Atlantic League—relocated their team to the township for the start of the 2001 season and renamed it the Lakewood BlueClaws. Two thousand fourteen was the BlueClaws' fourteenth season as a member of the South Atlantic League.

The Home of the BlueClaws—FirstEnergy Park

Having reached an agreement with the ownership of the Piedmont Boll Weevils to move their team to New Jersey, Lakewood Township embarked on the building of a new baseball stadium. Ground was broken in April 2000 and the stadium was ready for Opening Day of the 2001 season. An agreement was signed with FirstEnergy Corp. and the stadium had its name—FirstEnergy Park.

As shown in Fig. 3-1 LWD, FirstEnergy Park, which is one of the newest stadiums of the South Atlantic League, is a very attractive ballpark. It is equipped with all the amenities of a modern stadium: party and picnic areas, luxury suites, a large kids' play area, arcade, specialty food concessions, and a Tiki Bar. It has a wide elevated concourse and all of the 6,588 seats at the

Figure 3–1 LWD. FirstEnergy Park, Lakewood, NJ.

field level slope down from the concourse toward the edge of the ball field. Food concessions and the team store are conveniently located on the far side of the concourse along both the first base and third base sides of the infield.

A plus is that the action of the game can be viewed while standing at any point on the concourse. The Doctor Bernard's Kid Zone is located toward the left field end of the concourse, and a specialty food court is located at the right field end. There are no bleachers, but the stadium has grass berms behind both the left field and right field walls that offer general admission seating on the grass to watch the game.

Another attractive feature of the stadium is that the concourse allows you to walk completely around the ball field. There is some seating along the outfield stretch of the concourse and at a Tiki Bar where you can stop and get a different and interesting view of the ball field and game. In addition to the blue claw crab in the team logo, FirstEnergy Park has a bit of a New Jersey shore flavor. At various spots along the outfield concourse walkway there are oversized traditional lifeguard chairs. They offer a fun opportunity for children—or maybe even adults—to climb up and have a photo taken of them sitting in a gigantic lifeguard stand.

FirstEnergy Park is an excellent venue for attending a baseball game. Its suburban location is easy to drive to and there is plentiful parking when you arrive. It has all the concessions and facilities one might want and a pleasant family oriented stadium environment and atmosphere in which to enjoy watching a game. And yes, on some special occasions the furry, green Phillie Phanatic makes the trip over from Citizen Bank Park in Philadelphia to see his pal Buster and entertain the fans at FirstEnergy Park.

The South Atlantic League Years

As identified earlier, the BlueClaws are the only professional baseball team to call the township of Lakewood home. Also, as shown in Table 3–2(a) LWD, the BlueClaws have always been the A-level minor league affiliate of the Philadelphia Phillies. The Phillies, who play their home games just over 60 miles away at Citizens Bank Park in the southern part of Philadelphia, have a strong fan base in southern New Jersey. The proximity of the Lakewood BlueClaws to their major league affiliate offers Phillies fans the opportunity to see up and coming prospects as they pass through the A level of Philadelphia's minor league organization. The Phillies other minor league teams are listed in Table 3–2(b) LWD.

Even though professional baseball is relatively new to Lakewood, 2014 was the BlueClaws' fourteenth season as a member of the South Atlantic League. This ties them with the Kannapolis Intimidators (the team that replaced the Boll Weevils when they departed Kannapolis) as the team with the third longest period of continuous participation with their current major league affiliate.

During this period the BlueClaws have excelled. The Lakewood Blue-Claws, who have always been a member of the Northern Division of the Sally League, have made three playoff runs—2006, 2009, and 2010. They gained entry into the postseason by winning the division during the second half of the 2006 season, first half of the 2009 season, and both half seasons in 2010. The BlueClaws went on to win the South Atlantic League championship in each of those three seasons.

Name	MLB Affiliate	Years
Lakewood BlueClaws	Philadelphia Phillies	2001-today

Level	Team	Stadium	League
Rk	GCL Phillies	Carpenter Complex Clearwater, FL	Gulf Coast League
A-	Williamsport Crosscutters	Bowman Field Willamsport, PA	New York-Penn League
A	Lakewood BlueClaws	FirstEnergy Park Lakewood, NJ	South Atlantic League
A+	Clearwater Threshers	Bright House Field Clearwater, FL	Florida State League
AA	Reading Fightin Phils	FirstEnergy Stadium Reading, PA	Eastern League
AAA	Lehigh Valley IronPigs	Coca-Cola Park Allentown, PA	International League

Top: Table 3–2(a) LWD. Lakewood BlueClaws major league affiliation. *Above:* Table 3–2(b) LWD. Philadelphia Phillies minor league organization.

The 2006 Lakewood team's offense was led by outfielders Jeremy Slayden and Mike Spidale. Slayden led the regular field players in hits (124), doubles (44), slugging percentage (.510), total bases (204), and tied for first in runs batted in (81). As a journeyman minor league outfielder Mike Spidale batted .345 and had both the highest batting average and on-base percentage (.418) among the regular players on the team. However, Spidale's 361 plate appearances are 17 shy of the 378 required to officially be considered the team leader in offensive percentage stats, such as AVE or OBP. For this reason, Slayden, who batted .310, was the BlueClaws' official batting average leader. Spidale was the team leader in stolen bases (29)—a stat that does not have this PA restriction. Slayden led all players in the South Atlantic League in doubles for the season and ranked in the top 10 in the league in AVE, SLG, and OPS. With his 44 doubles and .501 slugging percentage, Slayden broke the existing BlueClaws all-time single season records for both of those offensive stat categories, and he remains Lakewood's leader in them today.

The ace of the pitching staff was left-handed starter Matt Maloney. Maloney topped the starting rotation with 16 wins and led the BlueClaws' regular starters in earned run average (2.03) and strikeouts (180). He also led all pitchers in the South Atlantic League in those three pitching statistic categories for the season. His 16 W, 180 SO, and 2.03 ERA set new BlueClaws all-time single-season team records that still stand today.

In the opening round of the playoffs Lakewood swept the Lexington Legends (Houston Astros) in the best-of-three series 2–0 to win their first Northern Division title. In game 2, Maloney went 7 innings and struck out 11 Legends batters to close out the series win for the BlueClaws. Lakewood moved on to face the Augusta GreenJackets (San Francisco Giants) in the South Atlantic League Championship Series. The BlueClaws took the best-of-five championship round of the playoffs 3 games to 1 to win their first league championship.

Again Maloney pitched the deciding game at FirstEnergy Park while Mike Spidale and Jeremy Slayden supplied the offense. In the bottom of the first inning, Spidale doubled and Slayden singled to knock in runs and put Lakewood on top 2–0. Next, Spidale and Slayden contributed singles to a rally in the top of the fifth that put the BlueClaws up 5–0. Maloney outdid his first round performance. He pitched a 9-inning complete game shutout and en route to his second playoff round victory struck out 12 GreenJackets batters. Maloney was traded by the Phillies to Cincinnati during the 2007 season for right-handed starter Kyle Lohse and made his major league debut with the Cincinnati Reds on June 6, 2009, at the age of 25.

The offense of the BlueClaws' 2009 South Atlantic League championship team was driven by three players: first baseman Jim Murphy, catcher Travis d'Arnaud, and center fielder Anthony Gose. Murphy and d'Arnaud supplied the power hitting. They were number 1 and number 2 in doubles, home runs, and RBIs on the team with d'Arnaud leading in two base hits and runs batted in. Murphy was number 1 with 14 HR, while d'Arnaud topped the team with 38 doubles and 71 RBI. However, Murphy also led the team in the on-base percentage (.393), slugging (.467), and on-base plus slugging percentage (.860) batting stat categories. Murphy also played the full 2011 season at Lakewood. That season he hit 22 homers, which tied the single-season record for the most home runs by a player in the BlueClaws uniform. Murphy remains the co-holder of the BlueClaws' all-time home run record today.

Gose supplied consistent hitting and speed on the base paths. He was the leader of the team in runs scored (72), hits (132), triples (9), and stolen bases (76). His 76 stolen bases led all players in the South Atlantic League by a wide margin. This total broke the BlueClaws' all-time record for the most stolen bases in a single season, and Gose remains the team's record holder in that offensive stat today.

The BlueClaws swept the Kannapolis Intimidators (Chicago White Sox) in the opening round of the playoffs 2 games to 0 on strong outings by starters Matt Way and Trevor May to become the 2009 Northern Division champions. Way pitched game 1 and gave up just 1 run on 7 hits in 7 complete innings. He walked 1 batter and struck out 7. Lakewood won the game 4–2. In game 2, May and 3 relievers combined to shut out the Intimidators on just 3 hits, while the BlueClaws staged a 14 hit offensive attack to win 9 to 0.

Lakewood met the Greenville Drive (Boston Red Sox) in the South Atlantic League Championship Series. Lakewood won their second SAL championship by beating the Drive in the best-of-five series 3 games to 1. In game 2 right-hander Jesus Sanchez, who led the Lakewood starters with 10 victories during the regular season, took the mound for the first time in the postseason. He threw six innings of 3 hit 0 run ball. Two relievers came on to shut down the Drive's offense the rest of the way. Sanchez got the win and the BlueClaws were off to a commanding 2–0 start in the championship series.

The series moved to Greenville, South Carolina, and the Drive bounced back by winning game 3. But, Lakewood closed out the series with a 5–1 victory in game 4 to win their second South Atlantic League Championship. Gose and d'Arnaud led the BlueClaws' offense during the postseason. Gose batted .407 and went 2 for 5 with 1 RBI and 3 stolen bases in the championship series finale; d'Arnaud batted .391 with 9 hits and 4 RBI in the six postseason games.

The Phillies traded Gose and d'Arnaud in separate deals. On December 16, 2009, d'Arnaud was sent to Toronto as part of a package for Roy Halladay. Over the next few years, the power hitting catcher worked his way up to the AAA level in the Blue Jays minor league organization. But Toronto traded d'Arnaud to the New York Mets after the 2012 season as part of a package that brought them Cy Young Award-winning knuckleballer R. A. Dickey. On August 17, 2013, d'Arnaud made his major league debut at the age of 24 as the catcher of the Mets. He was the New York Mets' 2014 season Opening Day catcher.

On July 29, 2010, Gose was sent to Houston in a package for right-handed starter Roy Oswalt, but on that same day Houston traded him to Toronto for corner infielder Brett Wallace. Gose made his major league debut in the Blue Jays uniform in an away game at Yankees Stadium on July 17, 2012, at the age of 21. He entered the game in the top of the seventh inning as a pinch hitter, but ground out. He took over in right field and came to bat a second time in the top of the ninth. In that plate appearance the speedster got a bunt single—his first hit at the major league level. Toronto traded Gose to the Detroit Tigers during the 2014 off season.

The BlueClaws' 2010 playoff run began against the Hickory Crawdads

(Texas Rangers) and they won that series 2 games to 1 to capture the Northern Division championship. Lakewood faced the Greenville Drive (Boston Red Sox) for the second season in a row in the South Atlantic League championship round and again beat them 3 games to 1 to win their third South Atlantic League title.

The 2010 postseason was all about pitching for the BlueClaws. Four pitchers, Trevor May, Brody Colvin, Jonathan Pettibone, and Julio Rodriguez, made starts, and they all had excellent outings. In the three division series games, Lakewood outscored Hickory 14 runs to 2. Both BlueClaws victories were shutouts.

In the championship series, they dropped the opening game at Greenville but then went on to win three in a row. Game 3 of the series at FirstEnergy Park in Lakewood was a momentum changer. The BlueClaws won a 2–1 walk-off victory. On that day, second baseman Keoni Ruth drove in Lakewood's first run in the bottom of the fourth inning to tie the game at 1 run each. With two down in the bottom of the ninth, third baseman Jeremy Barnes singled to drive in the game winning run and the BlueClaws took a 2–1 lead in the series. During the playoffs, Ruth and Barnes led the Lakewood offense—Ruth batted .333 for the series and Barnes .286.

Pettibone notched a victory in both the division and championship series. In the division series' deciding game 3, he threw 7 shutout innings and allowed the Hickory offense just 1 hit in leading Lakewood in a 6–0 victory. Pettibone struck out 9 and walked just 1. In the league championship series, he again pitched the series finale, this time throwing five innings of 7 hit 2 run ball. The BlueClaws won 4–2 to take home the SAL championship. Pettibone made his major league debut on April 22, 2013, made 18 starts for the Philadelphia Phillies during the season, and ended the season with a 5W:4L record. After pitching briefly in Philadelphia and for the Phillies' AAA affiliate, the Lehigh Valley IronPigs, in the International League in April and May 2014, Pettibone was shut down for the balance of the season due to a shoulder injury.

Successful Major Leaguers Who Played in Lakewood

Lakewood is another city that has had a professional baseball team which has participated in the South Atlantic League for a relatively short number of years. In this case it is a single team—the BlueClaws—that has been affiliated with the same major league club—the Philadelphia Phillies. Even though 2014 was just the fourteenth season that the BlueClaws have been a member of the league, the fans of the team and local Philadelphia fans have had the opportunity to see quite a few future Phillies players play the early years of their professional career at FirstEnergy Park.

Table 3–3 LWD shows that only two players who have been on a Lakewood BlueClaws roster have played at least ten seasons at the major league level. They are Ryan Howard and Gavin Floyd. Both of them played for the BlueClaws during the 2002 season and were called up at the end of 2004 when the rosters were expanded on September 1. Two thousand fourteen was the eleventh season that each of them played games in the major leagues. Today Howard is the star first baseman of the Phillies.

Howard played college ball at Missouri State University and was signed by the Phillies after the June 2001 Amateur Draft at the age of 21. During the 2002 season, Howard was the starting first baseman of the Lakewood Blue-Claws and led the team in most offensive stat categories. Table 3–4 LWD summarizes his batting statistics for that season. He led all field players on the team in hits, triples, home runs, runs batted in, total bases, bases on balls, on-base percentage, slugging percentage, and on-base plus slugging percentage. These stats ranked him in the top 10 among all regular players in the league for the 2002 season in seven offensive stat categories. His highest rankings were tied for number 3 with 19 home runs with one other player, tied for fourth with 87 RBIs with one other player, and number 4 in total bases.

Season	Player	Age at LWD	MiLB Season	Position	MLB Debut	Age at Debut	MLB Team	Seasons in MLB
2001	Carlos Ruiz	22	2	C	5/6/06	27	PHI	9+
2002	Ryan Howard	22	2	1B	9/1/04	24	PHI	11+
	Gavin Floyd	19	1	RHP	9/3/04	21	PHI	11+
2003	Cole Hamels	19	1	LHP	5/12/06	22	PHI	9+
	Alfredo Simon	22	3	RHP	9/6/08	27	BAL	7+
2004	Michael Bourn	21	2	CF	7/30/06	23	PHI	9+
	Kyle Kendrick	19	2	RHP	6/13/07	22	PHI	8+
2005	J. A. Happ	22	2	LHP	6/30/07	24	PHI	8+
	Carlos Carrasco	18	2	RHP	9/1/09	22	CLE	5+
2006	Josh Outman	21	2	LHP	9/2/08	23	OAK	6+
2007	Antonio Bastardo	21	2	LHP	6/2/09	23	PHI	6+
	Kyle Drabek	19	2	RHP	9/15/10	22	TOR	5+
2008	Domonic Brown	20	3	LF	7/28/10	22	PHI	5+
	Vance Worley	20	1	RHP	7/24/10	22	PHI	5+
2009	x							

Table 3–3 LWD. Lakewood SAL players that went on to have long major league careers.

G	AB	R	H	2B	3B	HR	RBI
135	493	56	138	20	6	19	87

TB	BB	SO	AVE	OBP	SLG	OPS
227	66	145	.280	.367	.460	.828

Table 3–4 LWD. Ryan Howard 2002 batting stats at Lakewood.

The Phillies called up Howard when the rosters expanded on September 1, 2004, and he made his debut as a pinch-hitter on that day. Since he had just 39 at bats at the major league level during the balance of the 2004 season, Howard retained his rookie status for the 2005 season. At mid-season he became the regular first baseman of the Phillies. In the months that followed he batted .288 with 22 home runs and 63 RBI. Howard received the National League Rookie of the Year Award for his play during his 2005 rookie season. The next season, 2006, he led the National League with 58 home runs and 149 RBI. That season he was voted to represent the league in the all-star game and after the season was selected as the National League Most Valuable Player (MVP). Since then Howard has twice more been a member of the National League All-Star Team.

Four other players listed in Table 3–3 LWD that became regular players for the Philadelphia Phillies are catcher Carlos Ruiz, left-handed starting pitcher Cole Hamels, right-handed starter Kyle Kendrick, and left-handed reliever Antonio Bastardo. Hamels and Kendrick were both key members of the Phillies' 2013 starting rotation and made 30 or more starts during the season. They were all back playing those same roles for the Phillies in 2014.

During the 2003 season, the 19-year-old Hamels got off to an excellent start at the A level. He went 6W:1L in 13 starts for the BlueClaws and pitched to both an exceptionally low 0.84 ERA and 0.763 WHIP. Hamels was promoted on July 28, 2003, to the Clearwater Thrashers—the Phillies' A+ level team in the Florida State League—where he made 5 more starts before the end of the season. Two thousand fourteen was the ninth consecutive season that Hamels was a member of the Phillies' starting rotation.

For the past few seasons, Antonio Bastardo has been a member of the Philadelphia Phillies bullpen and served as a lefty specialist and short reliever. During 2007 the 21-year-old Bastardo was a starter for the Lakewood Blue-Claws and went 9W:0L in 15 starts. He made his major league debut on June 2, 2009, at the age of 23 and won his first game as a starter. Bastardo made a total of five more appearances, four which were starts, before going on the DL. He did not make the transition to the reliever role until the 2010 season. Since then he has been a regular out of the bullpen for Philadelphia.

Right-handed pitcher Alfredo Simon took an unusual route to the major leagues. He was signed by the Philadelphia Phillies in the 1999 Amateur Draft and played in Lakewood for the BlueClaws at the age of 22 during the 2003 season. Simon went 5W:0L for the BlueClaws in a combination of fourteen relief and starting appearances. Philadelphia traded Simon to the San Francisco Giants in July 2004. After that he bounced around the minor league organizations of the Giants, Rangers, Orioles, Dodgers, and even the Phillies again between 2004 and 2008. As shown in Table 3–3 LWD, the 27-year-old Simon made his major league debut with the Baltimore Orioles on September 6, 2008. In that game he threw 1.2 innings in relief. Simon had waited almost a full ten seasons before making his major league debut. Since then, he has pitched mainly as a reliever for Baltimore and more recently the Cincinnati Reds. During the 2013 season, Simon made 63 relief appearances for the Reds, went 6W:4L; and pitched to a 2.87 ERA. Simon was elevated to Cincinnati's starting rotation to start the 2014 season, which was his seventh season in the majors. He got off to a great start and was selected to represent the Reds on the 2014 National League All-Star roster. Simon's pitching record was 12W:4L at the all-star break. However, he tailed off in the second half of the season and ended the year with a 15W:10L record.

In more recent years, a couple of young up and coming Phillies prospects who played in Lakewood have carved out roles on the Philadelphia Phillies' rosters. For example, Domonic Brown, who played center and right field for the 2008 BlueClaws, has made appearances with the Phillies over the last five seasons. Two thousand thirteen was a breakout year for Brown as the left fielder of the Phillies. He opened the season batting sixth in the Philadelphia order and as their left fielder. Brown went on to play in 139 games, bat .272 for the season, lead the team's offense in home runs (27) and runs batted in (83), and finish with a .494 slugging percentage. Brown was Philadelphia starting left fielder during the 2014 season.

Lefty reliever Jake Diekman has recently played a key role in the Philadelphia Phillies bullpen. He is not listed in Table 3–3 LWD because he has played at the major league level for only the last three seasons. Diekman was a reliever for the Lakewood BlueClaws during the 2009 season. He made his major league debut for the Phillies on May 15, 2012, versus the Astros at Citizens Bank Park. Diekman came in relief in the top of the tenth inning of a game tied at 3 all. He pitched a 1, 2, 3 inning in which he struck out two batters. In the bottom of the tenth, Hunter Pence hit a solo homer for a walk-off Phillies win. Diekman got his first win at the major league level in his debut.

Baseball Attractions Near Lakewood

• **Trenton Thunder Home Game at Arm & Hammer Park**, 1 Thunder Rd., Trenton, NJ 08611 (609) 394–3300
• **Yogi Berra Museum & Learning Center at Yogi Berra Stadium**, 8 Yogi Berra Dr., Little Falls, New Jersey 07424 (973) 655–2378
• **Jackie Robinson Statue**, 54 Journal Square Plaza, Jersey City, NJ 07306 (address is for Loew's Jersey Theatre across the street from the statue)

Attractions Near Lakewood

• **Jenkinson's Boardwalk**, 300 Ocean Ave., Point Pleasant Beach, NJ 08742 (732) 892–0600

Dining Near Lakewood

Brewpubs and Breweries

• **Basel T's Brewery and Italian Grill**, 183 Riverside Ave., Red Bank, NJ 07701 (732) 842–5990

Restaurants

• **Frankie's Bar and Grill**, 414 Richmond Ave., Point Pleasant Beach, NJ 08742 (732) 892–6000
• **Shrimp Box,** 75 Inlet Dr., Point Pleasant Beach, NJ 08742 (732) 899–1637
• **Red's Lobster Pot**, 57 Inlet Dr., Point Pleasant Beach, NJ 08742 (732) 295–6622
• **Jack Baker's Lobster Shanty**, 83 Channel Dr., Point Pleasant Beach, NJ 08742 (732) 899–6700
• **Jack Baker's Wharfside Restaurant,** 101 Channel Dr., Point Pleasant Beach, NJ 08742 (732) 892–9100
• **The Coal House**, 710 Arnold Ave., Point Pleasant Beach, NJ 08742 (732) 899–4400

- **Martell's Tiki Bar (located on the boardwalk)**, 308 Boardwalk, Point Pleasant Beach, NJ 08742 (732) 892–0131
  - **Woodchuck's BBQ**, 3009 Route 88, Point Pleasant, NJ 08742 (732) 714–1400
    - **Pizza Express**, 2408 Route 88, Point Pleasant, NJ 08742 (732) 295–1414
    - **Green Planet Coffee Company**, 700 Arnold Ave., Point Pleasant Beach, NJ 08742 (732) 899–2201
      - **Mueller's Bakery**, 80 Bridge Ave., Bay Head, NJ 08742 (732) 892–0442
      - **Hoffman's Ice Cream & Yogurt**, 800 Richmond Ave., Point Pleasant Beach, NJ 08742 (732) 892–0270

Lexington Legends

Whitaker Bank Ballpark
207 Legends Ln., Lexington, KY 40505
www.milb.com/index.jsp?sid=t495

Professional baseball had been played in Lexington, Kentucky, as early as 1885, but as shown in Table 3–1 LEX not often. In fact, in the one hundred and sixteen years prior to the Lexington Legends coming to town, there had been a team playing in the city during just fifteen baseball seasons. The city's first two ventures into professional baseball were with teams that lasted just one season. In 1885 a Lexington based team played in the independent Interstate League. This league consisted of six teams located in the states of Ohio, Kentucky, Pennsylvania, and New York. Lexington was the southernmost team, the only one that resided in Kentucky, and quite far (135 miles to 700 miles) from the other cities in the league. The league folded after its inaugural season.

In 1896, the city hosted another team, but this time in a league—the Blue Grass League—that had all of its teams in the state of Kentucky. At this time, the Blue Grass League was independent and had just four teams. The other towns that hosted teams were all very close to Lexington. In fact, the road trip to the farthest town, Maysville, Kentucky, was just 65 miles. But this turned out to be the last year that the independent version of this league operated, and that ended the first era of professional baseball in Lexington.

After a twelve year lapse, the Blue Grass League was reestablished in 1908 as a D-class minor league. Table 3–1 LEX shows that the Lexington Colts Baseball Club was a member of the league during its inaugural season. Lexington was centrally located among the other five members of the league, and the farthest team, which was the Shelbyville Grays in Shelbyville, Ken-

Team Name	1st Year	Years	Leagues
Lexington	1885	1	Interstate League
Lexington	1896	1	Blue Grass League
Lexington Colts	1908	5	Blue Grass League
Lexington Colts	1913	4	Ohio State League
Lexington Reds	1922	2	Blue Grass League
Lexington Studebakers	1924	1	Blue Grass League
Lexington Colts	1954	1	Mountain States League
Lexington Legends	2001	14	South Atlantic League

Table 3–1 LEX. Teams that have played in Lexington, KY (source: www.baseball-reference.com).

tucky, was less than 50 miles away. After five seasons of play, the league disbanded after the 1912 season. However, the Lexington Colts connected for the start of the 1913 season with the Ohio State League, which was entering its sixth consecutive year of operation. That season the league consisted of eight teams located in the states of Ohio, West Virginia, and Kentucky. The Colts played in this league for the next four seasons, but the league folded after the 1916 season. After hosting a professional baseball team in nine consecutive seasons, the city of Lexington was again left without a team.

As shown in Table 3–1 LEX, the city of Lexington briefly hosted a baseball team known as the Lexington Reds in the early 1920s. The Blue Grass League was reformed prior to the 1922 season. This variant of the league had six teams, including the Lexington Reds. Again, the league consisted of teams located only in Kentucky with Lexington at the center of the league. In fact, five of these six teams were in towns that fielded teams in the Blue Grass League during the 1912 season. The Reds played the 1922 and 1923 seasons, and then the team's nickname was changed to the Studebakers for the 1924 season. But this league lasted only those three seasons. This closed the chapter on Lexington's second short era of professional baseball.

Professional baseball did not return to Lexington for many years. In fact, baseball was played in the city for only one season between 1925 and the arrival of the Lexington Legends in 2001. During the 1954 season, a Lexington Colts team played in the C-class Mountain States League. This league, which fielded teams in Kentucky and Tennessee, ceased to operate after that season.

After close to a fifty year drought, professional baseball returned to Lexington for the 2001 season when the Houston Astros formed a South Atlantic

League A-level affiliate in the city. Prior to that season the Houston Astros dropped their A+ level team in the Florida State League—the Kissimmee Cobras. Even though they already had an A-level team—the Michigan Battle Cats in the Midwest League—they temporarily added a second A-level team— the Lexington Legends—to their minor league organization. This was the start of the current era of professional baseball in Lexington. The year 2014 was the Legends' fourteenth season in the city of Lexington as a member of the South Atlantic League.

The Home of the Legends—Whitaker Bank Ballpark

Since such a long time had elapsed without professional baseball having been played in Lexington, the city did not have a baseball facility to attract a team. Efforts to obtain city and state funding to construct a new stadium were unsuccessful. But in 1999 a group of local investors, Lexington Professional Baseball Company, LLC, provided financing for a stadium and start-

Figure 3–1 LEX. Whitaker Bank Ballpark, Lexington, KY.

up of a baseball team. Based on their commitment to build a new stadium, they reached agreement with the Houston Astros to establish an A-level affiliate of the South Atlantic League in Lexington.

A groundbreaking ceremony took place on February 7, 2000, at a site that is approximately 2 miles northeast of the heart of downtown Lexington. Naming rights were sold to Applebee's International, Inc., the owner of the popular restaurant chain, and the stadium named Applebee's Park was ready for Opening Day of the 2001 season. The new Astros minor league affiliate, called the Lexington Legends, had their home opener at Applebee's Park on April 9, 2001. The Legends beat the Hagerstown Suns 15–1 before a standing room only crowd. The long drought from professional baseball in Lexington was over. Figure 3–1 LEX shows the stadium, which was renamed Whitaker Bank Ballpark in 2011.

Whitaker Bank Ballpark has a modern design with a high grandstand building that ranges from midway down the right field line, around behind home plate, and then halfway down the left field line. The top level of the grandstand building houses luxury suites. A concourse with general concessions is located behind and under the grandstand seating area and does not permit a view of the field. Behind home plate is the Kentucky Ale Taproom which offers both inside and outside seating and an excellent view of the game from both of those seating options.

Access to the seats in the grandstand area is by a narrow walkway with field level box seats on the field side and access to elevated general seating areas that rise from the walkway toward the luxury suites at the top of the grandstand on the other side. There are also bleacher seats behind the left field wall and two lawn sitting area for overflow crowds. Overall the stadium can seat 5061 fans.

The South Atlantic League Years

As identified in Table 3–2(a) LEX, the Lexington Legends are the only South Atlantic League team to have played in the city of Lexington. From the team's origination in 2001 through the 2012 season, they were the A-level affiliate of the Houston Astros. However, after the 2012 season, Houston moved their A-level team to Davenport, Iowa, as the Quad City River Bandits in the Midwest League. The River Bandits had been the single-A affiliate of the Astros for a number of years in the mid–1990s. Table 3–2(a) LEX shows that the vacancy at Whitaker Bank Ballpark was immediately filled by the Kansas City Royals. The Royals relocated their Midwest League single-A

Name	MLB Affiliate	Years
Lexington Legends	Kansas City Royals	2013-today
Lexington Legends	Houston Astros	2001-2012

Level	Team	Stadium	League
Rk	AZL Royals	Surprise Stadium Surprise , AZ	Arizona League
Rk	Idaho Falls Chukars	Melaleuca Field Idaho Falls, ID	Pioneer League
Rk	Burlington Royals	Burlington Athletic Stadium Burlington, NC	Appalachian League
A	Lexington Legends	Whitaker Bank Ballpark Lexington, KY	South Atlantic League
A+	Wilmington Blue Rocks	Frawley Stadium Wilmington, DE	Carolina League
AA	Northwest Arkansas Naturals	Arvest Ballpark Springdale, AR	Texas League
AAA	Omaha Storm Chasers	Wener Park Papillion, NE	Pacific Coast League

Top: Table 3–2(a) LEX. Lexington Legends major league affiliations. *Above:* Table 3–2(b) LEX. Kansas City Royals minor league organization.

team, which was the Kane County Cougars in Geneva, Illinois, to Lexington as the Legends.

Lexington was a member of the Northern Division of the South Atlantic League from 2001 through 2008, but due to realignment it was transferred to the Southern Division to start the 2009 season and remains there today. While affiliated with the Astros and a member of the Northern Division, the Legends appeared three times in the South Atlantic League playoffs—2001, 2003, and 2006. During their 2001 inaugural season, the Legends won the Northern Division for the first half of the season with a 50W:20L record and had the best record in the league (92W:48L) for the full season. The Lexington team was an offensive juggernaut and led the South Atlantic League in almost every batting statistic category. For example, they scored a league leading 781 runs during the regular season—over 140 more than the next closest team. Moreover, the team compiled 1321 hits—150 more than the next best team—and led the league in doubles, home runs, runs batted in, batting average, on-base percentage, and even slugging percentage.

The Legends' 2001 offense was keyed by several players including left fielder Jon Topolski, shortstop Tommy Whiteman, second baseman Félix Escalona, and catcher John Buck. Today all four of these players are inductees of the Lexington Legends Hall of Fame. Topolski had a record setting season with the bat. A summary of his batting stats for the 2001 season appears in Table 3–3 LEX. He led all players on the Legends and in the South Atlantic League in five key batting stat categories: R (98), H (158), RBI (96), BB (75), and TB (271). He also led the team in home runs with 25. His 98 runs scored, 158 hits, 75 bases on balls, and 271 total bases are still today all-time Legends single-season offensive records. However, his hits record was tied by Jimmy Paredes in 2010 and walks record tied by Zach Johnson in 2012. So in those two stat categories he is a co-leader today.

The pitching staff was just as dominant. Four members of the starting rotation had double digit wins: Mike Nannini (15W:5L), Rodrigo Rosario (13W:4L), Tony Pluta (12W:4L), and Nick Roberts (10W:1L). Nannini's 15 victories during the 2001 season is the all-time single season record for the most wins by a pitcher in the Lexington Legends uniform. His 190.1 innings pitched also set the Legends' single season record for the most innings pitched. Moreover, that season Rosario set the Legends' all-time single season records for lowest ERA and WHIP. In 30 appearances, he pitched to a record setting 2.14 earned run average and .959 walks plus hits per inning pitched. All four of those records still stand today. Of these eight players, only Buck, Escalona, and Rosario went on to play in the majors.

In the first round of the playoffs Lexington beat the Hagerstown Suns (San Francisco Giants) to win their first Northern Division title. Due to the 9–11 attack in New York, the best-of-five South Atlantic League Championship

G	AB	R	H	2B	3B	HR	RBI
136	550	98	158	27	7	24	96

TB	BB	SO	SB	AVE	OBP	SLG	OPS
271	75	128	28	.287	.375	.493	.868

Table 3–3 LEX. Jon Topolski 2001 batting stats summary.

Series was terminated with Lexington up 2 games to 0 versus the Southern Division champion Asheville Tourists (Colorado Rockies). The Legends were awarded the South Atlantic League championship.

Lexington made their second run for the South Atlantic League title in 2003. However, during that season, the Lake County Captains (Cleveland Indians) won the Northern Division for both the first and second half seasons. In this case the opposing team in the Division Championship Series is a wild card team. The wild card was the team with the next best overall season record. The Legends' record for the 2003 season was 75W:63L, which was the second best to that of the Captains, and that punched them a ticket to the postseason. But Lexington's quest for their second Sally League title ended quickly when they lost in the first round to Lake County.

During the 2006 season, Lexington won the first half of the season with a 44W:25L record and went on to have a 75W:63L record for the overall season. However, the Legends' title run was again cut short when they were swept 2 games to 0 by the Lakewood BlueClaws (Philadelphia Phillies) in the Northern Division Championship Series.

As identified earlier, 2013 was the Legends' first season as the Kansas City Royals' single-A affiliate in the South Atlantic League. They finished the season with an overall 68W:70L record and placed sixth in the Southern Division during the first half season and fourth in the second half season. The Royals' other minor league affiliates are listed in Table 3–2(b) LEX.

Successful Major Leaguers Who Played in Lexington

Lexington has been engaged with the South Atlantic League since 2001, and before that professional baseball was not played in the city for many years. In spite of this, fans of the Legends have still had the opportunity to see a number of players who have gone on to have successful major league careers. Table 3–4 LEX lists eleven of those players. However, since the Lexington Legends have been affiliated with the Kansas City Royals just since the 2013 season, these players all came up through Houston's minor league organization and most of them made their major league debuts with the Astros.

As shown in Table 3–4 LEX, catcher John Buck was signed by the Houston Astros at the age of 17 and played his fourth season of professional ball for the Lexington Legends at Applebee's Park. He was the starting catcher and one of the power hitters in the Legends' batting order during their 2001 South Atlantic League Championship season.

Season	Player	Age at LEX	MiLB Season	Position	MLB Debut	Age at Debut	MLB Team	Seasons in MLB
2001	John Buck	20	4	C	6/25/04	23	KCR	11+
2002	Wandy Rodriguez	23	2	LHP	5/23/05	26	HOU	10+
2003	x							
2004	Matt Albers	21	3	RHP	7/25/06	23	HOU	9+
2005	Hunter Pence	22	2	RF	4/28/07	24	HOU	8+
	Ben Zobrist	24	2	2B	8/1/06	25	TBR	9+
	J. C. Gutiérrez	21	3	RHP	8/19/07	24	HOU	6+
	Troy Patton	19	2	LHP	8/25/07	21	HOU	6+
	Felipe Paulino	21	3	RHP	9/5/07	23	HOU	6+
2006	x							
2007	Chris Johnson	22	2	3B	9/9/09	24	HOU	6+
	Bud Norris	22	2	RHP	7/29/09	24	HOU	6+
2008	Fernando Abad	22	3	LHP	7/28/10	24	HOU	5+
2009	x							

Table 3–4 LEX. Lexington SAL players that went on to have long major league careers.

Buck was traded by the Astros to the Kansas City Royals on June 24, 2004, and made his major league debut the next day—June 25—at Kauffman Stadium, Kansas City, Missouri. On that day he was behind the plate for the Royals and caught 20-year-old right-handed starter Zack Greinke, who made his major league debut with Kansas City earlier in that season. Buck went on to play during six seasons in Kansas City. Since then he has played for a number of other teams and finished the 2013 season as a member of the Pittsburgh Pirates. Buck made a brief appearance in a 2013 postseason playoff game for the Pirates. He was signed by the Seattle Mariners during the offseason as their backup catcher for the 2014 season.

Two of the most successful players in the list of Table 3–4 LEX, Hunter Pence and Ben Zobrist, both played in Lexington during the 2005 season. Pence played college ball before being selected in the June 2004 amateur draft and was signed by the Astros at the age of 21. He got off to a great start for the Legends in 2005. In late July when he was promoted to the Salem Avalanche in the Carolina League (A+ level), Pence was batting .338 with 25 home runs. Even though Pence played about two-thirds of the season in Lexington, his 25 home runs led the team for the season. He was the starting center fielder for the Northern Division in the 2006 South Atlantic League All-Star Game.

Pence made his major league debut with the Astros on April 28, 2007, at Minute Maid Park in Houston. He started in center field, went 1 for 3 with the bat, and scored 1 run. Pence became Houston's starting right fielder the next season and played that position until he was traded to the Philadelphia Phillies just before the 2011 season trading deadline. Pence made his first postseason appearance that season, but the Phillies lost in the first round. Philadelphia traded him to the San Francisco Giants just before the 2012 trading deadline. The acquisition of Pence helped the Giants win both the National League Championship and 2012 World Series.

During the 2013 offseason, Pence was re-signed by the Giants to a five-year contract. He played in the Giants outfield during each of the 162 regular season games during both the 2013 and 2014 seasons. Again in 2014, Pence played a key role in San Francisco's postseason and World Series victory. For the World Series, he led or was tied for the lead among all regular players on the team in nine offensive stats: H (12 hits—tied with Pablo Sandoval), 2B (3—tied with Pablo Sandoval), HR (1—tied with Gregor Blanco), RBI (5), R (6), AVE (.444), OBP (.500), SLG (.667), and OPS (1.167). Pence was a member of the National League All-Star Team in 2009, 2011, and 2014.

Zobrist, another college baseball player, was also selected by Houston at the June 2004 amateur draft and signed to a contract. He started in 2005, which was his second season of professional ball, as the Legends shortstop. Zobrist represented the team as the starting shortstop of the SAL Northern Division All-Star Team and after the all-star break was promoted to the Salem Avalanche in the Carolina League (A+ level). However, the Astros traded Zobrist to the Tampa Bay Devil Rays on July 12, 2006. The Rays called him up by the end of the month and he made his major league debut at Tropicana Field in Tampa, Florida, versus the Detroit Tigers on August 1. Two thousand fourteen is Zobrist's ninth season playing for Tampa and he is signed to play with the Rays through 2015. He is a switch-hitter and normally plays second base, but he also has frequently filled in at short and right field. Zobrist was a member of the American League All-Star Team in 2009 and 2013. He has made postseason appearances with Tampa Bay in 2008, 2010, 2011, and 2013. This included a trip to the World Series in 2008 when the Rays lost to the Phillies.

During recent seasons, fans of the Lexington Legends have also had the opportunity to see a few up and coming players of the Houston Astros. For example, J. D. Martinez had a standout season as the right fielder of the Legends in 2010. In 88 games prior to being promoted to the Corpus Christi Hooks (Texas League, AA level), he had a team leading .362 batting average and also led all regular players on the team in on-base percentage (.433), slugging percentage (.598), and on-base plus slugging percentage (1.030). Martinez's 2010 stats bested the Legends' all-time single season record for each of those offensive categories. Today he remains the Legends' record holder in AVE, OBP, SLG, and OPS. Martinez made his major league debut with the Astros on July 30, 2011, at Miller Park in a game versus the Milwaukee Brewers. He entered the game in the top of the eighth inning as a pinch-hitter. Martinez delivered with an RBI double in his first major league at-bat. He signed with the Detroit Tigers for the 2014 season and took over as a regular in their outfield.

Two other players from Lexington's 2010 team, Jose Altuve and Jose Cisnero, have taken on a more significant role for the Astros. Altuve made his major league debut in the Houston uniform on July 20, 2011. On that day he played second base and batted in the two hole in Houston's batting order. He went 1 for 5 with the bat as the Astros won by a score of 3 runs to 2 in 11 innings. During the 2012 season Altuve took over as Houston's regular second baseman. Since then he has evolved to become a key member of their offensive attack. Two thousand fourteen was a breakout season for Altuve. He led the American League in three offensive stats: hits (255), batting average (.341), and stolen bases (56). Altuve represented the Astros on both the 2012 and 2014 National League All-Star teams and in 2014 received the Silver Slugger award for American League third baseman.

Cisnero, who made his major league debut in 2013, appeared in 28 games as a reliever that season. He started the 2014 season as a regular from the Astros bullpen but had Tommy John surgery on his elbow in May and was out for the balance of the season. Within the next few years some of the Kansas City Royals prospects that Lexington fans have seen take the field at Whitaker Bank Ballpark will be promoted to the majors.

Baseball Attractions Near Lexington

- **Louisville Slugger Museum and Factory**, 800 W. Main St., Louisville, KY 40202 (877) 775–8443
- **Louisville Bats Home Game at Louisville Slugger Field**, 401 E. Main St., Louisville, KY 40202 (855) 228–8497

Attractions in Lexington

- **Historic Victorian Square Shop & Entertainment Complex**, 401 W. Main St., Lexington, KY 40507 (859) 252–7575
- **Lexington Visitors Center—Suite 104 Victorian Square**, 401 W. Main St., Lexington, KY 40507 (859) 233–7299

- **Kentucky Horse Park**, 4089 Iron Works Pkwy., Lexington, KY 40511 (859) 233–4303
- **Keeneland Thoroughbred Racing-Tour**, 4201 Versailles Rd., Lexington, KY 40510 (859) 254–3412
- **The Red Mile Harness Racing**, 1200 Red Mile Rd., Lexington, KY 40504 (859) 255–0752
- **Mary Todd Lincoln House Tour**, 578 W. Main St., Lexington, KY 40507 (859) 233–9999

Dining in Lexington

BREWPUBS AND BREWERIES

- **Lexington Beerworks**, 213 N. Limestone St., Lexington KY 40509 (859) 317–8137

DOWNTOWN RESTAURANTS

- **Dudley's on Short**, 259 W. Short St., Lexington, KY 40507 (859) 252–1010
- **Nick Ryan's Saloon**, 157 Jefferson St., Lexington, KY 40508 (859) 233–7900
- **Saul Good Restaurant & Pub**, 123 N. Broadway Rd., Lexington, KY 40507 (859) 252–4663
- **Mellow Mushroom**, 503 S. Upper St., Lexington, KY 40508 (859) 281–6111
- **Sweet Spot**, 126 N. Broadway Rd., Lexington, KY 40507 (859) 317–2952

Rome Braves

State Mutual Stadium
755 Braves Blvd., Rome, GA 30161
www.mvilb.com/index.jsp?sid=t432

I am on one of my longer trips today—en route from Durham to northwest Georgia to see a home game of the Rome Braves—a member of the South Atlantic League's Southern Division. Rome is an interesting city that is nestled between the banks of the Etowah and Oostanaula rivers in the foothills of the Appalachian Mountains. The historic downtown district is located at the point where the two rivers join to form the Coosa River. Today the Rome Braves play the visiting Augusta GreenJackets in an evening game at State Mutual Stadium.

Rome has been involved with professional baseball since the early 1900s. However, over that long span of years, teams have played in the city only during four decades. In fact, baseball has been played in the city during just 24 seasons over the last 105 years. Table 3–1 ROM summarizes the baseball clubs that have represented the city of Rome, the baseball leagues they played in, and the number of years they were a member of that league. The first teams played in the city between 1910 and 1921. Note that those teams had the nicknames Romans or Hillies. During this early era, the teams located in the city played D-class ball—the rank used to identify the lowest level minor league baseball teams at that period of time.

The team's nicknames remained somewhat consistent during those early years of professional baseball in the city, but the leagues with which they were affiliated changed frequently. From 1910 through 1912, the Rome Romans played in the Southeastern League. During the 1910 inaugural season, the league fielded six teams that were located in four states—Alabama, Georgia, North Carolina, and Tennessee. The footprint of the league ranged over 300 miles from the northernmost team, the Johnson City Soldiers in Tennessee, to the most southern team, the Gadsden Steel Workers in Alabama. At that time, that was a long traveling distance for the teams of a D-level league.

By the next season the makeup of the league had changed drastically. The one team in North Carolina and three from Tennessee departed and were replaced by new teams located in Alabama. The team from Rome remained but took on a new name—the Rome Hillies—just for the 1911 season. The Hillies were the only team not located in Alabama still playing their games in the Southeastern League. For the 1912 season, the team's name was switched back to the Rome Romans.

Team Name	1st Year	Years	Leagues
Rome Romans	1910	1	Southeastern League
Rome Hillies	1911	1	Southeastern League
Rome Romans	1912	1	Southeastern League
Rome Romans	1913	1	Appalachian League
Rome Romans	1914	4	Georgia-Alabama League
Rome	1920	2	Georgia State League
Rome Red Sox	1950	2	Georgia-Alabama League
Rome Braves	2003	12	South Atlantic League

Table 3-1 ROM. Teams that have played in Rome, GA (source: www.baseball-reference.com).

The Southeastern League disbanded prior to the 1913 season. For this reason, the Rome Romans connected with the Appalachian League for that season. In that new league, they joined former Southeastern League teams from Knoxville, Tennessee; Johnson City, Tennessee; and Morristown, Tennessee, who had all moved to the Appalachian League for the 1911 season. Rome was the only city from Georgia to host a team in this league. Moreover, the other teams of the league were centrally located around Knoxville, Tennessee, and four of the other six towns associated with teams of the league were further north than Knoxville. Now the Romans were the southernmost team and over 280 miles from the most northern team in Bristol, Virginia.

After playing just one season in the Appalachian League, the Romans disengaged with the struggling league and joined the Georgia-Alabama League. Here Rome was the most northern team in the league, but two of the other teams also resided in the state of Georgia. They remained a member of this league from 1914 through the 1917 season. For that season, the league had contracted to six teams. But the 1917 season was short lived—the Rome Romans played just eighteen games before the league folded. That season marked the downfall of the Romans' reign in Rome, Georgia.

Professional baseball was not played again in Rome until the 1920 season. In that year, the city fielded a team that joined teams from three other Georgia cities that participated in the final year of the Georgia-Alabama League—Griffin, Lindale, and LaGrange—in a new league: the Georgia State League. With all teams located in Georgia, Rome was located about 100 miles from the farthest team—the Lindale Pepperelles. But this league lasted just two seasons. The collapse of this league after the 1921 season ushered in the end of the early era of baseball in the city of Rome. No professional baseball would be played again in the city for many years.

The Washington Senators, who had four D-level teams during the 1949 season, added a fifth team at that level in the city of Rome and as a member of a new variant of the earlier Georgia-Alabama League for the 1950 season. This event ended a twenty-nine year drought during which professional baseball was not played in the city. Even though the team was called the Rome Red Sox, it was an affiliate of the Senators.

Not all of the teams in this new Georgia-Alabama League were associated with a major league club. In fact, during 1950 only three of the eight teams in the league formally represented a major league team. Even though the Red Sox played both the 1950 and 1951 seasons in Rome, they were a participant in the Washington Senators minor league organization for only the first year. For the 1951 season, the league contracted from eight to six teams and the

Rome Red Sox operated as an independent team. By July two teams shut down leaving the league with just four active teams. The league disbanded after the 1951 season. This short stay of the Red Sox ended the second era of baseball in Rome.

Again, there was a very long period—this time fifty-one years—during which professional baseball was not played in Rome. During the 2001 off-season, the Atlanta Braves committed to relocate their South Atlantic League single-A team, the Macon Braves, to Rome for the 2003 season. The city reciprocated by building a new ball field, which was eventually named State Mutual Stadium. Two thousand fourteen was the Rome Braves' twelfth season in Rome and as the A-level affiliate of the Atlanta Braves.

The Home of the Braves—State Mutual Stadium

The building of State Mutual Stadium was critical to the Atlanta Braves' decision to move their A-level affiliate to Rome. The Macon Braves had played at historic Luther Williams Field for the past 12 seasons; however, the stadium was 79 years old and lacked many of the facilities offered by more modern ballparks. With the agreement in place for a new stadium in Rome, the Braves committed to relocate their South Atlantic League affiliate to the city. Ground was broken for the new stadium in April 2002 and the facility was ready for the Rome Braves' 2003 home Opening Day game.

The 2003 Rome Braves team had future Atlanta Braves right fielder Jeff "Frenchy" Francoeur and catcher Brian McCann on its roster. The R–Braves played their home opener against the Savannah Sand Gnats (New York Mets) at State Mutual Stadium on April 11, 2003. The Braves rallied for a 4–3 come-from-behind victory over Savannah. During the Rome Braves' inaugural season, Francoeur and McCann, who were both 19 years old at the time, were selected as Sally League Southern Division All-Stars.

The ballpark is located approximately 3 miles north of the historic downtown district of Rome. Figure 3–1 ROM shows the main entrance to the 5105-seat ballpark. Since the stadium is recently built, it has many of the attributes of newer parks, such as a concourse that circles the field so that you can walk around the complete field. The seats back up and rise from the field level toward the front part of the building structure. At the top are the press box and luxury suites. A number of rows of field level box seats run from mid-left field around the perimeter of the infield and part way down the right field line. These lower level seats are separated from the general seating area that rises to the luxury box level by a narrow walkway. A plus is that there

Figure 3–1 ROM. State Mutual Stadium, Rome, GA.

are no bleachers—all seating is in individual seats. But there is only a very small overhanging roof at the top by the luxury boxes so most seats are not protected from the sun or rain.

This seating configuration is unlike that in many of the new stadiums that have a wide concourse above the seating area with concessions from which you can view the game. At State Mutual Stadium the concessions are located in the front part of the building complex, below and behind the seating structure that overlooks the infield. In addition, down the right field line you will find Bubba's Barbeque—an interesting concession with picnic table seating. In the open area by the concessions, there is a series of posters that review the history of baseball in northwest Georgia and one that highlights former R–Braves that have played in the major leagues, such as Brian McCann, Jason Heyward, Freddie Freeman, and Craig Kimbrel.

Tom-toms and the tomahawk chop? Yes, just like at Atlanta Braves home games, the tradition also plays an important role in Rome Braves games at State Mutual Stadium.

The South Atlantic League Years

Unlike most of the other current South Atlantic League cities, Rome has had only one team—the Rome Braves—that played in the city. Moreover, as shown in Table 3-2(a) ROM, they have always been affiliated with a single major league club—the Atlanta Braves. The construction of State Mutual Stadium was the key to luring Atlanta to relocate its single-A affiliate to the city for the 2003 season. Even though the city of Rome was a latecomer to the South Atlantic League, it is tied with Greensboro, North Carolina, for fifth among the current fourteen cities for the longest continuous run of years with its current major league affiliate. As mentioned earlier, 2014 is the Rome Braves' twelfth consecutive season as the single-A team of the Atlanta Braves. Atlanta's other minor league teams are listed in Table 3-2(b) ROM.

The Rome Braves have always been a member of the Southern Division of the South Atlantic League. Since joining the league in 2003, they have made three postseason appearances—2003, 2006, and 2012. In their inaugural season in the league and at State Mutual Stadium, they won the South Atlantic League Championship. The R–Braves finished in first place during

Name	MLB Affiliate	Years
Rome Braves	Atlanta Braves	2003-today

Level	Team	Stadium	League
Rk	GCL Braves	Champion Stadium Lake Buena Vista, FL	Gulf Coast League
Rk	Danville Braves	Legion Field Danville, VA	Appalachian League
A	Rome Braves	State Mutual Stadium Rome, GA	South Atlantic League
A+	Carolina Mudcats	Five County Stadium Zebulon, NC	Carolina League
AA	Mississippi Braves	Trustmark Park Pearl, MS	Southern League
AAA	Gwinnett Braves	Coolray Field Lawrenceville, GA	International League

Top: Table 3-2(a) ROM. Rome Braves major league affiliation. *Above:* Table 3-2(b) ROM. Atlanta Braves minor league organization.

the second half of the season with a 42W:28L record to earn a slot in the postseason playoffs.

As mentioned earlier, the offense of the 2003 team was led by the righty-lefty hitting tandem of outfielder Jeff Francoeur and catcher Brian McCann. This power hitting duo led the regular players on the team in most power hitting stats. Table 3–3 ROM shows a comparison of their batting stats. Note that they ranked number one and number two in home runs, runs batted in, total bases, and slugging percentage.

During the regular season, the starting rotation included five pitchers who all eventually played at the major league level: Kyle Davies (RHP), Blaine Boyer (RHP), Anthony Lerew (RHP), Dan Meyers (LHP), and Jose Capellan (RHP). All five of these pitchers eventually made their major league debut with the Atlanta Braves. Blaine Boyer pitched during five seasons in Atlanta and made over 175 relief appearances in the Braves uniform.

With strong starting efforts from pitchers Lerew and Davies, the Braves beat the Hickory Crawdads (Pittsburgh Pirates) 2 games to 1 in the first round of the playoffs to clinch the Southern Division title. They went on to face the Northern Division winners, the Lake County Captains (Cleveland Indians), in the best-of-five league championship series. Again the Braves prevailed and won the series 3 games to 1.

After splitting the first two games of the South Atlantic League Championship Series on the road at Classic Park, Eastlake, Ohio, the Braves came home to win game 3 by a score of 3–1 and take a 2 game to 1 lead. Jeff Francoeur contributed an RBI double to get the team on the scoreboard and starter Matt Wright got the win. The Braves won the South Atlantic Championship

Player	AB	R	H	2B	3B	HR	RBI
Francoeur	524	78	147	26	9	14	68
Team Rank	#1	#1	#1	#3	#1	#1	#2
McCann	424	40	123	31	3	12	71
Team Rank	#3	#7	#3	#1	T-#4	#2	#1

Player	TB	AVE	OBP	SLG	OPS
Francoeur	233	.281	.325	.445	.769
Team Rank	#1	#4	#5	#2	#3
McCann	196	.290	.329	.462	.791
Team Rank	#2	#2	#4	#1	#1

Table 3–3 ROM. Summary of Jeff Francoeur and Brian McCann 2003 batting stats.

in front of their hometown crowd at State Mutual Stadium when Jonathan Schuerholz, son of the then-general manager and current president of the Atlanta Braves John Schuerholz, knocked in the game winning run with a sacrifice fly for a 4–3 victory in game 4.

The Rome Braves made another run for the South Atlantic League title in 2006. That season they placed first in the Southern Division for the first half of the season with a 42W:28L record. The Braves played the Augusta GreenJackets (San Francisco Giants) for the Southern Division title but lost the best-of-three series 2 games to 0.

Rome did not return to the postseason until 2012. In that season they won the second half of the season with a 44W:24L record. But again, their run for the league championship ended quickly when they lost to the Asheville Tourists (Colorado Rockies) in the division championship series. During the 2012 regular season, R–Braves third baseman Kyle Kubitza hit 9 triples to tie the team's all-time single season three-base hit record. However, he also walked 73 times to break the Rome Braves' all-time BB record. Kubitza remains the R–Braves' all-time team leader in bases on balls and co-leader in triples today.

Successful Major Leaguers Who Played in Rome

Because the Atlanta Braves A-level affiliate has been in Rome only since 2003, there are not many former Rome Braves players who have played ten or more years at the major league level. Earlier I identified Jeff Francoeur and Brian McCann as members of Rome's 2003 roster. But, 2014 was the tenth major league season for both of them. Fans of the Rome Braves had the opportunity to see these eventual Atlanta Braves starters play their early ball at State Mutual Stadium and lead the team to its only South Atlantic League Championship.

Table 3–4 ROM shows that during the 2003 season Francoeur and McCann were each 19 years old and playing their second season of professional ball. Both played the complete season in Rome. Interestingly, Francoeur and McCann made their major league debuts with the Atlantic Braves a month apart during the summer of 2005.

As mentioned earlier, both of these players had an excellent season with the bat and led the team in many offensive stats. Francoeur, who played right field five seasons in Atlanta before being traded, was ranked in the top 10 among all players in the South Atlantic League during the 2003 season in four batting statistic categories—number 2 in both hits (147) and triples (9),

Season	Player	Age at ROM	MiLB Season	Position	MLB Debut	Age at Debut	MLB Team	Seasons in MLB
2003	Jeff Francoeur	19	2	RF	7/7/05	21	ATL	10+
	Brian McCann	19	2	C	6/10/05	21	ATL	10+
2004	Martín Prado	20	2	3B	4/23/06	22	ATL	0+
	Jarrod Saltalamacchia	19	2	C	5/2/07	22	ATL	8+
	Charlie Morton	20	3	RHP	6/14/08	24	ATL	7+
2005	Yunel Escobar	22	1	SS	6/2/07	24	ATL	8+
2006	Elvis Andrus	17	2	SS	4/6/09	20	TEX	6+
2007	Tyler Flowers	21	2	C	9/3/09	23	CHW	6+
	Kris Medlen	21	2	RHP	5/21/09	23	ATL	5+
2008	Freddie Freeman	18	2	1B	9/1/10	20	ATL	5+
	Jason Heyward	18	2	RF	4/5/10	20	ATL	5+
	Craig Kimbrel	20	1	RHP	5/7/10	21	ATL	5+
2009	Mike Minor	21	1	LHP	8/9/10	22	ATL	5+

Table 3–4 ROM. Rome SAL players that went on to have long major league careers.

number 3 in total bases (233), and tied for number 5 in runs scored (78). That season, Francoeur set the Rome Braves' all-time single season record for triples. His record, which was 9 triples, remained the team's record until the 2012 season when it was tied by Kyle Kubitza. So today Francoeur and Kubitza are the co-holders of that R–Braves batting record.

McCann made his debut behind the plate for the Atlanta Braves in Oakland on June 10, 2005, and went 2 for 3 versus the A's pitching. The next day he hit his first home run at the major league level. Soon he was Atlanta's starting catcher and on his way to evolve into one of the Braves' star players. During the 2006 season, he was selected for the National League All-Star Team and at the end of the season received the Silver Slugger Award that is given to the best offensive player at each position in the National League and American League. Today McCann is one of the top catchers in the major leagues. He was a National League All-Star in seven of his nine seasons with the Braves, including 2013, and received five Silver Slugger awards. McCann became a free agent after the 2013 season and during the offseason signed a 5-year, $85 million contract to play for the New York Yankees.

Another player listed in Table 3–4 ROM who played in Rome and then went on to become a regular player for the Atlanta Braves is Martín Prado. Prado is a versatile player and appeared at both infield and outfield positions for the Braves. He hit for both average and power. After seven seasons with Atlanta, Prado was traded during the 2012 offseason to Arizona in the deal

G	AB	R	H	2B	3B	HR	RBI
130	491	70	155	33	7	18	95

TB	BB	SO	SB	AVE	OBP	SLG	OPS
256	46	84	5	.316	.378	.521	.899

Table 3–5 ROM. Freddy Freeman 2008 batting stats summary.

that brought outfielder Justin Upton to the Braves. At the 2014 trading dead-line, the Diamondbacks traded him to the New York Yankees where he fin-ished the season.

More recently the young stars of the Atlanta Braves, such as first base-man Freddie Freeman, right fielder Jason Heyward, and closer Craig Kimbrel, have all played their A-level ball for the Rome Braves. Table 3–4 ROM shows that they all played their fifth season in the majors with the Atlanta Braves in 2014. In fact, the table shows that all three of them were also on the Rome roster at the same time—the 2008 season. Freeman led the Rome Braves team in seven offensive stat categories during that season. A summary of his 2008 batting stats is given in Table 3–5 ROM. Freeman ranked in the top 5 in the SAL in eight of them: fourth in H (155), fifth in 2B (33, tied with 1 other), second in 3B (7, tied with 3 others), fourth in RBI (95), fifth in AVE (.316), third in TB (256), second in SLG (.521), and third in OPS (.899). During that season, Freeman set four of the R–Braves' all-time offensive stat records that still stand today. He is the team's all-time leader in hits, runs batted in, total bases, and slugging percentage. Freeman took over as the starting first baseman of the Atlanta Braves during the 2011 season. He has represented the Braves on both the 2013 and 2014 National League All-Star teams.

During 2008, Jason Heyward also had a standout season with the bat for the Rome Braves. He led the team in runs scored, walks, batting average, and on-base percentage and ranked in the top 5 in the league for three batting stats: fifth in R (88), third in AVE (.323), and tied for fourth in OBP (.388). That season, Heyward also set two of the R–Braves' all-time single season offensive records. His 88 runs scored and .323 batting average still rank him number 1 today among all players who have worn the R–Braves uniform in those two offensive stat categories.

Heyward opened the 2010 season as the starting right fielder of the Atlanta Braves and went on to have an exceptional rookie season in the field and with the bat. He ranked number 1 or number 2 on the Braves in ten offensive stats. Heyward was the Atlanta Braves' leader in triples (5), stolen bases (11), walks (91), on-base percentage (.393), and on-base plus slugging percentage (.849). In addition to his excellent speed and batting eye, Heyward demonstrated some power. He hit 29 doubles, 18 home runs, drove in 72 runs, and batted with a .456 slugging percentage, which ranked him number 2 on the team in each of those batting stats. Based on his play during the first half of the 2010 season, he was selected to represent the Atlanta Braves on that season's National League All-Star Team. Heyward had continued to hit at the top of the Braves batting order and start in right field. He was the recipient of a Rawlings Gold Glove Award as an outstanding outfield defender in the National League for the 2012 season. Heyward, who would have been eligible for free agency after the 2015 season, was traded to the St. Louis Cardinals for right-handed starter Shelby Miller during the 2014 offseason.

Craig Kimbrel's road to the major leagues was a little unusual in that he never started a game at the minor league level. All of his relief appearances were short and at all levels of the minors he primarily pitched in the role of a closer. Kimbrel took over as the Atlanta closer for the 2011 season and saved 46 games for the Braves. He was selected as a National League All-Star that season and was an all-star again in 2012, 2013, and 2014. For the 2013 season, he notched a league leading 50 saves. Early in the 2014 season, Kimbrel broke the Atlanta Braves' all-time saves record of 154 that was held by John Smoltz since 2004. He finished 2014 with 47 saves—his fourth straight season with more than 40 saves.

Baseball Attractions Near Rome

- **Gwinnett Braves Home Game at Coolray Field**, 2500 Buford Dr., Lawrenceville, GA 30043 (678) 277–0300
- **Ivan Allen Jr. Braves Museum and Hall of Fame at Turner Field**, 755 Hank Aaron Dr. SE, Atlanta, GA 30315 (404) 614–2310
- **Hank Aaron, Ty Cobb, and Phil Niekro Statues in Monument Grove at Turner Field**, 755 Hank Aaron Dr. SE, Atlanta, GA 30315 (404) 614–2310

Attractions in Rome

- **Historic Downtown Rome,** 210 Broad St., Rome, GA 30161
- **Rome Area History Museum**, 305 Broad St., Rome, GA 30161 (706) 235–8051

Dining in Rome

Downtown Restaurants

- **Partridge Restaurant**, 330 Broad St., Rome, GA 30161 (706) 235–0030
- **Curlee's Fish House & Oyster Bar,** 227 Broad St., Rome, GA 30161 (706) 204–8173
- **Jefferson's Restaurant**, 340 Broad St., Rome, GA 30161 (706) 378–0222
- **Mellow Mushroom**, 238 Broad St., Rome, GA 30161 (706) 234–9000
- **HoneyMoon Bakery**, 228 Broad St., Rome, GA 30161 (706) 232–0611

Savannah Sand Gnats

William L. Grayson Stadium
1401 East Victory Dr., Savannah, GA 31404
www.milb.com/index.jsp?sid=t543

Today I am traveling to see a game at one of the historic ballparks of the South Atlantic League—William L. Grayson Stadium in Savannah, Georgia. My route has taken me across the Savannah River into the historic, scenic city on the southern bank of the river. As mentioned in the section of this chapter on the Augusta GreenJackets, Savannah is the only other city of a current South Atlantic League team that hosted a professional baseball team as early as 1884. But as in Augusta during the late 1800s, the teams quickly came and went and they participated in a variety of different leagues.

Just like Augusta, Savannah fielded a team in the Georgia State League in 1884. As shown in Table 3–1 SAV, that team was called the Savannah Dixies. The league did not operate in 1885 but resumed play again for the 1886 season. For that season, the Dixies were joined by a second Savannah team, the Savannah Oglethorpes, and that expanded the league from six teams to seven—all located in the state of Georgia. But during 1886 Savannah was actually the host city for five baseball teams. They included two teams in the Southern League of Colored Base Ballists—the Savannah Broads and Savannah Lafayettes. The fifth Savannah team was a member of the Southern Association. All of those teams played in their league for just that one season. Table 3–1 SAV shows that a single team played in Savannah during the 1887 baseball season and that it was a member of the Southern League. But that season brought to a close the play of baseball during the 1880s.

The play of professional baseball did not resume in the city of Savannah until it reengaged with the Southern Association in 1893 and fielded a team called the Savannah Electrics or Rabbits in that season and the Savannah

Team Name	1st Year	Years	Leagues
Savannah Dixies	1884	2	Georgia State League
Savannah	1886	1	Southern Association
Savannah Broads	1886	1	Southern League of Colored Base Ballists
Savannah Lafayettes	1886	1	Southern League of Colored Base Ballists
Savannah Oglethorpe	1886	1	Georgia State League
Savannah	1887	1	Southern League
Savannah Electrics/Rabbits	1893	1	Southern Association
Savannah Modocs	1894	1	Southern Association
Savannah	1898	1	Southern League
Savannah Pathfinders	1904	2	South Atlantic League
Savannah Indians	1906	7	South Atlantic League
Savannah Colts	1913	3	South Atlantic League
Savannah Indians	1926	3	Southeastern League
Savannah Indians	1936	15	South Atlantic League
Savannah A's	1954	2	South Atlantic League
Savannah Red Legs/Reds	1956	4	South Atlantic League
Savannah Pirates	1960	1	South Atlantic League
Savannah White Sox	1962	1	South Atlantic League
Savannah Senators	1968	2	Southern League
Savannah Indians	1970	1	Southern League
Savannah Braves	1971	1	Dixie Association
Savannah Braves	1972	12	Southern League
Savannah Cardinals	1984	12	South Atlantic League
Savannah Sand Gnats	1996	19	South Atlantic League

Table 3–1 SAV. Teams that have played in Savannah, GA (source: www.baseball-reference.com).

Medocs the next season. During those years, the Southern Association spanned five southern states, Alabama, Georgia, Louisiana, South Carolina, and Tennessee, and was classified as B-level league. But this connection lasted just those 2 seasons and then professional baseball ceased to be played in the city until 1898 when a Savannah team played for one season in the Southern League. With the close of the 19th century, the first era of baseball in the city of Savannah, Georgia, came to an end. During the span of years from 1884 to 1899, professional baseball had been played in the city during just six of the sixteen baseball seasons.

The 20th century ushered in a new era of baseball for the city of Savannah. Most of the teams during this period were connected to one league—the original South Atlantic Leagues. In 1904 the Sally League fielded six teams—three in Georgia, two in South Carolina, and one in Florida. The Savannah Pathfinders was the name of the city's first South Atlantic League team and it represented Savannah in the league during the 1904 and 1905 seasons.

This new engagement with the South Atlantic League resulted in a more stable relationship that led to the regular play of minor league baseball in the city of Savannah during the next half century. Over the next fifty-nine years, there were a number of different teams: the Savannah Indians, Savannah Colts, Savannah A's, Savannah Red Legs or Reds, Savannah Pirates, and Savannah White Sox, but all of them as members of the South Atlantic League. Teams played a varying number of years with the Indians playing the most— 22 seasons. Between 1904 and 1962, Savannah was the home city of a team that played in the original South Atlantic League during 35 of the 59 seasons. Of the 24 seasons that Savannah did not host a Sally team, the league was not active during ten of them. Note in Table 3–1 SAV that, during this period of Savannah's baseball history, the Savannah Indians did play a three season stint from 1926 through 1928 in another league—the Southeastern League.

During the South Atlantic League years, the teams played at the A, B, or C level of professional baseball's minor league system. Moreover, during the later years the Savannah teams were affiliated with major league clubs— Philadelphia Athletics, Cincinnati Reds, Pittsburgh Pirates, and Chicago White Sox. For instance, the Savannah Indians were the A-class affiliate of the Philadelphia Athletics for eight seasons from 1946 through 1953 and then again as the Savannah A's in 1954 and 1955.

Through these teams of the late 1950s and early 1960s, baseball fans in Savannah had the opportunity to see a number of future major leaguers in action: pitcher Art Ditmar (Philadelphia Athletics), center fielder Curt Flood (Cincinnati Reds), shortstop Leo Cardenas (Cincinnati Reds), second baseman Cookie Rojas (Cincinnati Reds), first baseman Donn Clendenon (Pittsburgh Pirates), and left fielder Don Buford (Chicago White Sox). The team identified with each of these players is the one for which he made his major league debut. Many of them went on to have their best years and longest tenure with another ball club. For example, Curt Flood made his major league debut with the Reds on September 9, 1956, but played twelve of his fifteen seasons in the majors for the St. Louis Cardinals. Fans of the Savannah teams even got to see basketball Hall of Famer Dave DeBusschere pitch for the Savannah White Sox during the 1962 season.

Partway through the 1962 season the Savannah White Sox relocated to

Lynchburg, Virginia. That bought a temporary end to the play of minor league baseball in Savannah. However, prior to the 1968 season the city connected with a very old friend—the Southern League. After lying dormant for 75 baseball seasons, a new Southern League was formed in 1964 and associated with major league baseball as an AA-level minor league organization. Savannah hosted the Savannah Senators for the 1968 and 1969 seasons in this league and the Savannah Indians in 1970.

When the Atlanta Braves moved their AA affiliate from Shreveport, Louisiana, to the city as the Savannah Braves in 1971 a lasting relationship was formed. Actually, during the first season, the Southern League was inactive. So the Savannah Braves played in the Dixie Association for that season and then transitioned to the Southern League to start the 1972 season. Savannah remained the home of the Atlanta Braves AA affiliate for thirteen seasons. During those years, baseball fans in Savannah had the opportunity to see a number of Atlanta's up-and-coming prospects including: catcher Bruce Benedict (1976), right fielder Dale Murphy (1976), second baseman Glenn Hubbard (1977), and reliever Steve Bedrosian (1979).

Prior to the 1984 season, the Atlanta Braves relocated their AA team in the Southern League to Greenville, South Carolina. This event ended another era of baseball in Savannah—that associated with the original South Atlantic League. However, it opened the door for the modern South Atlantic League era.

With the departure of the Braves at the end of 1983, the St. Louis Cardinals moved their South Atlantic team—the Macon Redbirds—to Savannah to fill the void. The city of Savannah was engaged with the modern South Atlantic League. St. Louis named their new single-A team the Savannah Cardinals and set up shop at William L. Grayson Stadium for the next twelve seasons. In 1995 the Cards left but were replaced by the Los Angeles Dodgers, who renamed the team the Savannah Sand Gnats. Since then the Sand Gnats major league affiliate has changed a number of times, but 2014 was the nineteenth season in which a Savannah Sand Gnats team has played in today's South Atlantic League.

The Home of the Sand Gnats—William L. Grayson Stadium

William L. Grayson Stadium, the home of today's New York Mets South Atlantic League affiliate, the Savannah Sand Gnats, was built in 1926. The stadium was the home of all of the teams that played in the city starting with the 1926 Savannah Indians of the Southeastern League—the A's, Reds, Pirates,

White Sox, Senators, Braves, and Cardinals. This ballpark, which is normally just referred to as Grayson Stadium, is the second oldest of the historic stadiums of today's South Atlantic League—just 2 years younger than McCormick Field in Asheville, North Carolina.

Grayson Stadium is an in-city ball field which is located just a few miles south of the city's downtown riverfront historic district. Savannah is an interesting city in which to attend a baseball game and at the same time visit the attractive downtown to view its historic sites. Grayson Stadium is located on the grounds of Daffin Park—an interesting tree-lined park area with a lake. The stadium underwent renovation and modernization in 1941 and more recently in 2009 to keep it in tune with the needs of modern baseball. Figure 3–1 SAV shows the stadium as it appears today. Fans enter through the large archway in the traditional brick grandstand structure.

The stadium, which has a seating capacity of 4000, is a comfortable place to view a baseball game. It has a traditional covered grandstand behind home plate. Surrounding the inner part of the infield diamond are field level box seats. There is a narrow walkway between the rows of box seats and the gen-

Figure 3–1 SAV. William L. Grayson Stadium, Savannah, GA.

eral admission seats that rise up under the grandstand roof. The area in the upper section that is located right behind home plate is reserved seating, not general admission seating. Fans in the box and reserved seating sections have individual traditional plastic stadium seats. Very large fans are mounted to the bottom side of the grandstand roof to circulate the air on hot, steamy summer evenings. There is a second general admission seating area located on the first base side of the infield. Fans in the general admission seating areas have bleacher like bench seats, but with a back rest.

Even though the stadium is within the city, because of its park location the view seen looking out from the grandstand area across the infield and up over the outfield walls is a relaxing treed background. Traditional baseball stadium food and drink concessions are located in the lower level of the grandstand structure through which you enter the stadium. One local specialty that is served here is boiled peanuts. The ballpark also has an attractive combination bar and restaurant that offers deck seating—the Landshark Landing—located toward the right field corner. This area offers seating at tables on several deck levels with a great close-up outfield view of the game. Down the left field line is a large picnic area.

I found the stadium easily accessible, with adequate parking, and an enjoyable environment to take in a baseball game.

The South Atlantic League Years

As mentioned earlier, the modern South Atlantic League era of baseball in Savannah began when the St. Louis Cardinals relocated their prior South Atlantic League A-level affiliate to the city in 1984. During the thirty-one baseball seasons that modern South Atlantic League teams have played in Savannah, they have gone to the postseason eight times and brought home five Southern Division championships and four South Atlantic League titles.

Table 3–2(a) SAV shows that the Savannah team was the affiliate of the St. Louis Cardinals from 1984 through 1995. During the Savannah Cardinals' stint in the city, the team made four postseason appearances. The Cardinals won a playoff berth in their inaugural season, 1984. However, they lost in the first round to the Charleston Royals (Kansas City Royals). But they again advanced to the postseason in 1990, 1993, and 1994. In 1990 the Cardinals again fell short of a South Atlantic League title. They beat the Columbia Mets (New York Mets) in the first round of the playoffs to win the team's first Southern Division title but lost to the Charleston Wheelers (Cincinnati Reds) in the best-of-five South Atlantic League Championship Series.

Name	MLB Affiliate	Years
Savannah Sand Gnats	New York Mets	2007-today
Savannah Sand Gnats	Washington Nationals	2005-2006
Savannah Sand Gnats	Montreal Expos	2003-2004
Savannah Sand Gnats	Texas Rangers	1998-2002
Savannah Sand Gnats	Los Angeles Dodgers	1995-1997
Savannah Cardinals	St. Louis Cardinals	1984-1995

Level	Team	Stadium	League
Rk	GCL Mets	Tradition Field Port St. Lucie, FL	Gulf Coast League
Rk	Kingsport Mets	Hunter Wright Stadium Kingsport, TN	Appalachian League
A-	Brooklyn Cyclones	MCU Park Brooklyn, NY	New York-Penn League
A	Savannah Sand Gnats	William L. Grayson Stadium Savannah, GA	South Atlantic League
A+	St. Lucie Mets	Tradition Field Port St. Lucie, FL	Florida State League
AA	Binghamton Mets	NYSEG Stadium Binghamton, NY	Eastern League
AAA	Las Vegas 51s	Cashman Field Las Vegas, NV	International League

Top: Table 3-2(a) SAV. Savannah teams' major league affiliations. *Above:* Table 3-2(b) SAV. New York Mets minor league organization.

But 1993 and 1994 were a different story. In both seasons the Savannah Cardinals came home with the South Atlantic League Championship title. The 1993 Cardinals team had future major leaguers Joe McEwing in the outfield and Mike Busby on the mound. McEwing played in the majors during nine seasons with the St. Louis Cardinals, New York Mets, Kansas City Royals, and Houston Astros, while Busby pitched during four seasons for the St. Louis Cardinals. The Savannah Cardinals won the Southern Division in both halves of the season and for that reason got a bye in the Division Championship round. With the Southern Division Championship under their belt and a little extra rest, they faced off against the Northern Division champion Greensboro Hornets (New York Yankees) in the finals and won the best-of-five series to take home Savannah's first South Atlantic League championship.

During the 1994 season, second baseman Jeff Berblinger led the Savannah Cardinals in seven offensive stats: R (86), H (142), 2B (27), 3B (7), SB (24), AVE (.296), and OBP (.390). He ranked in the top 10 among all regular players in the league in runs, hits, batting average, on-base percentage and even a stat category in which he ranked second on the team—on-base plus slugging percentage.

Right-hander Matt Arrandale led the Savannah starting rotation with 15 wins in 19 starts for an overall 15W:3L record. He also led all regular starters in strikeouts with 121, lowest ERA (1.76), and lowest WHIP (.998). He ranked number 2 in the South Atlantic League in wins for the season and first in both earned run average and walks plus hits per inning pitched among pitchers who pitched more than 112 innings. However, Arrandale was promoted to the St. Petersburg Cardinals in the Florida State League—A+ level—prior to the end of the season. The team's closer was Craig Grasser. He saved a league high 34 games for the Cardinals that season. Berblinger made his major league debut for the St. Louis Cardinals on September 7, 1997, but appeared in only seven games at the major league level. Arrandale and Grasser never got the call to the majors.

The Savannah Cardinals opened the 1994 postseason by beating the Columbus Red Stixx (Cleveland Indians) to become the Southern Division champions. Then they faced the Northern Division champs—Hagerstown Suns—in the championship round. The Cardinals swept the Suns 3 games to 0 to win the South Atlantic League Championship in a second consecutive year.

The list in Table 3-2(a) SAV shows that when the St. Louis Cardinals departed after the 1994 season, the city engaged with the Los Angeles Dodgers. Along with the change in major league affiliation came a new name for the team—the Savannah Sand Gnats. Prior to that the Dodgers did not have a single-A level team but had two A+ teams—the San Bernardino Stampede in the California League and Vero Beach Dodgers in the Florida State League.

In 1996, while a member of the Dodgers minor league organization, the Sand Gnats made another postseason run. This team had future major league pitcher Greg Gagne in the starting rotation. He went 7W:6L for the season and led the team with 131 strikeouts. Also, the Sand Gnats third baseman was current major leaguer Adrian Beltre. But Beltre was promoted mid-season to the San Bernardino Stampede and did not participate with the team in the postseason.

Outfielder Eric Stuckenschneider had a record setting season with the bat. He led the regular players on the team in nine offensive categories: R (111), 2B (28), HR (16 tied), BB (111), SB (50 tied), TB (218), OBP (.424), SLG (.464), and OPS (.888). Moreover, he led all players in the South Atlantic League in runs scored and bases on balls for the 1996 season. His 111 runs scored, 50 stolen bases, 111 bases on balls, and .424 on-base percentage all set Sand Gnats all-time single season batting records that still stand today. However, that same season, teammate Jose Pimentel also stole 50 bases. So Stuckenschneider and Pimentel share that record. Stuckenschneider advanced to the AAA level but was never promoted to the majors.

During that period, the teams of the South Atlantic League were organized into three divisions: Northern, Central, and Southern. The playoffs structure was a round robin tournament between the eight teams with the best overall season record. Savannah's record was 72W:69L, which was the 7th best in the league. The Sand Gnats worked their way through the ladder of championship contenders to meet the Delmarva Shorebirds in the finals. Savannah prevailed! They won the series 3 games to 1 to take home their third South Atlantic League title.

But the Dodgers stayed in Savannah for only 2 seasons and over the years that followed the team's affiliation changed frequently. Table 3–2(a) SAV shows that the Dodgers were replaced by the Texas Rangers for the 1998 through 2002 seasons, Montreal Expos for 2003 and 2004, and Washington Nationals for 2005 and 2006. But when the New York Mets moved their A-level team from Hagerstown to Savannah prior to the 2007 season things stabilized.

After the 1996 SAL Championship win, there was a thirteen season drought before the Savannah Sand Gnats returned to the playoffs. But since becoming a Mets affiliate, they have reached the postseason three times— 2010, 2011, and 2013. Savannah won the Southern Division during the first half of the 2010 season with a 42W: 28L record to gain entry into the playoffs. However, their postseason run was short. They got swept 2 games to 0 in this first round by the Southern Division second half season winner—the Greenville Drive (Boston Red Sox).

In 2011 the Sand Gnats again won the first half season to get another postseason berth. In the Division Championship Series round of the playoffs, they faced off against the Augusta GreenJackets (San Francisco Giants)—the second half season winner of the Southern Division. They took the series with the GreenJackets 2–1 to become the 2011 Southern Division champions and advance to the league championship series. In the best-of-five championship round, the Sand Gnats met the Greensboro Grasshoppers (Florida Marlins). Savannah got out to a 2–1 lead, but then the Grasshoppers came back to win the final two games of the series and take the South Atlantic League title.

After winning the first half of the 2013 season with a 43W:26L record, the Savannah Sand Gnats returned to the postseason for a third try at winning the South Atlantic League title. This season the Sand Gnats' starting rotation was led by 20-year-old right hander Gabriel Ynoa. With a 15W:4L record, Ynoa led the team and the South Atlantic League in wins. Ynoa broke two longstanding Sand Gnats all-time single season pitching records. His 15 wins broke the prior record of 12 wins that was set by righty starter Matt Kosderka in 1999. Moreover, Ynoa's 2013 WHIP, which was 1.025, bested the prior walk plus hits per inning pitched record of 1.107, which was set by right-handed starter Dean Mitchell in 1997.

Savannah's offense got a lift when they picked up second baseman Dilson Herrera in a trade with the Pittsburgh Pirates for the last week of the regular season and their playoff run. He was one of the top second basemen in the league and also ranked as one of the Pirates' MLB Top 20 Prospects.

Again they faced the Augusta GreenJackets in the first round and pre-vailed. Ynoa opened the series on the mound for Savannah and went 7.2 innings in leading them to a 10–2 game 1 victory. In game 2 left-hander Steven Matz threw 7 scoreless innings of 1 hit ball. Savannah won 5–0 and took the Southern Division title in a 2 games to 0 sweep.

The Sand Gnats faced the Hagerstown Suns—the Northern Division champions—in the South Atlantic League Championship Series. After the Sand Gnats and Suns split games 1 and 2 of the series at Hagerstown, the series moved to Savannah. Hagerstown had to face Gabriel Ynoa in game three. Savannah's offense got started early. In the bottom of the second inning, second baseman Dilson Herrera led off and walked and advanced to third on first baseman Cole Frenzel's single to right, but Frenzel moved up to sec-ond on the throw to third. Next, left fielder Stefan Sabol hit a sacrifice fly to knock in Herrera with the first run of the game. Frenzel, who had advanced to third base on the throw to the plate, scored when third baseman Jeff Reynolds lined a single up the middle. The Sand Gnats had broken out to a 2–0 lead after just two innings of play. Savannah added 2 more runs in the bottom of the fourth inning and solo runs in the fifth and sixth frames to extend their lead to 6–0.

Meanwhile, Ynoa was having an excellent outing. He scattered just 4 hits and a walk over 7 scoreless innings and struck out 5 on his way to his second postseason win. The Sand Gnats won 6–0 and broke out to a 2–1 series lead.

The next day, Steven Matz pitched another gem for Savannah. This time he threw 5.2 scoreless innings; allowed 2 hits and gave up 2 walks, while striking out 9. The Sand Gnats got only 2 hits off excellent Suns pitching. However, in the bottom of the fourth inning Hagerstown pitcher Dakota Bacus walked Brandon Nimmo (CF), Dilson Herrera (2B), and Cole Frenzel (1B) to load the bases and then gave up a 1 out double to left fielder Stefan Sabol. Nimmo and Herrera raced home on the hit and Savannah had the winning margin on the scoreboard.

Relievers Paul Sewald, Jeuyrs Familia, and Beck Wheeler shut down the Suns the rest of the way to preserve a Sand Gnats 2–0 victory. Matz got his second playoff win and Wheeler his first playoff save. This victory sealed the Sand Gnats' fourth South Atlantic League Championship.

When Savannah took the field as the New York Mets' single A franchise in the South Atlantic League in April 2014, it was the twentieth season with the Sand Gnats moniker. A list of the New York Mets' other minor league teams is given in Table 3–2(b) SAV.

Successful Major Leaguers Who Played in Savannah

Savannah is one of several current host cities of a South Atlantic League team that can claim a long, rich history of minor league baseball. As noted earlier, a number of great players played their early ball in Savannah prior to the modern South Atlantic League era. For example, Curt Flood of the St. Louis Cardinals, Leo Cardenas of the Cincinnati Reds, and Dale Murphy of the Atlanta Braves, who all played in fifteen or more seasons at the major league level, all played for Savannah teams. But in the modern South Atlantic League years local fans and those of the Cardinals, Dodgers, Rangers, Expos, Nationals, and Mets have seen many up-and-coming prospects of their favorite ball club play on the field of William L. Grayson Stadium and then go on to be successful in the major leagues.

Table 3–3 SAV lists twenty-one baseball players who took the field in a Savannah uniform during the modern South Atlantic League years and went on to have successful major league careers. Again my criterion is that a player who reached the majors prior to the 2000 season has to have appeared in major league games during a minimum of 10 baseball seasons. On the other hand, for those who debuted in the majors from 2000 through 2009 the criteria is that they must have played in each of the last five seasons and currently be an active major league player. Next I will look at a few of those players and their rise and success in the major leagues.

Season	Player	Age at SAV	MiLB Season	Position	MLB Debut	Age at Debut	MLB Team	Seasons in MLB
1984	x							
1985	x							
1986	Bernard Gilkey	19	2	LF	9/4/90	23	STL	12
1987	x							
1988	x							
1989	Mark Clark	21	2	RHP	9/6/91	23	STL	10
1990	x							
1991	John Mabry	20	1	1B	9/23/94	23	STL	14
1992	x							
1993	Jay Witasick	20	1	RHP	7/7/96	23	OAK	12
1994	Eli Marrero	20	2	C	9/3/97	23	STL	10
1995	x							
1996	Adrian Beltre	17	1	3B	6/24/98	19	LAD	17+
	Eric Gagne	20	1	RHP	9/7/99	23	LAD	10
1997	x							
1998	Travis Hafner	21	2	1B	8/6/02	25	TEX	12
	Carlos Pena	20	1	1B	9/5/01	23	TEX	14+
	Joaquin Benoit	20	2	RHP	8/8/01	24	TEX	13+
1999	x							
2000	x							
2001	Edwin Encarnacion	18	2	3B	6/24/05	22	CIN	10+
	Laynce Nix	20	2	CF	7/19/03	22	TEX	11
	C. J. Wilson	20	1	LHP	6/10/05	24	TEX	10+
2002	x							
2003	Roger Bernadina	19	2	LF	6/29/08	24	WSN	7+
2004	x							
2005	Ian Desmond	19	2	SS	9/10/09	23	WSN	6+
	Ryan Zimmerman	20	1	3B	9/1/05	20	WSN	10+
2006	Justin Maxwell	22	1	CF	9/5/07	23	WSN	6+
	Marco Estrada	22	2	RHP	8/20/05	25	WSN	7+
	John Lannan	21	2	LHP	7/26/07	22	WSN	8+
	Craig Stammen	22	2	RHP	5/21/09	25	WSN	6+
2007	Josh Thole	20	3	C	9/3/09	22	NYM	6+
2008	x							
2009	x							

Table 3–3 SAV. Savannah SAL players that went on to have long major league careers.

First, I will single out Adrian Beltre. Note in Table 3–3 SAV that he is the player who passed through Savannah on his way to the majors who has played the most seasons at the major league level—seventeen. Since Beltre is still under contract with the Texas Rangers through the 2016 season, he will be closing in on a 20 year career. But Beltre's path to the majors is also interesting. Beltre played his first season of professional ball in 1996 at the age of 17 as the third baseman of the Savannah Sand Gnats. Beltre played in just 68 games for Savannah before being promoted to Los Angeles' A+ team in the California League—the San Bernardino Stampede. While with the Sand Gnats he hit with power and for average. In just 244 official at-bats he hit 16 home runs—enough to tie him for the team lead for the season. Moreover, he batted .307 with a high .406 on-base percentage. His .406 OBP along with a high .586 slugging percentage (SLG) resulted in an excellent .992 on-base percentage plus slugging percentage (OPS).

Beltre spent the next season—1997—again playing A+ ball, but this time he was stationed with the Vero Beach Dodgers in the Florida State League. Again he stood out—24 HR, .317 AVE, .407 OBP, and .561 SLG. He struggled some in the field, but continued to play third base. With Vero Beach he made 37 errors in just 121 games and had a very poor .895 fielding percentage.

For the start of the 1998 season, Beltre was promoted to the Dodgers' AA team, the San Antonio Missions in the Texas League. Again he was ripping the cover off the ball. In late June of that season, Beltre got the call to the majors. At that point he had never played in a game at the AAA level and had appeared in just a little over 300 minor league games.

In a home game versus the Los Angeles Angels on June 24, 1998, Beltre made his debut at the age of 19 as Los Angeles' third baseman. During that game he batted eighth in the Dodgers order and went 2 for 5 with a single and a double, collecting 1 RBI in the process. Beltre doubled to knock in the Dodgers' first run and tie the game at 1 all in his first major league at-bat. The Dodgers won the game in the eleventh inning and Beltre played a role in that too. His second hit, an infield single with one down in the bottom of the eleventh, advanced Dodgers first baseman Matt Luke to third. Luke crossed the plate with the winning run when the next batter, left fielder Trent Hubbard, hit a walk-off single.

Over the last seventeen seasons, Beltre has played third base and batted in the middle of the order for the Dodgers, Mariners, Red Sox, and Rangers. The four-time American League All-Star worked hard on his fielding and has received four Gold Glove Awards for his play at third base. He has played the hot corner in over 2300 major league games and has a lifetime fielding percentage over .959 at the position.

Travis Hafner took kind of the slow route to the majors. He was playing baseball at Cowley County Community College in Kansas when drafted by the Texas Rangers in the June 1996 Amateur Draft. However, he did not sign with the Rangers until a full year later—June 2, 1997, the day before his 20th birthday. Hafner played his first season of professional baseball at the rookie level with the GCL Rangers.

To start the 1998 season, he was assigned to the Savannah Sand Gnats. Hafner played both first base and third base that season, but he had a soft season with the bat. He hit just .237. Hafner returned in 1999 to play a second full season in Savannah. That season he focused on playing first base and turning his offense around. Hafner succeeded. He led the team in almost every batting stat category: R (94), H (140), 2B (30), HR (28), RBI (111), BB (67), SLG (.546), OPS (.933), and TB (262). His home runs, runs batted in, slugging percentage, and on-base percentage plus slugging percentage led all players in the South Atlantic League. In fact, Hafner set the Sand Gnats' all-time single season record in each of those four power hitting stats and total bases. Today Hafner is still the Sand Gnats' all-time leader in HR, RBI, SLG, OPS, and TB.

In the three seasons that followed, Hafner advanced one level at a time—A+, AA, and AAA. While playing for the Oklahoma RedHawks—the Rangers' AAA team in the Pacific Coast League—in 2002, he was batting .342 with 21 home runs. At the beginning of August he got the call to the majors and made his debut on August 6 in an away game versus Detroit as a pinch-hitter and struck out.

The next day Hafner made his first start. He was the Rangers' designated hitter and batted seventh in their lineup. He went 2 for 5 with a single and a triple, scored 1 run, and had 1 RBI. In the top of the fifth inning, Hafner tripled in a run to tie the score at 2–2. Then in the top of the eleventh he singled and later scored the game-winning run as the Rangers rallied for five runs to take a 7–2 lead.

At the end of the 2002 season it looked like Travis Hafner's major league career was set to take off. However, during the offseason he was traded to the Cleveland Indians. But instead Hafner was back in the minors to start the 2003 season, this time with the Indians' triple-A team—the Buffalo Bisons in the International League. But this stay was short. Soon he was back with Cleveland splitting time between first base and designated hitter. In 2004 Hafner took over as the Indians' regular DH. Hafner went on to play ten seasons in Cleveland. Another facet of Hafner's career that is interesting is that he appeared in 1183 regular season games and in all but 72 of them he was a designated hitter.

One last player from the list in Table 3–3 SAV whose route to the majors was unusual is third baseman/outfielder Ryan Zimmerman, of the Washington Nationals. Zimmerman played college ball at the University of Virginia prior to being selected as the number 4 pick in the first round of the 2005

Amateur Draft. He signed with the Washington Nationals on June 18 of that season and was on the field playing third base for the Savannah Sand Gnats just three days later on June 21. During his first four games with the Sand Gnats he went 8 for 17 at the plate with 2 doubles, 1 triple, 2 home runs, and 6 RBI.

After playing in just those few games, he was promoted to the Nationals' AA affiliate in the Eastern League, the Harrisburg Senators. Zimmerman played just 63 games at the AA level before being called up by the Nationals when the major league rosters were expanded on September 1, 2005. He spent just 71 days in the minor leagues and played in a total of 67 games at that level before making his major league debut.

On the day he was called up, Zimmerman pinch-hit in the top of the seventh inning in a game versus the Atlanta Braves at Turner Field in Atlanta. He struck out looking. After making a few pinch-hitting appearances and defensive substitutions, he finally got his first start in a home game versus the Florida Marlins at Robert F. Kennedy Stadium. But in his debut he played shortstop, not third base. On that day Zimmerman hit sixth in the Nationals batting order and went 1 for 4 on the day.

As shown in Table 3–3 SAV, 2014 was Zimmerman's tenth season in the majors. He took over as Washington's starting third baseman in 2006. Since then Zimmerman won Silver Slugger Awards for the National League third baseman in 2009 and 2010, the Golden Glove Award for National League third baseman in 2009, and was selected to represent Washington on the 2009 National League All-Star team. During the 2014 season, Zimmerman began to also play left field and a little first base for the Nats.

Attractions in or Near Savannah

- **Historic Riverfront Plaza**, 115 E. River St., Savannah, GA 31401
- **Savannah Harbor Riverboat Cruise**, 9 E. River St., Savannah, GA 31401 (800) 786–6404
- **Old Town Trolley Tours (Welcome Center/Parking)**, 234 Martin Luther King Jr. Blvd., Savannah, GA 31401 (912) 233–0083
- **Ships of the Sea Maritime Museum**, 41 Martin Luther King Jr. Blvd., Savannah, GA 31401 (912) 232–1511
- **Georgia State Railroad Museum**, 655 Louisville Rd., Savannah, GA 31401 (912) 651–6823
- **Wormsloe Historic Site**, 7601 Skidaway Rd., Savannah, GA 31406 (912) 353–3023

- **Mighty Eighth Air Force Museum**, 175 Bourne Ave., Pooler, GA 31322 (912) 748–8888

Dining in Savannah

BREWPUBS AND BREWERIES

- **Moon River Brewing Company**, 21 W. Bay St., Savannah, GA 31401 (912) 447–0943

DOWNTOWN RESTAURANTS

- **Fiddlers Crab House**, 131 W. River St., Savannah, GA 31401 (912) 644–7172
- **Bernie's Oyster House**, 115 E. River St., Savannah, GA 31401 (912) 236–1827
- **Huey's A Southern Café**, 115 E. River St., Savannah, GA 31401 (912) 234–7385
- **Bayou Café**, 14 N. Abercorn St., Savannah, GA 31401 (912) 233–6411
- **Kevin Barry's Irish Pub**, 117 W. River St., Savannah, GA 31401 (912) 233–9626
- **Vic's Coffee House**, 15 E. River St., Savannah, GA 31401 (912) 721–6299
- **Leopold's Ice Cream**, 212 E. Broughton St., Savannah, GA 31401 (912) 234–4442

West Virginia Power

Appalachian Power Park
601 Morris St., Charleston, WV 25301
www.milb.com/index.jsp?sid=t525

The West Virginia Power's home stadium, Appalachian Power Park, is located in Charleston—the capital city of West Virginia. Based on population, Charleston is the largest city in the state. Similar to a number of other historic cities that host teams of the South Atlantic League, Charleston is on the banks of a river. In this case rivers, since it is located at the confluence of the Kanawha and Elk rivers. Today Charleston is the center of West Virginia's government and business.

Table 3–1 WV shows that Charleston has hosted a number of professional baseball teams in a variety of leagues over the last century. Note that during

Team Name	1st Year	Years	Leagues
Charleston Senators	1910	1	Virginia Valley League
Charleston Senators	1911	2	Mountain States League
Charleston Senators	1913	4	Ohio State League
Charleston Senators	1931	12	Middle Atlantic League
Charleston Senators	1949	3	Central League
Charleston Senators	1952	9	American Association
Charleston Marlins	1961	1	International League
Charleston Indians	1962	3	Eastern League
Charleston Charlies	1971	13	International League
Charleston Wheelers	1987	8	South Atlantic League
Charleston AlleyCats	1995	10	South Atlantic League
West Virginia Power	2005	10	South Atlantic League

Table 3-1 WV. Teams that have played in Charleston, WV (source: www.baseball-reference.com).

the first half of the 20th century a team called the Charleston Senators represented the city. In fact, a Charleston Senators team played on and off during thirty-one of the fifty-one baseball season between 1910 and 1960. The moniker Senators honored the members of the state's government that meets in the city. The team first appeared on the scene as a member of the Virginia Valley League in 1910. That league was made up of six teams that were all located less than 100 miles either north or west of Charleston. Five of the teams were located in West Virginia, but one was in eastern Kentucky. Like many leagues of its day, this league folded after its inaugural season and the Senators were in search of another league to join for the 1911 season.

The Senators played in two other leagues during the 1910 decade—the Mountain States League and Ohio State League. For the 1911 season, they joined teams from five other towns that had participated in the Virginia Valley League as members of the Mountain States League for its inaugural season. This league included a sixth team—the Ironton Nailers—that resided in Ohio. The Mountain States League lasted just two seasons.

Next, the Senators entered into an engagement with a league that had existed for a number of years—the Ohio State League. During the 1912 season, this league had six teams all located in the state of Ohio. However, for the 1913 season it added teams in Kentucky and West Virginia to expand to eight teams. The Charleston Senators resided at the southeast corner of the footprint of the league with all of the other teams located either directly west or to the northwest. The farthest teams, which were located in Lexington, Kentucky, and Hamilton, Ohio, were close to 200 miles away.

Over the next few baseball seasons the Ohio State League shrank and eventually folded after the 1917 season. This brought an end to the first era of baseball in Charleston. During this first decade of baseball, the leagues in which the Charleston Senators played were all classified at the D level of minor league baseball.

Professional baseball did not return to the city for more than a decade. Note in Table 3–1 WV that in 1931 a Charleston Senators team played its first season in the Middle Atlantic League. This league had teams in West Virginia, Maryland, and Pennsylvania. Charleston was located to the southwest with all of the other teams in towns or cities to either the north or northeast and a number of them were farther than 200 miles away. The connection between the Senators and the Middle Atlantic League lasted through the 1942 season. During this twelve season stretch, the team was first affiliated with the Detroit Tigers as their C-level minor league team and later with the Cleveland Indians. However, after the 1942 season, the league suspended play during the World War II years. When the league resumed play in 1946 it was without a team in Charleston.

But baseball was not dormant in Charleston for long. Prior to the 1949 season, a Charleston Senators team joined the Central League, which was in its second year of operation. This Senators team was an A-level affiliate of the Cincinnati Reds. The footprint of this league covered a much broader area. It had three teams in Michigan, one in Ohio, and one in Indiana. Charleston set the southeast boundary of the league and was located over 500 miles from the farthest team—the Muskegon Clippers—in northwest Michigan.

The 1949 Senators had two players who went on to have extended careers playing for the Cincinnati Reds—left-handed pitcher Joe Nuxhall and outfielder Wally Post. At this point in baseball history, it was not uncommon that players under the age of 18 were playing on the minor league teams of major league clubs. That is the case for both Nuxhall and Post. In fact, Joe Nuxhall holds a special place in Major League Baseball history, having made his major league debut on June 10, 1944, at the age of 15 for the Birmingham Barons in the Southern Association. Nuxhall That was during World War II, and there was a shortage of players due to the war. Cincinnati called him up and he pitched two-thirds of an inning in relief. Till today and probably forever, he will remain the youngest player to have ever appeared in a major league game. Nuxhall was recalled by Cincinnati in 1952 at the age of 23 and went on to have a sixteen-year major league career. He pitched during fifteen of those seasons for the Reds.

After the 1951 season, the Central League disbanded. Part way through the 1952 season, the Chicago White Sox relocated their AAA team in the American Association—the Toledo Sox—to Charleston as the Charleston Senators. Over the next nine baseball seasons, the Senators were the AAA affiliate of the Chicago White Sox, Detroit Tigers, and then the Washington Senators in the American Association. During this period, the baseball fans in Charleston had the opportunity to see many ballplayers who went on to play at the major league level. In fact, often they ended up being called up during the current season or very next season. For example, in 1956, when the Senators were affiliated with the Detroit Tigers, Jim Bunning was a key member of Charleston's starting rotation. The next season, 1957, Bunning was on the opening day roster of the Detroit Tigers; he went 20W:8L for the season and was selected as a member of the American League All-Star Team. Bunning went on to pitch in the majors for the Tigers, Phillies, Pirates and Dodgers over a seventeen-year career. While a starter for Philadelphia, he threw a perfect game versus the New York Mets at Shea Stadium in New York. Bunning was a seven time All-Star and was inducted into the Baseball Hall of Fame in 1996.

But this stint in the American Association ended when the Washington team relocated to Minnesota as the Twins for the 1961 season. That was the end of the reign of a team known as the Charleston Senators. But the end of the Charleston Senators ushered in a new era of baseball in Charleston—a period when teams from higher levels of Major League Baseball's minor league organizations continued to play in the city. Midway through the 1961 season professional baseball was already back in Charleston. The St. Louis Cardinals' International League affiliate, the San Juan Marlins, got into financial trouble. So the Cardinals relocated the team to the city of Charleston for the balance of that season.

The Cleveland Indians moved their A-level affiliate in the Eastern League—the Reading Indians—from Pennsylvania to Charleston as the Charleston Indians for the 1962 season. Two pitchers from the 1962 club—lefty Tommy John and righty Luis Tiant—would go on to have very long and successful major league careers. These two pitchers threw to a 21-year-old Duke Sims, journeyman catcher who went on to play for five major league clubs over an eleven-season major league career. Tiant won 229 games over 19 seasons and Tommy John won 288 games over twenty-six seasons. John might be best known for the fact that he was the first pitcher to have undergone ulnar collateral ligament (UCL) reconstruction surgery by Dr. Frank

Jobe, which is more commonly known today as Tommy John surgery. John had the surgery after his twelfth season pitching in the majors and sat out the 1975 season to recover. He returned to the mound in 1976 and then went on to pitch in fourteen more seasons.

In the next season, 1963, the Eastern League was reclassified by Major League Baseball to the AA level, moving Charleston up one notch in stature. But the Indians stayed only through 1964 and after that the city of Charleston was again without a team for a number of years.

Charleston did not wait long for a new baseball team. In preparation for the 1971 season, the Pittsburgh Pirates relocated their International League team from Columbus, Ohio, to Charleston. That team was named the Charlies and brought triple-A baseball back to the city. The Charlies were a fixture in the city for the next sixteen seasons, but not all those years were as a member of the Pirates' minor league system. However, there was a seamless transition from the Pirates to the Houston Astros in 1977, to the Texas Rangers in 1980, and finally to the Cleveland Indians in 1981.

Fans of baseball got to see a continuous stream of future major leaguers play on the field of Watt Powell Park in Charleston: outfielders Richie Zisk and Dave Parker of the Pirates, outfielder Terry Puhl of the Astros, and outfielder Von Hayes of the Indians. Also, during the 1974 season, three players, Tony LaRussa, Art Howe, and Ken Macha, who all went on to be mangers at the major league level, played at the same time for the Charleston Charlies. But the string of years of AAA ball in the city ended when the Indians relocated their team to Old Orchard Beach, Maine, for the 1984 season.

Again the play of professional baseball lapsed for a number of years in the city of Charleston. But the door reopened prior to the 1987 season. The modern South Atlantic League set up a co-op team in the city—the Charleston Wheelers. It was a team made up of players from a number of different major league clubs. In the years to come, the team's name evolved from the Wheelers to the Charleston AlleyCats to today's West Virginia Power. During this progression, the major league affiliation changed frequently and included the Chicago Cubs, Cincinnati Reds, Milwaukee Brewers, and Pittsburgh Pirates from the National League and the Kansas City Royals and Toronto Blue Jays of the American League.

Since 2009, the West Virginia Power has been the A-level affiliate of the Pittsburgh Pirates and 2014 was the sixth season that the team was part of their minor league system. This six-year stretch is the longest engagement between the city of Charleston and a single major league club during the South Atlantic League years.

The Home of the Power—Appalachian Power Park

The teams that played baseball in the city of Charleston during the second half of the 20th century and early 2000s played their games at Watt Powell Park. This stadium was built in 1948 and named after Walter "Watt" Powell, a former player and manager of the Charleston Senators. The stadium was located in Kanawha City, which is approximately two miles from the heart of Charleston's capital district, but on the southern bank side of the Kanawha River. This stadium was the home of the Charleston Wheelers and Charleston AlleyCats teams of the South Atlantic League.

Prior to the 2004 season, ground was broken for a new downtown Charleston stadium. The Milwaukee Brewers had taken over the Sally League franchise after the 2004 season and the team had been renamed the West Virginia Power for the coming season. The new ballpark was ready for the 2005 season—the inaugural season of both the West Virginia Power and the new stadium called Appalachian Power Park.

Figure 3–1 WV, which is taken from behind home plate, shows that the

Figure 3–1 WV. Appalachian Power Park, Charleston, WV.

stadium is designed with an open air feel. There is no grandstand that covers the seats to provide shade or protect from inclement weather. Instead, a very wide elevated concourse rings the ball field from the left field corner to the right field corner. Play on the field can be viewed from almost any point on the concourse. Seating areas extend from the concourse down toward the field level and are close to the field for a good view of the game. The view from behind home plate is interesting—first with historic buildings right beyond the outfield wall and then extending up to tree-covered hills in the distance.

However, there is one spot on the concourse from which you can't view the game. That is from directly behind home plate. At that point there is a small building on the field side of the concourse that serves as a press box. On the back side of the building, which faces the concourse, you will find the Charleston Baseball Wall of Fame. Here there are plaques to honor former players and a number of individuals who played an important role relative to professional baseball in Charleston. Plaques on the wall feature former players Jim Bunning, Trevor Hoffman, Dave Parker, Joe Nuxhall, Tommy John, Art Howe, Tony LaRussa, Kent Tekulve, and Ryan Braun.

To the far side of the concourse down the first base line and extending to the right field corner is first a newly constructed building that houses a number of concessions followed by an attractive historic warehouse building that has been restored as part of the stadium. There is also a building with additional concessions located on the back side of the third base side of the concourse. Because of the open concourse, you can view the game while waiting to buy food. There are a number of luxury suites on the second floor of the first base side concession building with seating on the inside and an outdoor balcony. Finally, behind the outfield wall there is a large children's play area called the H&H Enterprises Fun Zone. There is something at the ballpark for everyone. Overall I found Appalachian Power Park a casual and friendly place to enjoy a baseball game.

The South Atlantic League Years

Two thousand fourteen was the twenty-eighth consecutive season that the city of Charleston has been the home of a team in the modern South Atlantic League. As pointed out earlier, the team's name and affiliation have changed a number of times. Table 3–2(a) WV shows that the team's name has been the Charleston Wheelers, Charleston AlleyCats, and today the West Virginia Power. The South Atlantic League teams of Charleston have been

Name	MLB Affiliate	Years
West Virginia Power	Pittsburgh Pirates	2009-today
West Virginia Power	Milwaukee Brewers	2005-2008
Charleston AlleyCats	Toronto Blue Jays	2001-2004
Charleston AlleyCats	Kansas City Royals	1999-2000
Charleston AlleyCats	Cincinnati Reds	1995-1998
Charleston Wheelers	Cincinnati Reds	1990-1994
Charleston Wheelers	Chicago Cubs	1988-1989
Charleston Wheelers	Multiple teams	1987

Level	Team	Stadium	League
Rk	GCL Pirates	Pirate City Complex Bradenton, FL	Gulf Coast League
Rk	Bristol Pirates	DeVault Memorial Stadium Bristol, VA	Appalachian League
A-	Jamestown Jammers	Russell E. Diethrick, Jr. Park Jamestown, NY	New York-Penn League
A	West Virginia Power	Appalachian Power Park Charleston, WV	South Atlantic League
A+	Bradenton Marauders	McKechnie Field Bradenton, FL	Florida State League
AA	Altoona Curve	Peoples Natural Gas Field Altoona, PA	Eastern League
AAA	Indianapolis Indians	Victory Field Indianapolis, IN	International League

Top: Table 3–2(a) WV. Charleston teams' major league affiliations. *Above:* Table 3–2(b) WV. Pittsburgh Pirates minor league organization.

quite successful. Over the years they have appeared in the league playoffs during eight seasons and won the Northern Division Championship five times, but they took home the South Atlantic League Championship Title only once.

Note in Table 3–2(a) WV that in 1988 the Chicago Cubs added the Wheelers to their minor league organization. This gave them three A-level teams. After the 1989 season the Cubs dropped two of the A-level clubs, and one of them was the Wheelers. But the timing was just right as the Cincinnati Reds relocated their current South Atlantic League team from Greensboro, North Carolina, to Charleston as the Wheelers. This began a 9-year relationship between the Reds and the city of Charleston.

During this Cincinnati Reds period, the Wheelers won the 1990 South Atlantic League title. They swept the Fayetteville Generals (Detroit Tigers) 2–0 in the opening round of the playoffs to win the Northern Division title. In the championship round, they played the Southern Division champion Savannah Cardinals (St. Louis Cardinal) and the outcome was similar. The Wheelers took the series 3–0 to win the city's first and, as it turns out, only South Atlantic League Championship. During the 1990 season, future star reliever Trevor Hoffman played at either shortstop or third base for Charleston, not as a pitcher, but then went on to become one of the greatest major league closers of all time.

The Reds' Wheelers returned to the postseason in 1991 and 1992 and won the Northern Division title in both years. During the 1991 season, Charleston won the Northern Division during both the first half and second half of the season to earn a bye in the division championship series. They posted the best record in the league for the season, 92W:50L, but got swept 3–0 by the Columbia Mets (New York Mets) in the best-of-five championship round. In 1992 the Wheelers beat the Spartanburg Phillies (Philadelphia Phillies) in the division championship round but were again swept in the finals. This time they lost to the Myrtle Beach Hurricanes (Toronto Blue Jays).

In 1995 and still under the Reds' watch, the team was renamed the Charleston AlleyCats. Other notable players who played for the Wheelers or AlleyCats and then went on to make their major league debuts with Cincinnati are infielder Pokey Reese (1992), catcher Jason LaRue (1996), and pitchers Kevin Jarvis (1992), Brett Tomko (1995), and B. J. Ryan (1998).

When Cincinnati left the city, the AlleyCats became the SAL affiliate of the Kansas City Royals from 1999 to 2000 and then the Toronto Blue Jays from 2001 to 2004. During the 2004 season, the Blue Jays' AlleyCats made the postseason but were swept by the Hickory Crawdads (Pittsburgh Pirates) in the first round. Here are a few of the players who played for the Charleston AlleyCats and went on to make their major league debuts with the Toronto Blue Jays: outfielder Alex Rios (2001), infielder Ryan Roberts (2004) and pitchers Dustin McGowan (2002), Brandon League (2003), and Shaun Marcum (2004).

In sync with the opening of a new downtown stadium—Appalachian Power Park—in 2005, Charleston's team was renamed the West Virginia Power and transitioned to become the SAL A-level franchise of a new major league club—the Milwaukee Brewers. In 2007 the Power won the Northern Division during the first half of the season by eleven games with a 48W:20L record. This gained them entry into the South Atlantic League play-offs.

The 2007 team had a potent offense that was led by three players: right fielder Chuckie Caufield, first baseman Andrew Lefave, and left fielder Stephen Chapman. The West Virginia Power led all other teams in the league in runs scored, hits, runs batted in, batting average, on-base percentage, and on-base percentage plus slugging percentage. Caufield was a table-setter. He led the team in R (100), H (149), and 2B (32). His runs scored and hits ranked him in the top 10 among all players in the South Atlantic League in those two offensive statistics. Moreover, his 100 runs scored broke the Power's all-time single season record for that batting stat category. Caufield still holds that record today.

Lefave was the best overall hitter on the club. He led all regular players on the team in AVE (.345), OBP (.432), SLG (.525), and OPS (.957). In fact, his .345 batting average and .432 on-base percentage ranked him number 1 in the league in both of those important offensive stat categories. Similar to Caufield, that season Lefave set new all-time single season offensive records for a player in the West Virginia Power uniform. Lefave broke the prior records for batting average, on-base percentage, and on-base percentage plus slugging percentage, and he still holds those three records today.

Chapman was the team's power hitter. He led the team with 24 home runs, 89 runs batted in, and 228 total bases. He ranked in the top 10 among all players in the South Atlantic League for the season in each of those stat categories. Chapman's 24 home runs set the West Virginia Power all-time single season record for that offensive power-hitting stat. He is still the Power's all-time home run leader today.

The West Virginia Power faced the Hickory Crawdads (Pittsburgh Pirates) in the first round of the playoffs—the Northern Division Championship Series. They beat Hickory 2–1 to take home the Northern Division title. In the South Atlantic League Championship Series they faced the Southern Division champion Columbus Catfish (Tampa Bay Rays) but were swept in three games. The team's weakness was its pitching. Relative to the sixteen teams that played in the league that season, the Power's pitching staff ranked eleventh in the league in strikeouts, ninth in earned run average, and eighth in walks plus hits per inning pitched.

After winning the Northern Division in the second half of the 2008 season with a 45W:25L record, West Virginia went back to the postseason for the second straight year. That season Steffan Wilson, who played first base and third base for the Power, supplied the power for the batting order. He led the team with 91 runs scored, 19 home runs, and 100 runs batted in. Wilson's 100 RBI set the Power's all-time single season record for that offensive stat and he still holds the team's RBI record today.

The starting rotation was headed by right hander Evan Anundson. He threw a team high 145 innings during his 28 starts and led the team in wins with 12. His 12 victories tied him for third in that pitching stat in the South Atlantic League for the season. Anundson's 145 IP ranked sixth in the league. Both his innings pitched and wins set new all-time single season records for the Power and those totals remain the team record today.

Again the Power won the Northern Division title, this time with a 2 game to 1 victory over the Lake County Captains (Cleveland Indians). However, they were turned away for the second season in a row in the championship round. They lost the SAL Championship Series 3 games to 0 to the Augusta GreenJackets (San Francisco Giants).

Since 2009, the West Virginia Power has been the single-A affiliate of the Pittsburgh Pirates. They did not make a playoff appearance while representing the Pirates until the 2013 season. By winning the Northern Division during the second half of the season with a 45W:25L record, the Power got to take on the first half season division winner—the Hagerstown Suns. But this time they lost in the first round of the playoffs 2 games to 1. A listing of the Pittsburgh Pirates' other minor league affiliates is given in Table 3–2(b) WV.

Successful Major Leaguers Who Played in Charleston

Since 1987 fans of the South Atlantic League teams that played their games in Charleston, the Charleston Wheelers, Charleston AlleyCats, and West Virginia Power, have had the opportunity to see many players tune their baseball skills on the fields of Watt Powell Park or Appalachian Power Park. I mentioned a few of them in earlier sections, for example, Trevor Hoffman, Brett Tomko, B. J. Ryan, and Ryan Braun. Table 3–3 WV lists more than twenty players who played their A-level ball as members of the rosters of the Wheelers, AlleyCats, or Power.

The table shows that Trevor Hoffman, who played for the Charleston Wheelers in 1990, is the player in this list who had the longest major league

Season	Player	Age at WV	MiLB Season	Position	MLB Debut	Age at Debut	MLB Team	Seasons in MLB
1987	x							
1988	Alex Arias	20	2	SS	5/12/92	24	CHC	11
	Matt Walbeck	18	2	C	4/7/93	23	CHC	10
1989	x							
1990	Trevor Hoffman	22	2	P	4/6/93	25	FLA	18
	Dan Wilson	21	1	C	9/7/92	23	CIN	14
1991	x							
1992	Kevin Jarvis	22	2	RHP	4/6/94	24	CIN	12
1993	Chad Fox	22	2	RHP	7/13/97	26	ATL	10
1994	x							
1995	Brett Tomko	22	1	RHP	5/27/97	24	CIN	14
1996	Jason LaRue	22	2	C	6/15/99	25	CIN	12
1997	x							
1998	B. J. Ryan	22	1	LHP	7/28/99	23	CIN	11
1999	Jeremy Affeldt	20	3	LHP	4/6/02	22	KCR	13+
2000	x							
2001	Alex Rios	20	2	RF	5/27/04	23	TOR	11+
2002	Dustin McGowan	20	3	RHP	7/30/05	23	TOR	7+
2003	Brandon League	20	3	RHP	9/21/04	21	TOR	11+
	Erik Kratz	23	2	C	7/17/10	30	PIT	5+
2004	Ryan Roberts	23	2	3B	7/30/06	25	TOR	9+
	Shaun Marcum	22	2	RHP	9/6/05	23	TOR	8+
2005	Ryan Braun	21	1	LF	5/25/07	23	MIL	8+
	Alcides Escobar	18	2	SS	9/3/08	21	MIL	7+
	Yovani Gallardo	19	2	RHP	6/18/07	21	MIL	8+
2006	Michael Brantley	19	2	CF	9/1/09	22	CLE	6+
	Lorenzo Cain	20	2	CF	7/16/10	24	MIL	5+
	Joe Thatcher	24	3	LHP	7/26/07	25	SDP	8+
2007	Jeremy Jeffress	19	2	RHP	9/1/10	22	MIL	5+
2008	Jonathan Lucroy	22	2	C	5/21/10	23	MIL	5+
2009	x							

Table 3-3 WV. West Virginia SAL players that went on to have long major league careers.

career—eighteen seasons. Earlier I pointed out that Hoffman's minor league career got off to an unexpected start—he played infield during his first two seasons of professional ball and shortstop and third base for the Wheelers during the 1990 season. In 1991, Hoffman began a second season of A-level ball, but with the Cedar Rapids Reds in the Midwest League. It was during that season that he transitioned to pitching.

Hoffman did not begin as a starter and then convert to a reliever. At

Cedar Rapids he made 27 appearances—all in relief. He finished 25 of those 27 games and recorded 12 saves. Later in the season he was promoted to AA—the Chattanooga Lookouts in the Southern League—and saved 8 more games. Hoffman quickly progressed to AAA in 1992.

His major league career took unexpected twists and turns, too. During the 1992 offseason, Hoffman was selected by the Florida Marlins in the expansion draft and was a member of their 1993 inaugural season opening day roster. He made his major league debut on April 6, 1993, at the age of 25 versus the Los Angeles Dodgers at the Marlins' home field, Joe Robbie Stadium. Hoffman pitched to just 1 batter—the last batter in the top of the ninth inning—and struck him out. It was not a save opportunity. Florida was losing at the time and went on to lose the game 4–2. Hoffman got the first save of his major league career more than three weeks later on April 29, 1993, when he pitched the ninth inning in a Marlins 6–5 victory over the Atlanta Braves at Atlanta-Fulton County Stadium.

But Hoffman's major league career took another turn when he was traded to the San Diego Padres on June 24, 1993—just 71 games into his rookie season. The deal brought Gary Sheffield and Rich Rodriguez to the Marlins in exchange for Hoffman and two minor leaguers. Hoffman finished the season in the Padres bullpen. The next season he took over as San Diego's full time closer and history was in the making. On September 24, 2006, he recorded his 478th save to tie Lee Smith's all-time saves record. Two days later in St. Louis he saved his 479th game to take sole possession of Major League Baseball's all-time saves record.

Hoffman pitched in sixteen seasons as the Padres' closer and then finished up his career with the Brewers in 2009 and 2010. When he pitched his last game on September 29, 2010, at the age of 42 he had 601 saves, which was still the all-time major league saves record. During his eighteen-season major league career Trevor Hoffman never started a game; instead, he pitched in 1035 games as a reliever.

The first crop of players that were members of the 2005 West Virginia Power team and are still playing in the majors includes Ryan Braun, Alcides Escobar, and Yovani Gallardo. As shown in Table 3–3 WV, they were all called up by the Milwaukee Brewers. Braun and Gallardo are key players for the Brewers today. Gallardo is the number one starter in the Brewers' rotation. He has made 30 or more starts in each of the last five seasons and pitched and won their 2014 Opening Day game. During the 2005 season, a 19-year-old Gallardo went 8W:3L in 26 pitching appearances for the Power. His ERA that season, which was 2.74, set the all-time single season record for the lowest earned run average for a pitcher in the West Virginia Power uniform.

For a pitcher to qualify as the team or league leader in ERA, he must pitch a minimum of .8 innings per league game or 112 innings during a 140 game season. Two thousand fourteen was Gallardo's eighth consecutive season as a member of the Brewers' starting rotation. He was selected to represent Milwaukee on the 2010 National League All-Star Team.

Ryan Braun, who was signed at the age of 21 after playing college ball at the University of Miami, made a brief stop on the road to the major leagues to play for the West Virginia Power. During the 2005 season, his first season of pro ball, he played in 37 games for the Power. Braun was on the express route to the majors. He had played in just 199 minor league games before getting the call from the Brewers. In the minors Braun played only the third base position. He made his debut as the Milwaukee Brewers third baseman and number two batter on May 25, 2007. Braun had a great rookie season with the bat. He led the team with a .342 batting average and .692 slugging percentage. For his excellent play during the 2007 season, Braun was voted the National League Rookie of the Year.

However, during his rookie season, Braun made 26 errors at third base and had a rather low .895 fielding percentage. On Opening Day of the 2008 season, he batted cleanup but made the move to left fielder. Since then Braun has been Milwaukee's starting left fielder and a mainstay of their offense. He was selected to represent the Brewers on the National League All-Star Team five consecutive seasons from 2008 through 2012. Moreover, Braun was voted the Most Valuable Player in the National League for his play during the 2011 season. He is under contract to play with the Brewers through the 2020 season.

Table 3–3 WV shows that current Kansas City Royals outfielder Lorenzo Cain played for the Power during the 2006 season. As their starting right fielder, Cain had an outstanding season with the bat. He led all regular players on the team in hits (162), double (36), and batting average (.307). His 162 hits that season broke the existing all-time hits record for a player in the West Virginia Power uniform. He remains the record holder for the Power in that batting stat today.

Cain was traded by the Milwaukee Brewers to the Kansas City Royals during the 2010 offseason and made his major league debut in the Royals uniform on July 16, 2010. Two thousand fourteen was a breakout year for him. During the regular season, Cain had 142 hits, 29 doubles and a team leading .301 batting average in 133 games. He was a key contributor in both the field and at the plate in Kansas City's 2014 postseason run to their first World Series appearance in 29 years. During the American League Championship Series versus the Baltimore Orioles he batted .533 and received the Most Valuable Player award for his play. In the World Series, he made a number of exceptional diving and leaping catches in center and right field as well as batting .308.

Since the Pittsburgh Pirates have been engaged with the West Virginia Power since only 2009, none of the players who played for the team during those years have yet appeared in games at the major league level for the last five seasons. However, some of them are beginning to contribute for the Pirates. For example, during the 2013 season Starling Marte, who played center field in Charleston in 2009, took over as Pittsburgh's starting left fielder. He was Pittsburgh's 2013 Opening Day left fielder, and the speedster went on to lead the team in triples (10) and stolen bases (41) for the season. Two thousand fourteen was his third season playing at the major league level.

Attractions in Charleston

- **West Virginia State Capitol Building**, 1811 Washington St., Charleston, WV 25311
- **Capitol Street Historic District Shops and Restaurants**, 200–290 Capitol St., Charleston, WV 25301
- **Capital Market and Tourist Center**, 800 Smith St., Charleston, WV 25301 (304) 344–1905
- **Magic Island Park**, 101 Kanawha Blvd., W. Charleston, WV 25302
- **Avampato Discovery Museum at Clay Center**, 1 Clay Square, Charleston, WV 25301 (304) 561–3570

Dining in Charleston

Downtown Restaurants

- **Fifth Quarter Restaurant**, 201 Clendenin St., Charleston, WV 25301 (304) 345–3933
- **Pies and Pints**, 222 Capitol St., Charleston, WV 25301 (304) 342–7437
- **Taylor Books Café,** 226 Capitol St., Charleston, WV 25301 (304) 342–1461
- **Ellen's Homemade Ice Cream**, 225 Capitol St., Charleston, WV 25301 (304) 343–6488
- **Musical Grounds European Coffeehouse at Capital Market**, 800 Smith St., Charleston, WV 25301 (304) 344–1905
- **Soho's Italian Restaurant at Capital Market**, 800 Smith St., Charleston, WV 25301 (304) 720–7646

4

The Perfect Hub for South Atlantic League Travel

Located in east-central North Carolina, Durham is a thriving city with a population of over 225,000, is the home of a number of renowned universities, including Duke University, and boasts an economy supported by a broad base of industrial and medical related companies and facilities. Durham is a city that blends the old with the new and is ranked as one of the best places to live or do business in the United States.

Economic Evolution of Durham, North Carolina

From the mid–1800s and continuing for over a hundred years the North Carolina economy was primary agricultural and evolved to where it was heavily based on the growing of tobacco and manufacturing of tobacco products. The farming region in this part of North Carolina was not rich enough to support a wide range of crops but was satisfactory for growing tobacco. Combining the type of crop harvested in this area with a flue-curing process developed in North Carolina produced a very desirable grade of tobacco know as brightleaf tobacco.

In the late 1870s, the Blackwell Tobacco Company of Durham created a company trademark using a bull's head in an effort to differentiate their smoking tobacco from those of their competitors. Their product, which was named Bull Durham, was the first nationally distributed brand of tobacco and its trademark with the bull's head became one of the most recognized symbols in the world. In this way, the city of Durham—at this point already one of the key cities for the growing tobacco industry in North Carolina— got its first nickname as the "Bull City." In 1898, the American Tobacco Company bought out the Blackwell Tobacco Company and the Bull Durham brand.

The predominant industry of Durham remained tobacco through the middle of the 20th century and Durham kept its title as the Bull City. However, in the mid–1950s, driven by a number of universities—Duke University, North Carolina State University, and the University of Carolina at Chapel Hill—the state of North Carolina created Research Triangle Park (RTP). This was the catalyst that ignited the evolution of the economy of the region in a new direction.

These three universities are well known for their academic excellence, highly regarded medical programs, and advanced research capabilities. The primary goal of Research Triangle Park was to attract companies that were involved in industrial research to set up facilities where they could capitalize on cooperation with the universities and their research facilities. Another goal was that the job creation produced by the RTP would stem the drain of talented researchers and technologists from the state.

The idea of Research Triangle Park blossomed and grew. Today the park is the home to more than 170 companies that employ more than 40,000 people. They include a large contingent of companies—80 or more—that specialize in the fields of life sciences and biotechnology. RTP has become an economic driver for the whole Triangle region—Raleigh, Durham, and Chapel Hill—and has transformed the economy of Durham. Based on this plus excellent local university medical education programs and teaching hospitals, the city has taken on a new nickname—the "City of Medicine, USA."

Baseball and Durham, North Carolina

But what does all this have to do with baseball? Well! On the website of the Durham Bull Baseball Club, Bill Law, a team ambassador, states that he believes that Durham should be called "Baseball City, USA." So what is the link between Durham and baseball that would warrant such a designation?

I will expand on some of Bill Law's arguments for why Durham can also be called Baseball City, USA. Bill says:

• Durham is the home city of the best known minor league team in the country—the Durham Bulls.
• The movie *Bull Durham*, possibly the best sports movie and certainly the best baseball movie ever filmed, was shot in Durham.
• USA Baseball, the governing body for all amateur baseball from the Olympics on down, is headquartered in Durham.

- *Baseball America*, the prominent bi-weekly national baseball-only newspaper is published from Durham.
- Durham is home to two NCAA Division I baseball programs: the Duke University Blue Devils and North Carolina Central University Eagles.
- Miles Wolff, former owner of the Durham Bulls and *Baseball America*, remains an influential force in minor league baseball, with multiple baseball holdings that are headquartered out of Durham.

First I will comment on the Durham Bulls Baseball Club, the movie *Bull Durham*, and historic Durham Athletic Park. As noted by Law the Durham Bulls are one of the most recognized minor league baseball teams in the country. Part of the reason for this is that the Bulls baseball team and historic Durham Athletic Park played such a significant role in the popular 1988 movie *Bull Durham*. However, there is much more to the Durham Bulls story than that.

During the 115 years since 1900, the city of Durham, North Carolina, has played home to a baseball team for ninety-one of those baseball seasons and for all but four of them the team was named the Durham Bulls. Over this period, the team had been a member of five different leagues, including the Carolina League and International League, and played ball at the AAA, A+, A, B, C, and D levels. Today the Bulls are the Tampa Bay Rays' triple-A team in the International League.

More than 500 former players of the Durham Bulls have gone on to play in the major leagues. A large number of them had extended and very successful careers—John Franco (23 seasons), Fred McGriff (19 seasons), Andruw Jones (17 seasons), and Greg Luzinski (15 seasons) to name just a few. The list also includes a few superstars, for instance, Hall of Fame second baseman Joe Morgan and future Hall of Famer third baseman Chipper Jones. Even a number of today's major league top players, such as B. J. Upton and Carl Crawford, made stops in Durham on their way to "The Show."

Also historic Durham Athletic Park (DAP) is a baseball landmark in the city of Durham. Figure 4–1 shows the DAP and its signature tower crested with the Durham Bulls logo—a bull jumping through the Durham D. This stadium was completed for the 1926 season and served as home to all of Durham's minor league baseball teams through 1994. The ballpark was originally named El Toro Park but was renamed Durham Athletic Park in 1933.

Durham Athletic Park was the ball field where Nuke LaLoosh (Tim Robbins) pitched and journeyman minor league catcher Crash Davis (Kevin Costner) settled in behind the plate to attempt to receive his pitches. There are still many memories of the movie *Bull Durham* in the city and its surrounding communities. For instance, the bar in which Crash Davis and Nuke LaLoosh first

Figure 4-1. Historic Durham Athletic Park.

met and fought in the back alley—Mitch's Tavern—still stands. The tavern still proudly displays memorabilia from the shooting of the scene from the movie.

Also, two other ball fields which were used as sites for filming the movie still serve as the home of baseball teams today. The Wilson Tobs of the Coastal Plain League play their games at historic Fleming Stadium in Wilson, North Carolina. This stadium, which is shown in Fig. 4–2, was built in 1939. In the movie, Crash Davis and the team are in the midst of a seven game losing road trip when they arrive in town late in the evening for an away game the next day at Fleming Stadium. Tired from traveling and losing, one of the players, Deek, says "We need a night off just to stop our losing streak. We need a rainout." Crash replies "I can get us a rainout." Another player, Mickey, says "It's 90 degrees; there ain't been a cloud in the sky in weeks." Crash challenges them: "Hundred bucks says I can get us a rainout tomorrow." A fourth team member Tony says, "You're on." A plan for getting the next day's game cancelled had been hatched.

Later in the evening the players, led by Crash, break into Fleming Stadium and turn on the field's sprinkler system to soak the field and artificially create a rainout of the next day's game.

Figure 4–2. Historic Fleming Stadium.

The other ball field is Burlington Athletic Stadium (built in 1960), in Burlington, North Carolina, which currently is the home of the Kansas City Royals rookie level team in the Appalachian League—the Burlington Royals.

The DAP was replaced by a new stadium, Durham Bulls Athletic Park (DBAP), for the start of the 1995 season. It is the current home ball field of the Durham Bulls. This stadium is located in the American Tobacco Historic District. The ballpark is adjacent to the popular American Tobacco complex, which includes restaurants, shops, a performing arts center, and business offices. DBAP, which is shown in Fig. 4–3, is located at 409 Blackwell St.—a street named in memory of W. T. Blackwell and his tobacco company.

In the movie *Bull Durham*, there was a bull positioned above the left field fence that snorted steam whenever a player hit a home run. This was not part of the DAP; it was a prop just added for effect in the movie. However, a similar bull, shown in Fig. 4–4, exists and performs the same function in the new Bulls stadium.

Seeing the Bulls play a home game in Durham Bulls Athletic Park has been a tradition in Durham for so long that this has led to some confusion about the origins of the city's first nickname, "Bull City." As pointed out earlier that was driven by the success of the Bull Durham tobacco brand and its trademarked logo of a bull, not the Durham Bulls baseball club. Attending a home game of the Durham Bulls is a must do for any South Atlantic League baseball road trip.

Figure 4–3. Durham Bulls Athletic Park.

Figure 4–4. Snorting bull at Durham Bulls Athletic Park.

Bill Law accurately points out that Durham is home to two NCAA Division I baseball programs: the Duke University Blue Devils and North Carolina Central University Eagles. But the Triangle region's connection to college baseball is much stronger than that. Two of the nation's top ranked college baseball teams—the University of North Carolina Tar Heels and the North Carolina State University Wolfpack—play their home games at ball fields in cities of the Triangle. The Tar Heels baseball team's home field is Boshamer Stadium, Chapel Hill, North Carolina, while the home ballpark of the Wolfpack is Doak Field, Raleigh, North Carolina. Both of these teams are members of the Atlantic Coast Conference (ACC) of college baseball—one of the top ranked collegiate baseball conferences in the nation. In fact, the North Carolina Tar Heels were the 2013 conference champions.

The Duke University Blue Devils baseball team is also a member of the ACC. They play their home games at Jack Coombs Field in Durham. In the final National College Athletic Association (NCAA) rankings for the 2013 baseball season, the Tar Heels were ranked as the #1 college baseball team in the country, the Wolfpack #7, and the Blue Devils #79. How about adding a college baseball game played in the Triangle Region to your baseball road trip itinerary?

North Carolina is also the hub of the Coastal Plain League—one of the top ranked collegiate summer leagues in the country. Nine of the fourteen teams of this league play in North Carolina with many of them in towns formerly associated with South Atlantic League teams. Home games played by a number of teams from the Coastal Plain League can be easily attended as a day trip from Durham—another opportunity for diversifying your baseball road trip itinerary. How about attending a home game of the Wilson Tobs at historic Fleming Stadium as part of your South Atlantic League road trip?

Is Durham Really Baseball City, USA?

Well what is my conclusion? I am finished for now with assisting at building Bill Law's case for Durham to be nicknamed Baseball City, USA. I have expanded on a few of the points he made. However, I did not address USA Baseball, *Baseball America*, and the impact of Miles Wolff on professional baseball. They only strengthen Law's argument. Moreover, there is another factor he did not mention—the tobacco companies and their impact on the early days of professional baseball and today's baseball card industry. I think the case is pretty strong. As an enthusiastic fan of the sport of baseball, I conclude that in fact Durham is worthy of this designation, with an understanding that this moniker would

Figure 4–5. North Carolina Baseball Museum.

coexist with "City of Medicine." At the same time, I accept that maybe only avid fans of the sport would agree with this premise.

An excellent destination for another side trip out of Durham is the North Carolina Baseball Museum. This museum is unique in that it focuses on baseball leagues and teams that have been located in the state of North Carolina and players who are native to the state. Figure 4–5 shows a photo of the museum, which is located at Fleming Stadium in Wilson, North Carolina. The North Carolina Baseball Museum is an easy approximately 70 mile or 1 hour drive from Durham and is a highlight of any North Carolina baseball trip.

Attractions in or Near Durham

Baseball

• **North Carolina Baseball Museum at Historic Fleming Stadium,** 300 Stadium St., Wilson, NC 27893 (252) 296–3048
• **Historic Durham Athletic Park (DAP),** 28 Morris St., Durham, NC 27701

- **Durham Bulls Home Game at Durham Bulls Athletic Park**, 409 Blackwell St., Durham, NC 27701 (919) 687–6500
- **Carolina Mudcats Home Game at Five County Stadium,** 1501 NC Highway 39, Zebulon, NC 27597 (919) 267–2287
- **Burlington Royals Home Game at Burlington Athletic Stadium,** 1450 Graham St., Burlington, NC 27217 (336) 222–0223
- **Wilson Tobs Home Game at Fleming Stadium,** 300 Stadium St., Wilson, NC 27893 (252) 291–8627
- **North Carolina Tar Heels Home Game at Boshamer Stadium,** 235 Ridge Rd., Chapel Hill, NC 27599
- **North Carolina State University Wolfpack Game at Doak Field,** 1081 Varsity Dr., Raleigh, NC (919) 865–1510
- **Duke University Blue Devils Game at Jack Coombs Field,** 101 Whitford Dr., Durham, NC 27708 (919) 681–2583
- **USA Baseball Collegiate National Team Game at the USA Baseball National Training Complex (or another stadium in NC),** 200 Brooks Park Ln., Cary, NC (919) 459–0761

Non-Sports

- **Brightleaf Square Shopping and Dining,** 905 W. Main St., Durham, NC 27701 (919) 682–9229
- **American Tobacco Historic District Dining and Entertainment**, 318 Blackwell St., Durham, NC 27701 (919) 433–1566
- **Ninth Street District—Shopping, Dining, and Entertainment,** Ninth St. between Green St. and W. Main St., Durham, NC 27705
- **Museum of Life and Science,** 433 W. Murray Ave., Durham, NC 27704 (919) 220–5429
- **Sarah P. Duke Gardens,** 420 Anderson St., Durham, NC 27708 (919) 684–3698

Dining in or Near Durham

Brewpubs and Breweries

- **Bull City Burger and Brewery,** 107 E. Parrish St., Durham, NC 27701 (919) 680–2333
- **Boylan Bridge Brewpub**, 201 S. Boylan St., Raleigh, NC 27603 (919) 803–8927

- **Carolina Brewery**, 460 W. Franklin St., Chapel Hill, NC 27516 (919) 942–1800
- **Top of the Hill Restaurant & Brewery**, 100 E. Franklin St., Chapel Hill, NC 27514 (919) 927–8676

RESTAURANTS IN THE AMERICAN TOBACCO CAMPUS

- **Mellow Mushroom**, 410 Blackwell St., Durham, NC 27701 (919) 680–8500
- **Tobacco Road Sports Café**, 280 S. Mangum Street, Durham, NC 27701 (919) 937–9909
- **Tyler's Restaurant and Taproom**, 324 Blackwell St., Durham, NC 27701 (919) 433–0345

RESTAURANTS IN OR NEAR BRIGHTLEAF SQUARE

- **Alivia's Durham Bistro**, 900 W. Main St., Durham, NC 27701 (919) 682–8978
- **Fishmonger's Restaurant & Oyster Bar**, 806 W. Main St., Durham, NC 27701 (919) 682–0128
- **Satisfaction Restaurant and Bar**, 905 W. Main St., Durham, NC 27701 (919) 682–7397

OTHER RESTAURANTS IN OR NEAR DURHAM

- **Bullock's Bar-B-Cue**, 3330 Quebec Dr., Durham, NC 27705 (919) 383–3211
- **Elmo's Diner**, 776 9th St., Durham NC 27705 (919) 416–3823, and 200 N. Greensboro St., Carrboro, NC 27510 (919) 927–2909
- **Mitch's Tavern**, 2426 Hillsborough St., Raleigh, NC 27607 (919) 821–7771
- **The Pit Authentic Barbecue**, 328 W. Davie St., Raleigh, NC 27601 (919) 890–4500
- **Parker's Barbecue**, 2514 U.S. Highway 301, Wilson, NC 27893 (252) 237–0972
- **Dick's Hotdog Stand,** 1500 N. Nash St., Wilson, NC 27893 (252) 243–6313

The South Atlantic League Baseball Road Trip—Itinerary 1

The closeness of the teams of a lower level minor league, such as the South Atlantic League, offers a number of baseball travel opportunities. As suggested in the Introduction, the avid baseball enthusiast might be motivated to set a goal to attend a home game of each team in the league. The plan could be to do this all in one baseball season or over a number of seasons. A less aggressive approach might be to see as many of the teams as can be traveled to with day-trips from a centralized hub city and then possibly a few more teams with short overnight trips to stadiums that can be easily reached from the hub. Earlier I proposed Durham, North Carolina, as an interesting city with a rich baseball history that can be used as an enjoyable hub location for attending Sally League games.

Table 5–1 lists the stadium and its address for each of the teams of the South Atlantic League. Included in the table are the travel mileage and time to each team's stadium from the Durham hub. The reference origin from which all distances and times are measured is the Raleigh-Durham International Airport (RDU), which is actually located a short distance from Durham in the suburb city of Morrisville, North Carolina.

For the moment I am making the assumption that the goal is the South Atlantic League Baseball Road Trip—that is, to attend a game at the home stadium of each of the South Atlantic League teams. In this chapter and the one that follows, I will outline three different itineraries based on various day-trips and 2-game, 3-game, 4-game, and 5-game road trips that will offer alternative solutions for attending home games of the various SAL teams. These road trip plans or a blend of their elements may be employed to accomplish this goal.

If your goal is not to see a home game played by each of the teams in

Team	Stadium	Stadium Address	Miles*	Time*
Greensboro Grasshoppers	NewBridge Bank Park	408 Bellemeade St. Greensboro, NC	67	1 Hr 15 Min
Kannapolis Intimidators	CMC-NorthEast Stadium	2888 Moose Rd. Kannapolis, NC	131	2 Hr 13 Min
Hickory Crawdads	L. P. Frans Stadium	2500 Clement Blvd. NW Hickory, NC	166	2 Hr 48 Min
Asheville Tourists	McCormick Field	30 Buchanan Pl. Asheville, NC	238	3 Hr 58 Min
Greenville Drive	Fluor Field at the West End	945 S. Main St. Greenville, SC	255	4 Hr 20 Min
Charleston RiverDogs	Joseph P. Riley Jr. Park	360 Fishburne St. Charleston, SC	292	5 Hr 2 Min
West Virginia Power	Appalachian Power Park	601 Morris St. Charleston, WV	308	5 Hr 9 Min
Augusta GreenJackets	Lake Olmstead Stadium	78 Milledge Rd. Augusta, GA	313	5 Hr 1 Min
Hagerstown Suns	Municipal Stadium	274 Memorial Blvd. Hagerstown, MD	330	5 Hr 40 Min
Delmarva Shorebirds	Arthur W. Perdue Stadium	6400 Hobbs Rd. Salisbury, MD	333	6 Hr 4 Min
Savannah Sand Gnats	William L. Grayson Stadium	1401 E. Victory Dr. Savannah, GA	341	5 Hr 27 Min
Rome Braves	State Mutual Stadium	755 Braves Blvd. Rome, GA	456	7 Hr 39 Min
Lakewood BlueClaws	FirstEnergy Park	2 Stadium Way Lakewood, NJ	472	8 Hr 17 Min
Lexington Legends	Whitaker Bank Ballpark	207 Legends Ln. Lexington, KY	481	7 Hr 46 Min

Table 5–1. Travel distance and time chart from the hub city—Durham, NC.

the South Atlantic League, I can understand that, too! The road trip plans I am about to propose may be selectively applied to attend home games for your preferred teams or to see all of them play in a game, but not necessarily at home. Don't want to see a baseball game played by each of the teams in the SAL? That is okay, too. Later I will also examine some alternative lesser baseball road trip objectives.

But first here are some formulas for seeing a game played by each SAL team at its home stadium. In the planning of the baseball road trips outlined in this and the following chapter, I have grouped the SAL teams according to their general direction relative to Durham, North Carolina:

- Cities south of Durham: Charleston, South Carolina; Augusta, Georgia; and Savannah Georgia
- Cities west of Durham: Greensboro, North Carolina; Kannapolis, North Carolina; Hickory, North Carolina; Asheville, North Carolina; Greenville, South Carolina; and Rome, Georgia
- Cities northwest of Durham: Charleston, West Virginia; and Lexington, Kentucky
- Cities north of Durham: Hagerstown, Maryland; Salisbury, Maryland; and Lakewood, New Jersey.

Then, I used these general directions in the naming of the various baseball trips (for instance, Southern Road Trip and Northwestern Road Trip).

One-Game Day-Trips from the Durham Hub—Grasshoppers, Intimidators, and Crawdads

The travel information provided in Table 5–1 gives us a frame of reference that may be used to plan travel from the Durham, North Carolina, hub to each of the stadiums of the South Atlantic League. My assumption is that baseball teams within 200 miles with a one-way travel time of approximately 3 hours or less could be candidates for attending a game as a day-trip. Using this as my guide, the data in Table 5–1 suggests that home games of the Greensboro Grasshoppers, Kannapolis Intimidators, and Hickory Crawdads could be attended by making a day-trip from the Durham area. These teams are affiliates of the Miami Marlins, Chicago White Sox, and the Texas Rangers, respectively, and are all members of the Northern Division of the South Atlantic League.

Potentially the longer distances, such as Hickory and Kannapolis, could be planned around a date that offers a day game. This would allow for more travel time both before and after the game. Three teams down and eleven more to go!

Hickory too far? Maybe—2 hours and 48 minutes each way is kind of close to the travel time limit for a day trip. It's only realistic for a day game.

Two-Game Road Trip Plans Originating from Durham

   Games for the teams that require a trip between 200 and 350 miles could be attended by planning a short overnight stay away from the Durham area. Next I will outline a number of two-game baseball road trips that will get us to the home stadiums of most of the other teams of the South Atlantic League.

Southern Road Trip—RiverDogs and Sand Gnats

   I will assume that dates have been identified for when both the Charleston RiverDogs (New York Yankees) and Savannah Sand Gnats (New York Mets) are playing at home and plan a southern baseball road trip to attend games on consecutive days in those two cities. For the moment, I will assume that this route requires 1-night stays at or near both Charleston, South Carolina, and Savannah, Georgia.
   Table 5–2 outlines a travel plan for this southern road trip that first takes you to Charleston for a RiverDogs game at Joseph P. Riley Jr. Park and then

Teams	Origin/Destination	Miles*	Cum. Miles	Travel Time*	Cum. Time
Starting point	RDU, 2400 W. Terminal Blvd. Morrisville, NC	0	0	0 Hr 0 Min	0 Hr 0 Min
Charleston RiverDogs	Joseph P. Riley Jr. Park, 360 Fishburne St. Charleston, SC	295	295	4 Hr 41 Min	4 Hr 41 Min
Savannah Sand Gnats	William L. Grayson Stadium, 1401 E. Victory Dr. Savannah, GA	110	405	2 Hr 10 Min	6 Hr 51 Min
Ending point	RDU, 2400 W. Terminal Blvd. Morrisville, NC	340	745	5 Hr 24 Min	12 Hr 15 Min

Table 5–2. Charleston RiverDogs–Savannah Sand Gnats two-game southern road trip travel plan.

the next day continues south to Savannah to see the Sand Gnats play at their home ballpark, William L. Grayson Stadium. The table shows estimated travel distances and drive times for each leg of the route as well as the cumulative travel distance and drive time. By taking this 2-game trip you will log approximately 745 miles and spend a minimum of 12 hours and 15 minutes in the car. Based on the RiverDogs and Sand Gnats game schedules, the order in which the cities of these two SAL Southern Division teams are visited could possibly be reversed.

Both Charleston and Savannah are interesting tourist destinations. They offer a wide range of historic points of interest, a number of tourist attractions, a broad selection of dining experiences, and a variety of lodging opportunities. For more details on the attractions and amenities offered by these cities check the information provided in the Charleston and Savannah team profiles in Chapter 3.

Note from Table 5–2 that the distance between Joseph P. Riley Jr. Park in Charleston and William L. Grayson Stadium in Savannah is just 110 miles and is approximately a 2-hour, 10-minute drive. This fact suggests that there are some other possible variations for the trip plan. For instance, if you could attend a Savannah Sand Gnats day game, instead of an evening game, the Savannah leg of the trip could be done as a day-trip from Charleston. This would enable you to extend your stay in Charleston by another night.

If you can arrive in Charleston on the first day of the trip in time to attend a RiverDogs day game, another variation on the trip plan is possible. In this case, post game you could travel on to Savannah and have an extended stay there instead of remaining overnight in Charleston.

How about a day game in Charleston and a night game the same day in Savannah? Interesting idea! Yes—possible, but only if your starting point is not Durham. The trip needs to originate in a town or city closer to the one in which you plan to attend the day game, or maybe you could arrive in that city the evening before the first game. Two games in the same day—definitely an opportunity for two stadiums that are closer together, such as those in Asheville and Greenville or Asheville and Hickory.

Southwestern Road Trip—GreenJackets and Braves

Let's assume that the southern route was taken and games were already attended at Charleston and Savannah. Therefore, you are poised to take another road trip originating from the Durham hub. The next step could be another 2-day road trip that would take you to see a game of the Augusta GreenJackets

Teams	Origin/Destination	Miles*	Cum. Miles	Travel Time*	Cum. Time
Starting point	RDU, 2400 W. Terminal Blvd. Morrisville, NC	0	0	0 Hr 0 Min	0 Hr 0 Min
Augusta GreenJackets	Lake Olmstead Stadium, 78 Milledge Rd. Augusta, GA	313	313	5 Hr 1 Min	5 Hr 1 Min
Rome Braves	State Mutual Stadium, 755 Braves Blvd. Rome, GA	219	532	3 Hr 42 Min	8 Hr 43 Min
Ending point	RDU, 2400 W. Terminal Blvd. Morrisville, NC	456	988	7 Hr 38 Min	16 Hr 21 Min

Table 5-3. Augusta GreenJackets–Rome Braves two-game southwestern road trip travel plan.

(San Francisco Giants) at Lake Olmstead Stadium and then make a second stop for a Rome Braves (Atlanta Braves) game at State Mutual Stadium.

The southwestern trip, which is outlined in Table 5–3, is planned for this purpose. As shown in the table, the first leg of the trip takes you approximately 313 miles south of Durham to Augusta, Georgia, and the second leg travels 219 miles west to Rome, Georgia. Both the Augusta GreenJackets and Rome Braves, like the RiverDogs and Sand Gnats, are members of the Southern Division of the South Atlantic League.

Western Road Trip—Tourists and Drive

Assuming that you have already completed both the southern route and the southwestern route to attend games of the Charleston RiverDogs, Savannah Sand Gnats, Augusta GreenJackets, and Rome Braves, the next teams on the list to see might be the Asheville Tourists and Greenville Drive. The Drive is the South Atlantic League affiliate of the Boston Red Sox and the team in Asheville is a Colorado Rockies minor league club. Both the Drive and Tourists are members of the Southern Division of the SAL.

These cities, which are located west of Durham, are the target destinations of the western road trip route outlined in Table 5–4. The summary of

Teams	Origin/Destination	Miles*	Cum. Miles	Travel Time*	Cum. Time
Starting point	RDU, 2400 W. Terminal Blvd. Morrisville, NC	0	0	0 Hr 0 Min	0 Hr 0 Min
Asheville Tourists	McCormick Field, 30 Buchanan Pl. Asheville, NC	238	238	3 Hr 58 Min	3 Hr 58 Min
Greenville Drive	Fluor Field, 945 S. Main St. Greenville, SC	64	302	1 Hr 21 Min	5 Hr 19 Min
Ending point	RDU, 2400 W. Terminal Blvd. Morrisville, NC	255	557	4 Hr 18 Min	9 Hr 37 Min

Table 5–4. Asheville Tourists–Greenville Drive two-game western road trip travel plan.

estimated travel distances and times in Table 5–4 shows that the Greenville Drive's home, Fluor Field, and McCormick Field, where the Asheville Tourists play, are just 64 miles apart. This should permit an overnight stay to be made in either town. Also, the 1-hour and 21-minute drive time between stadiums should allow the opportunity to attend a day game of one team and an evening game of the other in the same day.

Northwestern Road Trip—Power and Legends

With the single day and two-game trips I have suggested so far, it is possible to make a plan for attending games at the home stadiums of all nine South Atlantic League teams that reside in North Carolina, South Carolina, and Georgia. The benefit of these short trips is that the goal of attending a game of each SAL team could be achieved over a period of time. Maybe all of them could be done as weekend road trips.

However, we are still left with attending home games of the five teams that play in states to the north of North Carolina: West Virginia Power, Charleston, West Virginia; Lexington Legends, Lexington, Kentucky; and the three northernmost teams—the Hagerstown Suns, Delmarva Shorebirds, and Lakewood BlueClaws. Planning a road trip to attend games in Charleston and Lexington is next on the agenda.

Teams	Origin/Destination	Miles*	Cum. Miles	Travel Time*	Cum. Time
Starting point	RDU, 2400 W. Terminal Blvd. Morrisville, NC	0	0	0 Hr 0 Min	0 Hr 0 Min
West Virginia Power	Appalachian Power Park, 601 Morris St. Charleston, WV	308	308	5 Hr 9 Min	5 Hr 9 Min
Lexington Legends	Whitaker Bank Ballpark, 207 Legends Ln. Lexington, KY	174	482	2 Hr 41 Min	7 Hr 50 Min
Ending point	RDU, 2400 W. Terminal Blvd. Morrisville, NC	482	964	7 Hr 45 Min	15 Hr 35 Min

Table 5–5. West Virginia Power–Lexington Legends two-game northwestern road trip travel plan.

The West Virginia Power and Lexington Legends are located northwest of the hub city of Durham, North Carolina, but are somewhat farther away than most of the teams in the southern and western cities. However, they are relatively close to each other and their cities are linked by an express highway. Table 5–5 outline a northwestern road trip route that may be taken to attend home games of these two teams. The first stop is for a game at the home of the West Virginia Power, Appalachian Power Park, in Charleston, West Virginia. The Power is the South Atlantic League affiliate of the Pittsburgh Pirates and a member of the Northern Division. The next day you can take the 174-mile, 2-hour and 41-minute ride to Whitaker Bank Ballpark in Lexington, Kentucky, to see the Legends play. The Lexington team is a member of the Southern Division and the single-A affiliate of the Kansas City Royals. The distance and time associated with this route suggest that an overnight stay should be made in each city.

Three-Game Northern Road Trip Plan—Suns, Blue-Claws, and Shorebirds

After making the northwestern trip to Charleston and Lexington, you will have attended home games of eleven of the fourteen teams of the SAL.

That leaves just three cities on the South Atlantic League Baseball Road Trip travel list: Hagerstown, Maryland; Salisbury, Maryland; and Lakewood, New Jersey. Although the home stadiums of the Hagerstown Suns, Delmarva Shorebirds, and Lakewood BlueClaws are somewhat aligned on a northern route from the Durham hub, they are all quite far away. Municipal Stadium, the home of the Hagerstown Suns, is the closest, but it still requires a 330-mile, 5-hour and 40-minute drive, and Lakewood is another 238 miles farther north. For this reason, it is not practical to plan attending a game at these three locations using 2-game trips. Instead, they should all be attended together in a single three-game road trip. In this section, I outline a northern 3-game trip that will complete a first itinerary for our South Atlantic League Baseball Road Trip adventure.

Table 5–6 outlines a solution for a 3-game northern road trip that originates in the Durham area and takes you to the stadiums of all three of these Northern Division teams—the Hagerstown Suns (Washington Nationals affiliate), Lakewood BlueClaws (Philadelphia Phillies affiliate), and Delmarva Shorebirds (Baltimore Orioles affiliate). This table shows that the travel dis-

Teams	Origin/Destination	Miles*	Cum. Miles	Travel Time*	Cum. Time
Starting point	RDU, 2400 W. Terminal Blvd. Morrisville, NC	0	0	0 Hr 0 Min	0 Hr 0 Min
Hagerstown Suns	Municipal Stadium, 274 Memorial Blvd. Hagerstown, MD	330	330	5 Hr 40 Min	5 Hr 40 Min
Lakewood BlueClaws	FirstEnergy Park, 2 Stadium Way Lakewood, NJ	238	568	4 Hr 7 Min	9 Hr 47 Min
Delmarva Shorebirds	Arthur W. Perdue Stadium, 6400 Hobbs Rd. Salisbury, MD	197	765	3 Hr 44 Min	13 Hr 31 Min
Ending point	RDU, 2400 W. Terminal Blvd. Morrisville, NC	333	1098	6 Hr 5 Min	19 Hr 36 Min

Table 5–6. Hagerstown Sun, Lakewood BlueClaws, and Delmarva Shorebirds three-game northern road trip travel plan.

tance to the first stop, which is in Hagerstown, Maryland, for a Suns game, and the return from the Shorebirds game in Salisbury, Maryland, are both over 300 miles. Because all of the cities are more than a 300-mile drive from Durham, you probably need to plan for three overnight stays and allocate four days to complete this route.

Summary for Itinerary 1

Once you have made this northern trip, the goal of the South Atlantic League Baseball Road Trip is complete. Table 5–7 summarizes the first itinerary that was created. Following it you can attend a home game of each of the fourteen teams of the SAL by making eight independent road trips—

Trip Number	Type	Team(s)	Miles*	Cum. Miles	Travel Time*	Cum. Time
1	1-Game	Greensboro Grasshoppers	67	67	1 Hr 15 Min	1 Hr 15 Min
2	1-Game	Kinnapolis Intimidators	131	198	2 Hr 13 Min	3Hr 28 Min
3	1-Game	Hickory Crawdads	166	364	2 Hr 48 Min	6 Hr 16 Min
4	2-Game	Charleston RiverDogs, Savannah Sand Gnats	745	1109	12 Hr 15 Min	18 Hr 31 Min
5	2-Game	Augusta GreenJackets, Rome Braves	983	2092	16 Hr 21 Min	34 Hr 52 Min
6	2-Game	Asheville Tourists, Greenville Drive	556	2648	7 Hr 53 Min	42 Hr 45 Min
7	2-Game	West Virginia Power, Lexington Legends	964	3612	15 Hr 35 Min	58 Hr 20 Min
8	3-Game	Hagerstown Suns, Lakewood BlueClaws, Delmarva Shorebirds	1098	4710	19 Hr 36 Min	77 Hr 56 Min

Table 5–7. Summary of the independent trips needed to complete Itinerary 1 for the South Atlantic League Baseball Road Trip.

three day trips, four 2-game trips, and one 3-game trip. The individual routes require you to travel a total of 4710 miles and at a minimum spend close to 78 hours behind the steering wheel. Too many miles? Too much time? In the next chapter I will look at some ways to reduce the distance and time.

Selecting the Dates of the Games for the Baseball Road Trips

Now that individual road trips for Itinerary 1 have been defined, the last step is to review the schedules of the individual teams to identify windows of time when all of the teams for which games are to be attended are playing at their home stadiums. But first, some general information about the organization of baseball league team schedules.

The home and away schedules of the teams of all baseball leagues tend to follow a pattern. For a smaller league like the South Atlantic League, there are typically two different base schedule patterns and possibly a variant or two on each of them. Usually about one-half of the teams in the league have home and away schedules that are similar to one base pattern. The other half of the teams follow a second base home-away schedule pattern, which is typ-

July						
Sun	Mon	Tues	Wed	Thur	Fri	Sat
	1 Home	2 Home	3 Home	4 @Away	5 @Away	6 @Away
7 @Away	8 Off	9 Home	10 Home	11 Home	12 Home	13 Home
14 @Home	15 @Home	16 Off	17 @Away	18 @Away	19 @Away	20 @Away
21 @Away	22 @Away	23 @Away	24 Off	25 Home	26 Home	27 Home
28 Home	29 Home	30 Home	31 Home			

July						
Sun	Mon	Tues	Wed	Thur	Fri	Sat
	1 @Away	2 @Away	3 @Away	4 Home	5 Home	6 Home
7 Home	8 Off	9 @Away	10 @Away	11 @Away	12 @Away	13 @Away
14 @Away	15 @Away	16 Off	17 Home	18 Home	19 Home	20 Home
21 Home	22 Home	23 Home	24 Off	25 @Away	26 @Away	27 @Away
28 @Away	29 @Away	30 @Away	31 @Away			

Top: Table 5–8(a). Schedule template #1—Asheville, Charleston, Kannapolis, and Lakewood. *Above:* Table 5–8(b). Schedule template #2—Delmarva, Greenville, Hickory, and Rome. *Following page top:* Table 5–8(c). Schedule template #3—Hagerstown, Lexington, and Savannah. *Following page bottom:* Table 5–8(d). Schedule template #4—Augusta, Greensboro, and West Virginia.

July						
Sun	Mon	Tues	Wed	Thur	Fri	Sat
	1 Home	2 Home	3 Home	4 @Away	5 @Away	6 @Away
7 @Away	8 Off	9 Home	10 Home	11 Home	12 Home	13 Home
14 @Home	15 @Home	16 Off	17 @Away	18 @Away	19 @Away	20 @Away
21 @Away	22 @Away	23 @Away	24 Off	25 Home	26 Home	27 Home
28 Home	29 @Away	30 @Away	31 @Away			

July						
Sun	Mon	Tues	Wed	Thur	Fri	Sat
	1 @Away	2 @Away	3 @Away	4 Home	5 Home	6 Home
7 Home	8 Off	9 @Away	10 @Away	11 @Away	12 @Away	13 @Away
14 @Away	15 @Away	16 Off	17 Home	18 Home	19 Home	20 Home
21 Home	22 Home	23 Home	24 Off	25 @Away	26 @Away	27 @Away
28 @Away	29 Home	30 Home	31 Home			

ically a mirror image of the first. That is, they are home when the other group of teams is away and vice versa. The pattern of the base schedules normally varies from month to month of the season.

I analyzed the July 2013 schedules of the South Atlantic League teams and found that all of them fit into one of the four home-away patterns shown in Tables 5–8 (a), (b), (c), and (d). Note that the two base patterns are those of Tables 5–8 (a) and (b). The table captions show that four of the SAL teams follow each of these base patterns. Notice that the teams (Asheville Tourists, Charleston RiverDogs, Kannapolis Intimidators, and Lakewood BlueClaws) that follow the pattern of Table 5–8 (a) start the month with a 3-game home stand and depart on a 4-game road trip on July 4. Four other teams, the Delmarva Shorebirds, Greenville Drive, Hickory Crawdads, and Rome Braves, follow the mirror image of that schedule, which is shown in Table 5–8 (b). Note that they all start the month on the road and return home on July 4. This pattern continues for the rest of the month. Whenever the teams using the schedule of Table 5–8 (a) go on the road, the teams following the schedule of Table 5–8 (b) start a home stand and vice versa.

The diagram of Table 5–8 (c) shows that three teams—the Hagerstown Suns, Lexington Legends, and Savannah Sand Gnats—follow a slight variation of the home-away schedule in Table 5–8 (a). The only difference between these two schedules is that the three teams that have the schedule shown in Table 5–8 (c) are away, not at home, on July 29 through July 31.

Similarly, the Augusta GreenJackets, Greensboro Grasshoppers, and West Virginia Power follow the schedule of Table 5–8 (d), which differs from that in Table 5–8 (b) in that these three teams are at home from July 29 through July 31, instead of away. In fact, the home-away schedules of Tables 5–8 (c) and (d) are mirror images of each other.

Once familiar with the similarities and differences of the schedules of the various teams, you are prepared to select the games required to implement the road trip. So I will demonstrate this process with a few examples. Let us begin by selecting games based on the July 2013 schedules to implement the Southern Road Trip of Table 5–2. This road trip is to travel south from the hub in Durham to see home games played by both the Charleston RiverDogs and Savannah Sand Gnats.

Note that the RiverDogs follow the schedule pattern of Table 5–8 (a) and the Sand Gnats that of Table 5–8 (c). That means with the exception of the last three days of the month of July both teams are at home the exact same days. Therefore, a trip could be made to see them play on consecutive days during three periods: July 1–3, July 9–15, or July 25–28. Moreover, the road trip could travel to the stadium of either team first.

As a second example, let us assume that you want to select games to implement the Western Road Trip of Table 5–4 to attend home games of the Greenville Drive and Asheville Tourists on consecutive days. This poses a small problem—the Tourists follow the schedule of Table 5–8 (a) and Drive the pattern of Table 5–8 (b). Therefore, they are never playing at home on the same day. The solution to this is that you have to catch a game of one team on the day before it departs on the road and a game of the other team on the next day as it arrives home. Reviewing these schedules shows that there is only one period in July during which games of these two teams can be attended on consecutive days—July 3 in Asheville and July 4 in Greenville. On the other hand, there are a number of other windows during which games could be attended with a day off between them. In fact for those periods, a game at either city could be attended first. For example, a home game of the Drive could be attended on July 7 followed by a Tourists game on July 9.

Having completed this exercise in analyzing the team schedules and selecting games to implement a two-day baseball road trip, you are equipped to plan your South Atlantic League Road Trip schedule and set out on the road.

Some Variation on the Travel Itineraries

Depending on your starting point and how you travel to the suggested hub city, Durham, North Carolina, there may be some opportunities for variations on these South Atlantic League Road Trip travel itineraries. If you are driving to Durham, instead of flying, you may be able to plan your travel dates to get a head start by attending some games on the way.

If traveling from the Northeast or one of the Mid-Atlantic States, you could potentially attend a Lakewood BlueClaws home game at FirstEnergy Park in Lakewood, New Jersey and Delmarva Shorebirds game at Arthur W. Perdue Stadium in Salisbury, Maryland, on the south-going trip and make a stop at Municipal Stadium in Hagerstown, Maryland, to see the Hagerstown Suns play a game on the return back north.

A similar strategy could be employed if you are traveling to the Durham area from the south, southwest, west, or northwest. For example, a trip originating in the south could potentially go through Savannah, Georgia, and Charleston, South Carolina, to attend games in those cities on your route to North Carolina. Maybe the return route back south could be planned to travel through Greenville, South Carolina, and Rome, Georgia, to take in Drive and Braves games on the way home.

6

The South Atlantic League Baseball Road Trip—More Itineraries

The design of Itinerary 1 for the South Atlantic League Baseball Road Trip focused on attending the games through a number of short trips. The benefit of this itinerary is that most of the trips could potentially be done over a weekend. But this has a disadvantage in that it results in a larger number of independent trips, which increases the miles traveled and driving time needed to attend a game at each of the fourteen stadiums of the South Atlantic League. Here I will devise two more itineraries that would allow you to do this more efficiently. The first of them—Itinerary 2—employs a series of 3-game road trips to visit all of the stadiums of the Sally League. Then, travel distance and time are further reduced by expanding the trip length to include 4 and 5 games in Itinerary 3. But extending the number of games attended per leg of the trip means that most of the time you may need to be on the road for three or more consecutive days and requires longer overnight stays away from home.

Additional Three-Game Road Trip Plans Originating from Durham—Itinerary 2

By using a number of 3-day road trips to attend games of the southern, western, and northwestern teams of the SAL, the South Atlantic League Baseball Road Trip can be completed with fewer independent trips, fewer miles on the road, and a shorter overall drive time.

Southern Road Trip—RiverDogs, Sand Gnats, and GreenJackets

Again, our route will begin toward the south, but this time planning a trip that takes in games of the Charleston RiverDogs, Savannah Sand Gnats, and Augusta GreenJackets. The cities in which these teams play are all conveniently located to each other and enable a little larger southern loop that knocks off these three teams in a single road trip.

The outline of the route for the 3-game southern road trip, which includes the city to city travel distances and times, is given in Table 6–1. Comparing this trip to the 2-day trip that included games in Charleston, South Carolina, and Savannah, Georgia (Table 5–2), shows that adding the western leg to attend a GreenJackets game at Lake Olmstead Stadium in Augusta, Georgia, adds just 146 miles (2 hours, 55 minutes) to the trip and in fact shortens the return trip to Durham by close to a half hour. But now it is no longer a weekend activity. You probably need either 3 or 4 days to complete the trip and possibly 3 overnight stays while out on the road.

Teams	Origin/Destination	Miles*	Cum. Miles	Travel Time*	Cum. Time
Starting point	RDU, 2400 W. Terminal Blvd. Morrisville, NC	0	0	0 Hr 0 Min	0 Hr 0 Min
Charleston RiverDogs	Joseph P. Riley, Jr. Park, 360 Fishburne St. Charleston, SC	295	295	4 Hr 41 Min	4 Hr 41 Min
Savannah Sand Gnats	William L. Grayson Stadium, 1401 E. Victory Dr. Savannah, GA	110	405	2 Hr 10 Min	6 Hr 51 Min
Augusta GreenJackets	Lake Olmstead Stadium, 78 Milledge Rd. Augusta, GA	146	551	2 Hr 55 Min	9 Hr 46 Min
Ending point	RDU, 2400 W. Terminal Blvd. Morrisville, NC	312	863	4 Hr 57 Min	14 Hr 43 Min

Table 6–1. Charleston RiverDogs, Savannah Sand Gnats, and Augusta GreenJackets three-game southern road trip travel plan.

Selecting the Games for the 3-Game Southern Road Trip

Before going on to plan the next 3-game road trip for Itinerary 2, I will again demonstrate how to select the games to implement a trip. The goal will be to find a window of days during which the southern road trip just outlined—RiverDogs, Sand Gnats, and GreenJackets—could be done by attending a home game of each team on consecutive days. To do this you need to refer back to the schedule templates of Tables 5–8 (a), (b), (c), and (d).

Earlier I showed that Charleston and Savannah followed the schedules of Tables 5–8 (a) and (c), respectively. That means that they are at home the same days of the month with the exception of the July 29 to 31 period. On the other hand, Augusta follows the schedule of Table 5–8 (d), which is the opposite of that for Savannah. Therefore, all three teams are never at home at the same time.

Reviewing the schedules shows that there are only two periods during the month of July when home games of these three teams could be attended on consecutive days. The first would be Charleston on July 2, Savannah on July 3, and Augusta on July 4. The other window of time is July 27 in Charleston, July 28 in Savannah, and July 29 in Augusta.

Western Road Trip—Tourists, Braves, and Drive

Just as an Augusta GreenJackets game was merged into the 2-game southern trip to Charleston and Savannah, a Rome Braves game can be added to the 2-game Tourists-Drive western road trip of Table 5–4. The travel plan that results is outlined in Table 6–2. The first game is attended in Asheville, a stop is added at State Mutual Stadium in Rome, Georgia, for a Braves game by traveling southward, and the return back to Durham is via Greenville. This shortens the last leg of the trip, the return to Durham, and at the same time contributes positively to reducing the overall driving distance and travel time for Itinerary 2. The city to city distances and times for this new, extended 3-game western loop are summarized in the table.

Northwestern Road Trip—Crawdads, Legends, and Power

Next I will convert the 2-game northwestern road trip of Table 5–5 that took us to see games of the West Virginia Power and Lexington Legends

Teams	Origin/Destination	Miles*	Cum. Miles	Travel Time*	Cum. Time
Starting point	RDU, 2400 W. Terminal Blvd. Morrisville, NC	0	0	0 Hr 0 Min	0 Hr 0 Min
Asheville Tourists	McCormick Field, 30 Buchanan Pl. Asheville, NC	238	238	3 Hr 58 Min	3 Hr 58 Min
Rome Braves	State Mutual Stadium, 755 Braves Blvd. Rome, GA	230	468	4 Hr 36 Min	8 Hr 34 Min
Greenville Drive	Fluor Field, 945 S. Main St. Greenville, SC	204	672	3 Hr 30 Min	12 Hr 04 Min
Ending point	RDU, 2400 W. Terminal Blvd. Morrisville, NC	255	927	4 Hr 18 Min	16 Hr 22 Min

Table 6–2. Asheville Tourists, Rome Braves, and Greenville Drive three-game western road trip travel plan.

into a 3-game trip by adding a stop in Hickory, North Carolina. This new route, which is outlined in Table 6–3, has a stop to attend a Crawdads game added as the first leg of the route and then continues on to Lexington, Kentucky, for game 2. The stop in Hickory offers two advantages. Since Hickory is right on the route between the hub in Durham, North Carolina, and Whitaker Bank Ballpark in Lexington, Kentucky, it breaks up the long drive between these two cities. Also, it eliminates the long day-trip that was used to attend a Crawdads game in the first travel itinerary.

The driving distances and times for this new road trip are given in the table. By reversing the order in which Power and Legend games are attended, the extra long return trip from Lexington, Kentucky, in the prior 2-game trip is eliminated. The return via Charleston, West Virginia, is still quite long, but the 308-mile, 5-hour and 6-minute drive is approximately 175 miles shorter than that from Lexington and about 2 hours, 45 minutes faster. Because of the long distances between these three ballparks, you probably need to allocate 4 days and 3 overnight stays to complete this road trip. This route could be taken in reverse order. That would lengthen the departure leg of the trip but has the advantage of shortening the return back to Durham after the game in Hickory.

Teams	Origin/Destination	Miles*	Cum. Miles	Travel Time*	Cum. Time
Starting point	RDU, 2400 W. Terminal Blvd. Morrisville, NC	0	0	0 Hr 0 Min	0 Hr 0 Min
Hickory Crawdads	L. P. Frans Stadium, 2500 Clement Blvd. NW Hickory, NC	166	166	2 Hr 49 Min	2 Hr 49 Min
Lexington Legends	Whitaker Bank Ballpark, 207 Legends Ln. Lexington, KY	362	528	5 Hr 50 Min	8 Hr 39 Min
West Virginia Power	Appalachian Power Park, 601 Morris St. Charleston, WV	174	702	2 Hr 42 Min	11 Hr 21 Min
Ending point	RDU, 2400 W. Terminal Blvd. Morrisville, NC	308	1010	5 Hr 6 Min	16 Hr 26 Min

Table 6–3. Hickory Crawdads, Lexington Legends, and West Virginia Power three-game northwestern road trip travel plan.

Summary for Itinerary 2

A summary of Itinerary 2 for the South Atlantic League Baseball Road Trip is given in Table 6–4. Here our earlier day-trips to Greensboro and Kannapolis and the 3-game northern trip to the teams in Maryland and New Jersey are combined with the three new 3-game road trips outlined in this chapter to form a more efficient route for attending a game at the stadium of each of the fourteen South Atlantic League teams. Comparing the overall cumulative travel distance for these 6 road trip routes to that of Itinerary 1 in Table 5–7 shows that the total drive distance is now 4096 miles, reduced by more than 600 miles. Similarly, the amount of windshield face time has dropped to 70 hours and 35 minutes—a decrease of approximately 7 hours. This confirms that extending all of the 2-game trips to include a game of a third team has successfully shortened the distance travelled and reduced the overall drive time.

Trip Number	Type	Team(s)	Miles*	Cum. Miles	Travel Time*	Cum. Time
1	1-Game	Greensboro Grasshoppers	67	67	1 Hr 15 Min	1 Hr 15 Min
2	1-Game	Kannapolis Intimidators	131	198	2 Hr 13 Min	3Hr 28 Min
3	3-Game	Charleston RiverDogs, Savannah Sand Gnats, Augusta GreenJackets	863	1061	14 Hr 43 Min	18 Hr 11 Min
4	3-Game	Asheville Tourists, Rome Braves, Greenville Drive	927	1988	16 Hr 22 Min	34 Hr 33 Min
5	3-Game	Hickory Crawdads, Lexington Legends, West Virginia Power	1010	2998	16 Hr 26 Min	50 Hr 59 Min
6	3-Game	Hagerstown Suns, Lakewood BlueClaws, Delmarva Shorebirds	1098	4096	19 Hr 36 Min	70 Hr 35 Min

Table 6–4. Summary of Itinerary 2—a shortened trip to complete the South Atlantic League Baseball Road Trip.

Four- and Five-Game Road Trip Plans Originating from Durham—Itinerary 3

In Itinerary 2 the 2-day independent road trips were extended to three games and because of that both the overall distance you need to travel and time it took to complete the South Atlantic League Baseball Road Trip decreased. This idea can be extended further by adding more games to make 4-game and 5-game road trips. However, with trips this long it will be harder to find periods during which the schedules of all the teams line up to permit you to attend the games on consecutive days. The benefits of the longer road trips could again be a shorter total drive distance and less windshield time. But if the complexity of scheduling games led to the need for days off between cities, the overall duration of the road trip would increase, not decrease. If your schedule permits some free days, this could also be a good thing. The free days could be focused on other tourist activities or visiting attractions along the route.

Next I will propose a new road trip—Itinerary 3—based on two longer road trips—a southwest trip that will travel to the stadiums of five teams and a northwest trip that attends games of 4 teams. These two longer trips will be used to plan a new itinerary, which will further reduce travel distance and potentially time.

Five-Game Southwest Road Trip Plan—RiverDogs, Sand Gnats, GreenJackets, Braves, and Drive

A five-game southwest road trip route is summarized in Table 6–5. This trip makes a larger loop that first takes you southeast from the city of Durham, North Carolina, through the South Atlantic League cities of Charleston, South Carolina, and Savannah, Georgia, and then swings west to Augusta and Rome, Georgia, and finally returns to the hub by going northeast through Greensville, South Carolina. During this trip you will attend home games of all the teams in South Carolina and Georgia: Charleston RiverDogs, Savannah Sand Gnats, Augusta GreenJackets, Rome Braves, and Greenville Drive.

Table 6–5 shows that this 5-game route is much more efficient than the combination of the earlier 3-game Charleston, Savannah, and Augusta road trip (Table 6–1) and the alternative southwestern 2-day Greenville-Rome road trip (Table A1–2) provided in the Appendix. For example, the overall distance traveled drops from 1778 miles for the two independent road trips to just 1229 miles (approximately 30 percent) for this single five-game route. The drive time is reduced by a similar percentage, which is a real plus, but as mentioned earlier it may be hard to schedule this trip without taking days off because all of the teams are not playing at home during your schedule. So even though the total drive time is decreased, the overall time that it takes to complete the trip may expand significantly.

Selecting the Games for the Five-Game Southwest Road Trip

For both Itinerary 1 and 2, I demonstrated how games could be selected using the July 2013 schedule templates for the South Atlantic League in Tables 5–8 (a) through (d). When I suggested the idea of planning these longer trips, I pointed out that it might be harder, but not necessarily impossible, to schedule the games of a 4-game or 5-game road trip on consecutive days. Therefore, the trip plan might result in one or more days off on the route. Here I will reanalyze the schedules of Table 5–8 in an attempt to plan the games for the 5-game southwest road trip of Table 6–5 on consecutive days.

Teams	Origin/Destination	Miles*	Cum. Miles	Travel Time*	Cum. Time
Starting point	RDU, 2400 W. Terminal Blvd. Morrisville, NC	0	0	0 Hr 0 Min	0 Hr 0 Min
Charleston RiverDogs	Joseph P. Riley Jr. Park, 360 Fishburne St. Charleston, SC	295	292	4 Hr 41 Min	4 Hr 41 Min
Savannah Sand Gnats	William L. Grayson Stadium, 1401 E. Victory Dr. Savannah, GA	110	405	2 Hr 10 Min	6 Hr 51 Min
Augusta GreenJackets	Lake Olmstead Stadium, 78 Milledge Rd. Augusta, GA	146	551	2 Hr 55 Min	9 Hr 46 Min
Rome Braves	State Mutual Stadium, 755 Braves Blvd. Rome, GA	219	770	3 Hr 42 Min	13 Hr 28 Min
Greenville Drive	Fluor Field, 945 S. Main St. Greenville, SC	204	974	3 Hr 30 Min	16 Hr 58 Min
Ending point	RDU, 2400 W. Terminal Blvd. Morrisville, NC	255	1229	4 Hr 18 Min	21 Hr 16 Min

Table 6–5. Charleston RiverDogs, Savannah Sand Gnats, Augusta GreenJackets, Rome Braves, and Greenville Drive five-game southwest road trip travel plan.

The figure captions for Table 5–8 show which teams follow each of the schedule formats. For example, the first two stops in this trip are Charleston, South Carolina, and Savannah, Georgia. The schedules for the RiverDogs and Sand Gnats are those in Tables 5–8 (a) and (c), respectively. Earlier, I showed how the 3-game southern road trip that went to these two cities plus Augusta, Georgia, could be done in either the time window from July 2–4 or July 27–29.

This 5-game trip tags on two more stops after Augusta. They are to see a game of the Rome Braves at State Mutual Stadium in Rome, Georgia, on day four and then the Greenville Drive at Fluor Field at the West End in Greenville, South Carolina, on day five. Both the Brave and Drive follow the schedule outlined in Table 5–8 (b). Note that like the Augusta GreenJackets, they arrive to start a 4-game home stand on July 4. This matches perfectly with the other three teams. So the game sequence is Charleston on July 2, Savannah on the 3rd, Augusta on the 4th, Rome on the 5th and Greenville on the 6th. During this period, the five games can be attended on consecutive days. However, the trip would not work for the late July series of dates because both the Braves and Drive are on the road before, during, and after that interval of days.

Four-Game Northwest Road Trip Plan—Crawdads, Tourists, Legends, and Power

The 4-game northwest road trip of Table 6–6 first travels west to attend games of the Hickory Crawdads and Asheville Tourists and then turns north

Teams	Origin/Destination	Miles*	Cum. Miles	Travel Time*	Cum. Time
Starting point	RDU, 2400 W. Terminal Blvd. Morrisville, NC	0	0	0 Hr 0 Min	0 Hr 0 Min
Hickory Crawdads	L. P. Frans Stadium, 2500 Clement Blvd. NW Hickory, NC	166	166	2 Hr 48 Min	2 Hr 48 Min
Asheville Tourists	McCormick Field, 30 Buchanan Pl. Asheville, NC	78	244	1 Hr 20 Min	4 Hr 8 Min
Lexington Legends	Whitaker Bank Ballpark, 207 Legends Ln. Lexington, KY	287	531	4 Hr 41 Min	8 Hr 49 Min
West Virginia Power	Appalachian Power Park, 601 Morris St. Charleston, WV	174	705	2 Hr 42 Min	11 Hr 31 Min
Ending point	RDU, 2400 W. Terminal Blvd. Morrisville, NC	308	1013	5 Hr 6 Min	16 Hr 37 Min

Table 6–6. Hickory Crawdads, Asheville Tourists, Lexington Legends, and West Virginia Power four-game northwest road trip travel plan.

toward Kentucky and West Virginia to take in games of the Lexington Legends and West Virginia Power.

This extended road trip route has the same positive impact on the overall miles traveled and drive time. Comparing the cumulative miles and travel time in Table 6–6 to the independent 2-day trips—the alternative western Hickory-Asheville road trip (Table A1–3, Appendix) and West Virginia-Lexington road trip (Table 5–5)—shows that again the reductions in distance and drive time are about 30 percent.

Summary for Itinerary 3

By combining the new southwest route and northwest route with the earlier northern route to Hagerstown, Lakewood, and Delmarva and day-trips to Greensboro and Kannapolis results in Itinerary 3 for the South

Trip Number	Type	Team(s)	Miles*	Cum. Miles	Travel Time*	Cum. Time
1	1-Game	Greensboro Grasshoppers	67	67	1 Hr 15 Min	1 Hr 15 Min
2	1-Game	Kannapolis Intimidators	131	198	2 Hr 13 Min	3Hr 28 Min
3	5-Game	Charleston RiverDogs, Savannah Sand Gnats, Augusta GreenJackets, Rome Braves, Greenville Drive	1229	1427	21 Hr 16 Min	24 Hr 44 Min
4	4-Game	Hickory Crawdads, Asheville Tourists, Lexington Legends, West Virginia Power	1013	2440	16 Hr 37 Min	41 Hr 21 Min
5	3-Game	Hagerstown Suns, Lakewood BlueClaws, Delmarva Shorebirds	1098	3538	19 Hr 36 Min	60 Hr 57 Min

Table 6–7. Summary for Itinerary 3—tuning the South Atlantic League Baseball Road Trip a little more.

Atlantic League Baseball Road Trip. A summary of the city to city and cumulative distances traveled and drive times for this new route is given in Table 6–7. Comparing these results to those of Itinerary 2 in Table 6–4 shows that the overall distance traveled has dropped by over 500 miles. Finally, the cumulative travel time dropped by almost 10 hours.

In this chapter and the prior chapter, I have outlined three independent itineraries that outline different options for planning your South Atlantic League Baseball Road Trip. Moreover, I demonstrated how the team schedules may be interpreted to select dates for the games of the individual road trip elements. It is time to plan your own South Atlantic League adventure. You could use one of the itineraries that I have outlined, combine segments of those itineraries, or create your own custom South Atlantic Baseball Road Trip itinerary and take to the road.

7

Baseball Road Trip Options for Fans of a Specific Team

Earlier I mentioned that I would make other baseball road trip suggestions that might appeal to a fan of a specific team. Also I pointed out that other leagues in addition to the South Atlantic League had teams accessible from the Durham, North Carolina, area. Three other leagues—the International League (AAA), Carolina League (A+), and Appalachian League (Rk) have teams located in North Carolina. Finally, a fourth league, the Eastern League (AA), has a team in Richmond, Virginia, which is near the northeastern border of North Carolina and a little more than 160 miles from Durham. Lists of the teams that play in each of these leagues and their affiliate major league clubs are given in Table 7–1 (a), (b), (c), and (d), respectively.

A number of the major league baseball clubs that have a minor league team in the South Atlantic League also have an affiliate in one or more of the other four leagues identified in Table 7–1. This would enable a fan of one of those teams to attend a game of more than one of the minor league affiliates of their favorite team as part of a baseball road trip from the Durham hub.

Teams from Other Leagues That Are Within a Day-Trip Driving Distance of Durham

In Table 7–2 I have listed the teams from each of these four leagues that are potentially close enough to Durham, North Carolina, to travel to as a day-trip. Again I have set the benchmark for being close enough for a day-trip as the team residing within 200 miles and a 3-hour drive of the hub city. Three of the teams, the Salem Red Sox, Pulaski Yankees, and Myrtle Beach Pelicans, slightly exceed this metric, but I have included them for a different

North Division		
Team	Location	Affiliation
Buffalo Bisons	Buffalo, NY	Toronto Blue Jays
Lehigh Valley IronPigs	Allentown, PA	Philadelphia Phillies
Pawtucket Red Sox	Pawtucket, RI	Boston Red Sox
Rochester Red Wings	Rochester, NY	Minnesota Twins
Scranton/Wilkes-Barre RailRiders	Moosic, PA	New York Yankees
Syracuse Chiefs	Syracuse, NY	Washington Nationals
South Division		
Team	Location	Affiliation
Charlotte Knights	Charlotte, NC	Chicago White Sox
Durham Bulls	Durham, NC	Tampa Bay Rays
Gwinnett Braves	Lawrenceville, GA	Atlanta Braves
Norfolk Tides	Norfolk, VA	Baltimore Orioles
West Division		
Team	Location	Affiliation
Columbus Clippers	Columbus, OH	Cleveland Indians
Indianapolis Indians	Indianapolis, IN	Pittsburgh Pirates
Louisville Bats	Louisville, KY	Cincinnati Reds
Toledo Mud Hens	Toledo, OH	Detriot Tigers

Northern Division		
Team	Location	Affiliation
Frederick Keys	Frederick, MD	Baltimore Orioles
Lynchburg Hillcats	Lynchburg, VA	Cleveland Indians
Potomac Nationals	Woodbridge, VA	Washington Nationals
Wilmington Blue Rocks	Wilmington, DE	Kansas City Royals
Southern Division		
Team	Location	Affiliation
Carolina Mudcats	Zebulon, NC	Atlanta Braves
Myrtle Beach Pelicans	Myrtle Beach, SC	Chicago Cubs
Salem Red Sox	Salem, VA	Boston Red Sox
Winston-Salem Dash	Winston-Salem, NC	Chicago White Sox

Top: Table 7–1(a). International League teams and their affiliations. *Above*: Table 7–1(b). Carolina League teams and their affiliations. *Following page top*: Table 7–1(c). Appalachian League teams and their affiliations. *Following page bottom*: Table 7–1(d). Eastern League teams and their affiliations.

East Division		
Team	Location	Affiliation
Bluefield Blue Jays	Bluefield, WV	Toronto Blue Jays
Burlington Royals	Burlington, NC	Kansas City Royals
Danville Braves	Danville, VA	Atlanta Braves
Princeton Rays	Princeton, WV	Tampa Bay Rays
Pulaski Yankees	Pulaski, VA	New York Yankees
West Division		
Team	Location	Affiliation
Bristol Pirates	Bristol, VA	Pittsburgh Pirates
Elizabethton Twins	Elizabethton, TN	Minnesota Twins
Greeneville Astros	Greeneville, TN	Houston Astros
Johnson City Cardinals	Johnson City, TN	St. Louis Cardinals
Kingsport Mets	Kingsport, TN	New York Mets

Eastern Division		
Team	Location	Affiliation
Binghamton Mets	Binghamton, NY	New York Mets
New Britain Rock Cats	New Britain, CT	Colorado Rockies
New Hampshire Fisher Cats	Manchester, NH	Toronto Blue Jays
Portland Sea Dogs	Portland, ME	Boston Red Sox
Reading Fightin Phils	Reading, PA	Philadelphia Phillies
Trenton Thunder	Trenton, NJ	New York Yankees
Western Division		
Team	Location	Affiliation
Akron RubberDucks	Akron, OH	Cleveland Indians
Altoona Curve	Altoona, PA	Pittsburgh Pirates
Bowie Baysox	Bowie, MD	Baltimore Orioles
Erie SeaWolves	Erie, NY	Detroit Tigers
Harrisburg Senators	Harrisburg, PA	Washington Nationals
Richmond Flying Squirrels	Richmond, VA	San Francisco Giants

reason, which I will explain shortly. Note from the table that stadiums of five of these ten teams are located less than 100 miles from our hub location, the Raleigh-Durham Airport. They are:

- Durham Bulls (AAA)—Tampa Bay Rays
- Carolina Mudcats (A+)—Atlanta Braves
- Burlington Royals (Rk)—Kansas City Royals

Team	Location	Distance-Time	League	Affiliate
Durham Bulls	Durham, NC	14 Mi 20 Min	International	TBR
Carolina Mudcats	Zebulon, NC	39 Mi 43 Min	Carolina	ATL
Burlington Royals	Burlington, NC	45 Mi 52 Min	Appalachian	KCR
Danville Braves	Danville, VA	70 Mi 1 Hr 28 Min	Appalachian	ATL
Winston-Salem Dash	Winston-Salem, NC	93 Mi 1 Hr 40 Min	Carolina	CHW
Salem Red Sox	Salem, VA	155 Mi 3 Hr 14 Min	Carolina	BOS
Charlotte Knights	Charlotte, NC	156 Mi 2 Hr 24 Min	International	CHW
Richmond Flying Squirrels	Richmond, VA	164 Mi 2 hr 47 Min	Eastern	SFG
Pulaski Yankees	Pulaski, VA	184 Mi 3 Hr 11 Min	Appalachian	NYY
Myrtle Beach Pelicans	Myrtle Beach, SC	208 Mi 3Hr 40 Min	Carolina	CHC

Table 7–2. Teams of other leagues located close to Durham.

- Danville Braves (Rk)—Atlanta Braves
- Winston-Salem Dash (A+)—Chicago White Sox

It should be possible to make a day-trip from Durham to attend a day or evening game at any of these locations.

For example, Table 7–2 shows that the Chicago White Sox, in addition to having their A-level affiliate the Kannapolis Intimidators of the South Atlantic League in Kannapolis, North Carolina, have their Carolina League (A+) team—the Dash—that plays their home games at BB&T Ballpark (Fig. 7–1) in Winston-Salem, North Carolina, and International League (AAA) team the Charlotte Knights in Charlotte, NC. A White Sox fan could add stops in a South Atlantic League road trip plan to attend home games of either or both of these teams. In fact, the distance between the home stadiums of the Intimidators and Knights is just 30 miles so it would be possible to plan to see games of these two teams on consecutive days or even one in the afternoon and the other in the evening of the same day.

Figure 7–1. BB&T Ballpark, home of the Winston-Salem Dash.

Another example is the Boston Red Sox, who have their A-level team—the Greenville Drive—in the SAL. Their A+ level team—the Salem Red Sox—is a member of the Carolina League. LewisGale Field in Salem, Virginia, where the Red Sox play their home games, is 155 miles from Durham and slightly over a 3 hour drive. If a day game is possible, this could be done as a day-trip. This is one reason it has been added to the list of teams close to Durham. However, there is a second. Salem is right on the route between Durham and Charleston, West Viriginia, and could be an extra stop by a Red Sox fan added to the northwestern road trip to take in games of the West Virginia Power and Lexington Legends.

Finally, the Pulaski Yankees, who play their home games in Pulaski, Virginia, are also positioned for a stop on the route between Durham and Charleston, West Virginia. Similar to the Salem Red Sox, their home stadium is located approximately mid-way between Durham and Charleston and offers another potential stop along the route of the northwestern road trip to attend home games of the Power and Legends.

Major League Teams with Minor League Affiliates in Multiple Leagues

The information listed in Table 7–3 shows that fans of most major league teams that have an affiliate that plays in the SAL could attend either a home game or away game of other teams from their favorite teams' minor league organization as part of their South Atlantic League road trip. This table identifies the major league clubs that have a team in the South Atlantic League

MLB Club	MiLB Affiliates	Level	League	Home-Away
BOS	Greenville Drive	A	South Atlantic	Home
	Pawtucket Red Sox	AAA	International	Away
	Portland Sea Dogs	AA	Eastern	Away
	Salem Red Sox	A+	Carolina	Home
PIT	West Virginia Power	A	South Atlantic	Home
	Indianapolis Indians	AAA	International	Away
	Altoona Curve	AA	Eastern	Away
	Bristol Pirates	Rk	Appalachian	Away
ATL	Rome Braves	A	South Atlantic	Home
	Gwinnett Braves	AAA	International	Away
	Carolina Mudcats	A+	Carolina	Home
	Danville Braves	Rk	Appalachian	Home
BAL	Delmarva Shorebirds	A	South Atlantic	Home
	Norfolk Tides	AAA	International	Away
	Bowie Baysox	AA	Eastern	Away
	Frederick Keys	A+	Carolina	Away
WSN	Hagerstown Suns	A	South Atlantic	Home
	Syracuse Chiefs	AAA	International	Away
	Harrisburg Senators	AA	Eastern	Away
	Potomac Nationals	A+	Carolina	Away
NYY	Charleston RiverDogs	A	South Atlantic	Home
	Scranton/Wilkes-Barre RailRiders	AAA	International	Away
	Trenton Thunder	AA	Eastern	Away
	Pulaski Yankees	Rk	Appalachian	Home

Above and following page: Table 7–3. Teams that have 2 or more minor league affiliates teams in the five baseball leagues accessible from Durham, NC.

MLB Club	MiLB Affiliates	Level	League	Home-Away
NYM	Savannah Sand Gnats	A	South Atlantic	Home
	Binghamton Mets	AA	Eastern	Away
	Kingston Mets	Rk	Appalachian	Away
KCR	Lexington Legends	A	South Atlantic	Home
	Wilmington Blue Rocks	A+	Carolina	Away
	Burlington Royals	Rk	Appalachian	Home
CHW	Kannapolis Intimidators	A	South Atlantic	Home
	Charlotte Knights	AAA	International	Home
	Winston-Salem Dash	A+	Carolina	Home
PHI	Lakewood BlueClaws	A	South Atlantic	Home
	Lehigh Valley IronPigs	AAA	International	Away
	Reading Fightin Phils	AA	Eastern	Away
SFG	Augusta GreenJackets	A	South Atlantic	Home
	Richmond Flying Squirrels	AA	Eastern	Home
COL	Asheville Tourists	A	South Atlantic	Home
	New Britain Rock Cats	AA	Eastern	Away

and one or more additional minor league affiliates in these other four leagues. The list includes the name of the minor league team, the league in which it plays, and the level of that league. Note that fans of the Boston Red Sox, Pittsburgh Pirates, Atlanta Braves, Baltimore Orioles, Washington Nationals, and New York Yankees could potentially attend games played by four of their favorite club's minor league teams. Similarly, fans of the New York Mets, Kansas City Royals, Chicago White Sox, and Philadelphia Phillies could each see games of three of their team's minor league affiliates.

As illustrated in Table 7–2, the stadiums of a number of these teams are located within a day-trip driving distance of Durham. Those teams have Home marked into the Home-Away column. As pointed out earlier, it is easy for the fan of that team's major league club to add a home game of that minor league team into a South Atlantic League baseball road trip.

This does not mean that one cannot attend a game of his favorite team's other affiliates in these leagues as part of a South Atlantic League road trip. Those teams would need to be seen when they traveled to play a game against another team in their league that is located within a day-trip's distance of Durham. In Table 7–3 those teams are identified with Away in the Home-Away column. For instance, the first choice for attending a game of one of the International League teams, such as the Gwinnett Braves (Atlanta Braves) or Syracuse Chiefs (Washington National), would be an away game versus the Durham Bulls at Durham Bulls Athletic Park.

In addition to seeing the Lexington Legends play a game at Whitaker Bank Park, a Kansas City Royals fan could attend a home game of the Burlington Royals at Burlington Athletic Stadium (Fig. 7–2) in Burlington, NC. Moreover, they could see the Wilmington Blue Rocks play an away game against the Carolina Mudcats at Five County Stadium in Zebulon, NC. The home stadium of both the Royals and Mudcats are conveniently located within 50 miles of the Durham hub.

Another opportunity is possible for fans of the Chicago White Sox. Three of its minor league teams are within day-trip traveling distance of the Durham hub. So a White Sox fan could easily attend home games of the Kannapolis Intimidators, Charlotte Knights, and Winston-Salem Dash as part of a South Atlantic League road trip.

The Red Sox also have other teams in some of these leagues. For example, Boston has their AAA team—the Pawtucket Red Sox, Pawtucket, Rhode Island—in the International League and AA team—the Portland Sea Dogs,

Figure 7–2. Burlington Athletic Stadium, home of the Burlington Royals.

Portland, Maine—in the Eastern League. Even though these teams' home stadiums are very far away from Durham, North Carolina, there are solutions for attending games played by them as part of one's South Atlantic League road trip. During the season the PawSox travel to North Carolina to play away games versus both the Durham Bulls and Charlotte Knights. Also, the Sea Dogs go to Richmond, Virginia, for away games against the Richmond Flying Squirrels. With a little schedule analysis and flexibility, it might be possible for a Red Sox fan to catch home games of the Greenville Drive and Salem Red Sox as well as away games of the PawSox and Sea Dogs from the Durham Hub.

That is the reason I added the Richmond Flying Squirrels (San Francisco Giants) into the list of teams close to Durham. A trip to attend a game at their stadium—The Diamond (Fig. 7–3) in Richmond, Virginia—enables a fan of any one of the major league clubs that has an affiliate in the Eastern League to include a game of that minor league team in their South Atlantic League travel plan.

A final question: Why did I include the Myrtle Beach Pelicans in the list

Figure 7–3. The Diamond, home of the Richmond Flying Squirrels.

of teams close to Durham in Table 7–2 if it is more than 200 miles from the hub city and the trip to its stadium would take more than 3 hours? The answer is that Myrtle Beach, South Carolina, which is an interesting beachside community, can easily be reached as a short side trip on the route traveled between Durham and Charleston, South Carolina. For this reason, a stop for a Pelicans game could be added as a stop on any of the Sally League southern route road trips that include attending a RiverDogs game.

Appendix: Additional Road Trip Travel Plans

Teams	Origin/Destination	Miles*	Cum. Miles	Travel Time*	Cum. Time
Starting point	RDU, 2400 W. Terminal Blvd. Morrisville, NC	0	0	0 Hr 0 Min	0 Hr 0 Min
Savannah Sand Gnats	William L. Grayson Stadium, 1401 E. Victory Dr. Savannah, GA	341	341	5 Hr 27 Min	5 Hr 27 Min
Augusta GreenJackets	Lake Olmstead Stadium, 78 Milledge Rd. Augusta, GA	146	487	2 Hr 55 Min	8 Hr 22 Min
Ending point	RDU, 2400 W. Terminal Blvd. Morrisville, NC	312	799	4 Hr 57 Min	13 Hr 19 Min

Table A 1–1. Savannah Sand Gnats–Augusta GreenJackets alternative two-game southern road trip travel plan.

Teams	Origin/Destination	Miles*	Cum. Miles	Travel Time*	Cum. Time
Starting point	RDU, 2400 W. Terminal Blvd. Morrisville, NC	0	0	0 Hr 0 Min	0 Hr 0 Min
Greenville Drive	Fluor Field, 945 S. Main St. Greenville, SC	255	255	4 Hr 20 Min	4 Hr 20 Min
Rome Braves	State Mutual Stadium, 755 Braves Blvd. Rome, GA	204	459	3 Hr 29 Min	7 Hr 49 Min
Ending point	RDU, 2400 W. Terminal Blvd. Morrisville, NC	456	915	7 Hr 38 Min	15 Hr 27 Min

Table A 1–2. Greenville Drive–Rome Braves alternative two-game southwestern road trip travel plan.

Teams	Origin/Destination	Miles‡	Miles	Time ‡	Time
Starting point	RDU, 2400 W. Terminal Blvd. Morrisville, NC	0	0	0 Hr 0 Min	0 Hr 0 Min
Hickory Crawdads	L.P. Frans Stadium, 2500 Clement Blvd. NW Hickory, NC	166	166	2 Hr 49 Min	2 Hr 49 Min
Asheville Tourists	McCormick Field, 30 Buchanan Pl. Asheville, NC	78	244	1 Hr 20 Min	4 Hr 9 Min
Ending point	RDU, 2400 W. Terminal Blvd. Morrisvile, NC	237		3 Hr 55 Min	8 Hr 4 Min

Table A 1–3. Hickory Crawdads–Asheville Tourists alternative two-game western road trip travel plan.

Bibliography

Websites

General Baseball

The Baseball Cube (Players, Teams, Seasons, Minors) http://www.thebaseball cube.com/

Baseball-Reference.com (minors/leagues, minors/teams, minors/players, minors/ affiliates, players, boxes) http://www. baseball-reference.com/

Leagues and Teams

The Official Site of the Class A South Atlantic League (Schedule, Scoreboard, Standings, Stats, News, Playoffs, Hall of Fame) http://www.milb.com/index.jsp? sid=l116

• The Official Site of the Asheville Tourists (Schedule, Stats and Scores, Roster, News, McCormick Field) http:// asheville.tourists.milb.com/index. jsp?sid=t573

• The Official Site of the Augusta GreenJackets (Schedule, Stats and Scores, Roster, News, Lake Olmstead Stadium) http://augusta.greenjackets. milb.com/index.jsp?sid=t478

• The Official Site of the Charleston RiverDogs (Schedule, Stats and Scores, Roster, News, The Joe) http://charleston. riverdogs.milb.com/index.jsp?sid=t233

• The Official Site of the Delmarva Shorebirds (Schedule, Stats and Scores, Roster, News, Perdue Stadium) http:// delmarva.shorebirds.milb.com/index. jsp?sid=t548

• The Official Site of the Greensboro Grasshoppers (Schedule, Stats and Scores, Roster, News, Ballpark) http:// greensboro.grasshoppers.milb.com/ index.jsp?sid=t477

• The Official Site of the Greenville Drive (Schedule, Stats and Scores, Roster, News, Fluor Field) http://greenville. drive.milb.com/index.jsp?sid=t428

• The Official Site of the Hagerstown Suns (Schedule, Stats and Scores, Roster, News, Municipal Stadium) http://hagers town.suns.milb.com/index.jsp?sid= t563

• The Official Site of the Hickory Crawdads (Schedule, Stats and Scores, Roster, News, L. P. Frans Stadium) http:// hickory.crawdads.milb.com/index.jsp? sid=t448

• The Official Site of the Kannapolis Intimidators (Schedule, Stats and Scores, Roster, News, CMC-NorthEast Stadium) http://kannapolis.intimidators.milb.com/ index.jsp?sid=t487

• The Official Site of the Lakewood BlueClaws http://www.milb.com/index. jsp?sid=t427 (Schedule, Stats and Scores, Roster, News, FirstEnergy Park) http:// lakewood.blueclaws.milb.com/index. jsp?sid=t427

• The Official Site of the Lexington Legends (Schedule, Stats and Scores, Roster, News, Whitaker Bank Ballpark) http://www.milb.com/index.jsp?sid= t495 http://lexington.legends.milb.com/ index.jsp?sid=t495

• The Official Site of the Rome Braves (Schedule, Stats and Scores, Roster, News,

State Mutual Stadium) http://rome. braves.milb.com/index.jsp?sid=t432

• The Official Site of the Savannah Sand Gnats (Schedule, Stats and Scores, Roster, News, Grayson Stadium) http:// savannah.sandgnats.milb.com/index. jsp?sid=t543

• The Official Site of the West Virginia Power (Schedule, Stats and Scores, Roster, News, Appalachian Power Park) http://westvirginia.power.milb.com/ index.jsp?sid=t525

The Official Site of Major League Baseball (Scores, News, Stats, Players) http://mlb. mlb.com/home

• The Official Site of the Atlanta Braves (Scores, Stats, Roster) http:// atlanta.braves.mlb.com/index.jsp?c_id= atl

• The Official Site of the Baltimore Orioles (Scores, Stats, Roster) http:// baltimore.orioles.mlb.com/index.jsp?c_ id=bal

• The Official Site of the Boston Red Sox (Scores, Stats, Roster) http://boston. redsox.mlb.com/index.jsp?c_id=bos

• The Official Site of the Chicago Cubs (Scores, Stats, Roster) http://chicago.cubs. mlb.com/index.jsp?c_id=chc

• The Official Site of the Chicago White Sox (Scores, Stats, Roster) http:// chicago.whitesox.mlb.com/index.jsp?c_ id=cws

• The Official Site of the Cincinnati Reds (Scores, Stats, Roster) http:// cincinnati.reds.mlb.com/index.jsp?c_ id=cin

• The Official Site of the Colorado Rockies (Scores, Stats, Roster) http:// colorado.rockies.mlb.com/index.jsp?c_ id=col

• The Official Site of the Houston Astros (Scores, Stats, Roster) http://houston. astros.mlb.com/index.jsp?c_id=hou

• The Official Site of the Kansas City Royals (Scores, Stats, Roster) http:// kansascity.royals.mlb.com/index.jsp?c_ id=kc

• The Official Site of the Los Angeles Dodgers (Scores, Stats, Roster) http:// losangeles.dodgers.mlb.com/index. jsp?c_id=la

• The Official Site of the Miami Marlins (Scores, Stats, Roster) http://miami. marlins.mlb.com/index.jsp?c_id=mia

• The Official Site of the Milwaukee Brewers (Scores, Stats, Roster) http:// milwaukee.brewers.mlb.com/index. jsp?c_id=mil

• The Official Site of the New York Mets (Scores, Stats, Roster) http://new york.mets.mlb.com/index.jsp?c_id=nym

• The Official Site of the New York Yankees (Scores, Stats, Roster) http:// newyork.yankees.mlb.com/index.jsp?c_ id=nyy

• The Official Site of the Philadelphia Phillies (Scores, Stats, Roster) http:// philadelphia.phillies.mlb.com/index. jsp?c_id=phi

• The Official Site of the Pittsburgh Pirates (Scores, Stats, Roster) http://pitts burgh.pirates.mlb.com/index.jsp?c_id= pit

• The Official Site of the San Diego Padres (Scores, Stats, Roster) http://san diego.padres.mlb.com/index.jsp?c_id=sd

• The Official Site of the San Francisco Giants (Scores, Stats, Roster) http:// sanfrancisco.giants.mlb.com/index.jsp?c_ id=sf

• The Official Site of the St. Louis Cardinals (Scores, Stats, Roster) http:// stlouis.cardinals.mlb.com/index.jsp?c_ id=stl

• The Official Site of the Tampa Bay Rays (Scores, Stats, Roster) http://tampa bay.rays.mlb.com/index.jsp?c_id=tb

• The Official Site of the Texas Rangers (Scores, Stats, Roster) http://texas.rangers. mlb.com/index.jsp?c_id=tex

• The Official Site of the Toronto Blue Jays (Scores, Stats, Roster) http:// toronto.bluejays.mlb.com/index.jsp?c_ id=tor

• The Official Site of the Washington Nationals (Scores, Stats, Roster) http:// washington.nationals.mlb.com/index. jsp?c_id=was Stadiums

Ballparks

Ballparkreviews.com http://www.ballpark reviews.com

Baseball Pilgrimages http://www.baseball pilgrimages.com/A/kannapolis.html

Digitalballparks.com http://www.digital ballparks.com/

Stadium Journey http://www.stadiumjour ney.com/

City Websites

Asheville, NC http://www.exploreasheville. com/, http://en.wikipedia.org/wiki/ Asheville,_North_Carolina

Augusta, GA http://www.visitaugusta.com/, http://en.wikipedia.org/wiki/Augusta,_ Georgia

Charleston, SC http://www.charlestoncvb. com/visitors/, http://en.wikipedia.org/ wiki/Charleston,_South_Carolina

Charleston, WV http://charlestonwv.com/ default.aspx, http://en.wikipedia.org/ wiki/Charleston,_West_Virginia

Greensboro, NC http://www.visitgreens boronc.com/, http://en.wikipedia.org/ wiki/Greensboro,_North_Carolina

Greenville, SC http://www.visitgreenville sc.com/, http://en.wikipedia.org/wiki/ Greenville,_South_Carolina

Hagerstown, MD http://www.maryland memories.org/index.shtml, http://en. wikipedia.org/wiki/Hagerstown,_Mary-land

Hickory, NC http://www.hickorymetro. com/, http://en.wikipedia.org/wiki/ Hickory,_North_Carolina

Kannapolis, NC http://www.cityofkanna polis.com/visiting/attractions/, http:// en.wikipedia.org/wiki/Kannapolis,_ North_Carolina

Lakewood, NJ http://www.visitnj.org/ lakewood, http://www.visitnj.org/point-pleasant-beach

Lexington, KY http://www.visitlex.com/, http://en.wikipedia.org/wiki/Lexing-ton,_Kentucky

Ocean City, MD http://www.ocean-city. com/

Point Pleasant Beach, NJ http://en.wiki pedia.org/wiki/Point_Pleasant_Beach,_ New_Jersey

Rome, GA http://romegeorgia.org/, http:// en.wikipedia.org/wiki/Rome,_Georgia

Salisbury, MD http://www.wicomicotour ism.org/, http://en.wikipedia.org/wiki/ Salisbury,_Maryland

Savannah, GA http://visitsavannah.com/? gclid=CKiMk8_nrL8CFcnm7Aod SEQA9A, http://en.wikipedia.org/wiki/ Savannah,_Georgia

Books

Epting, Chris. *Roadside America: The Lo-cations of America's Baseball Landmarks*, 2d ed. Santa Monica: Santa Monica Press, 2009.

Garner, Bob. *Bob Garner's Guide to North Carolina Barbecue*. Winston-Salem: John F. Blair, 2012.

Myers, Erik Lars. *North Carolina Craft Beer & Breweries*. Winston-Salem: John F. Blair, 2012.

Pahigian, Josh. *101 Baseball Places to See Before You Strike Out*. Guilford, CT: The Lyons Press, 2008.

Pahigian, Josh. *The Ultimate Minor League Road Trip*. Guilford, CT: The Lyons Press, 2007.

Spavins, Jim. *Japanese Baseball Road Trip Guide*. Self-published, 2011.

Web Articles

Haunss, Chip. "Power Send Crawdads Pack-ing." MiLB.com. http://www.milb.com/ news/article.jsp?ymd=20070909& content_id=301226&vkey=news_milb&fe xt=.jsp

Lasseter, Tom. "Stacked Legends Swamped SAL." *Lexington Herald-Leader* http:// www.astroland.net/2001legends.html

Law, Bill. "Baseball City USA." The Official Site of the Durham Bulls (durhambulls. com). http://www.milb.com/content/ page.jsp?ymd=20110520&content_id=19 314614&sid=t234&vkey=team4

Lewis, Julia. "Baseball Landmark Could Help Bring Development to Bull City." WRAL.com. http://www.wral.com/news/ local/story/1688158/

Luchter, P. S. "Professional Baseball in Lake-wood, NJ." luckyshow.org http://www.

luckyshow.org/baseball/BlueClaws. htm

Vitty, Cort. "Buzz Arlett." Society for American Baseball Research (SABR). http:// sabr.org/bioproj/person/4419031b

Web Documents

Asheville Tourists Baseball. ashevilleNC. com. http://www.ashevillenc.com/area_ info/baseball

Bull Durham Filming Locations. 80's Movies Rewind. http://www.fast-rewind. com/locations_bulldurham.htm

Bull Durham Script. The Internet Movie Script Database (IMSDb). http://www. imsdb.com/scripts/Bull-Durham.html

Bull Durham Tobacco & the Durham Bulls. North Carolina History Project. http://www.northcarolinahistory.org/ encyclopedia/810/entry/

"First half Shorebirds standings report (2006)." monoblogue. http://monoblo gue.us/2006/06/20/first-half-shorebirds-standings-report/

"Fleming Stadium celebrates 75th year." The Wilson Times. http://www.wilson times.com/News/Feature/Story/ 29847338---CELEBRATING-75-YEARS

"Hessman Becomes Eighth Minor Leaguer to Hit 400 Career Home Runs." Society for American Baseball Research (SABR). http://sabr.org/latest/hessman-becomes-eighth-minor-leaguer-hit-400-career-home-runs

High Point-Thomasville Hi-Toms. Baseball-Reference.com. http://www.base ball-reference.com/bullpen/High_Point-Thomasville_Hi-Toms

"Intimidators Rout Suns, Take 2–1 Lead." HeraldMail.com. http://articles.herald mail.com/keyword/kannapolis-intimi dators/featured/5

"Maloney is King Crab and BlueClaws are Champs." OurSports Channel http:// www.oursportscentral.com/services/ releases/?id=3377733

North Carolina State League. Baseball-Reference.com. http://www.baseball-reference.com/bullpen/North_Car olina_State_League

Salisbury Braves. Baseball-Reference.com. http://www.baseball-reference.com/ bullpen/Salisbury_Braves

"Sand Gnats Beat Shorebirds for S. Atlantic Title." The Baltimore Sun. http://articles. baltimoresun.com/1996–07–18/sports/ 1996262059_1_sand-gnats-savannah-sand-salisbury

South Atlantic League. Baseball-Reference. com. http://www.baseball-reference. com/bullpen/South_Atlantic_League

South Atlantic League Individual Batting Records. The Official Site of the Class A South Atlantic League. http://www.milb. com/content/page.jsp?sid=l116&ymd= 20071201&content_id=327181&vkey= stats

South Atlantic League Pennant Winners and Playoff Champions. The Official Site of the Class A South Atlantic League. http://www.milb.com/content/page. jsp?ymd=20080311&content_id=415 49800&fext=.jsp&vkey=news_l116&sid= l116

Tar Heel League. Baseball-Reference.com. http://www.baseball-reference.com/ bullpen/Tar_Heel_League

Western Carolina League. Baseball-Reference.com. *http://www.baseball-ref erence.com/bullpen/Western_Carolina_ League*

Western Carolinas League. Baseball-Reference.com. http://www.baseball-refer ence.com/bullpen/Western_Carolinas_ League

Index

5/16/16